R. Schnell

The Sociology-Philosophy Connection

Science and Technology Studies
Mario Bunge, Series Editor

The Sociology-Philosophy Connection

Mario Bunge

with a foreword by
Raymond Boudon

Transaction Publishers
New Brunswick (U.S.A.) and London (U.K.)

This book is printed on acid-free paper that meets the American National Standard for Permanence of Paper for Printed Library Materials.

Library of Congress Catalog Number: 99-25391
ISBN: 1-56000-416-9
Printed in the United States of America

Library of Congress Cataloging-in-Publication Data

Bunge, Mario Augusto.
    The sociology-philosophy connection / Mario Bunge ; with a foreword by Raymond Boudon.
        p. cm. — (Science and technology studies)
    Includes bibliographical references and index.
    ISBN 1-56000-416-9 (alk. paper)
    1. Sociology. 2. Philosophy. I. Title.
HM585.B85   1999
301—dc21   99-25391
                                                                                    CIP

Contents

Acknowledgements

Chapters 1 and 5 have been written especially for this volume. The others are thoroughly revised versions of previous publications. I thank Sage Publications, Inc. for permission to use, with modifications, the following papers published in *Philosophy of the Social Sciences*: "A critical examination of the new sociology of science," 21: 524–560 (1991); 22: 46–76 (1992); "The seven pillars of Popper's social philosophy," 26: 528–556 (1996); and "Mechanism and explanation," 27: 410–465 (1997). An earlier version of chapter 4 was read at the Symposium on Quantitative Methods in Social Science, held at the University of Siena in 1992, and published in the *Journal of Quantitative Linguistics* 2:1–10 (1994). I am grateful to Prometheus Books for allowing me to use the material in chapter 7, originally published in Paul Kurtz and Tim Madigan, eds., *Challenges to the Enlightenment: In Defense of Reason and Science*, pp. 25–42 (1994). And I am indebted to the New York Academy of Sciences for permission to reprint chapter 10, wich was read at the conference on the Flight from Science and Reason held in 1995 at the New York Academy of Sciences, and published in the *Annals of the New York Academy of Sciences* 775: 96–116 (1996).

Foreword

The sociology-philosophy connection is an old one. Durkheim considered that his sociology proposed a scientific solution to major problems raised by Kant and by Auguste Comte. Weber built some of his analyses on ideas drawn from Kant and from Nietzsche. Simmel is in many respects a neo-Kantian, but considers Marx seriously, though he rejects Marxism. After World War I and until the sixties, the connection seemed to have disappeared. The great sociological names of the time do not mention the great philosophical names. Parsons quotes and builds on Durkheim, Weber, Pareto, and Alfred Marshall, but never mentions Kant, Hegel, or Marx. Then, in the sixties and after, big philosophical names reappear in the social sciences. Michel Foucault presents himself as a faithful Nietzschean and inspired many sociologists. Surprisingly, the name of Heidegger appears frequently in contemporary sociological writings. Phenomenology, the name for a philosophical movement initiated around World War I in Germany becomes a label for a movement developed in the sixties in California.

A history of the connection philosophy-sociology remains to be written, This would be an interesting topic in the history of ideas.

Writing such a history is not Bunge's objective in his book. His work starts from the impression that the state of the social sciences is far from being satisfactory. And his main point is that philosophy of science is able to help, setting a diagnosis on the state of the patient and curing the disease. By so doing, he continues the special type of philosophy-sociology connection set up and brilliantly illustrated by philosophers of science such as Carl Hempel, Karl Popper, or Ernst Nagel.

One of Bunge's points is that sociologists underestimate the capacity of sociology to discover social laws and are much too skeptical about the existence of such laws.

Sociologists have not always been skeptical of laws. A major point in Popper's *Poverty of Historicism*[1] was that such great classical sociologists as Spencer or Marx, not to speak of modern Marxists or of sociologists inspired by neo-Darwinism, had too easily believed in the existence of historical trends. Durkheim proposed a number of laws, regarding the increase in the division of labor or the relations between the rates of suicide and a number of independent variables.

It must be recalled though that, in his *Les Causes du Suicide*, Halbwachs, a Durkheim student, had shown that some of the laws about suicide Durkheim had demonstrated had become false within a few years. Even possibly the most solid—at least most frequently invoked—economic law, the so-called "Phillips curve " relating unemployment and inflation, has turned out to be dependent on circumstancial variables, in other words to be false or true depending on the circumstances. "Technological advances are accompanied by unemployment " is an example of the laws mentioned by Bunge. It results from the "mechanism" that increased productivity destroys jobs. But the "mechanism" is at work only locally. Here and there, a machine destroys jobs. But, as it had to be devised and has to be maintained and modernized, it also creates jobs. So that the sign of the balance is an empirical question: technological advances can be accompanied by unemployment, but also by full employment, as in the three decades after World War II. "Social democracy is losing ground everywhere" because the welfare state has satisfied many socialist demands would be another law. All governments of the European community are presently social-democrat though, with the exception of Spain, for the first time. Even President Chirac, a Gaullist, was half-ironically complimented by Chancellor Schröder for being a genuine social-democrat.

There are social laws, but they are most of them vague and general and depending on all kinds of circumstancial variables. For these reasons, determining the laws of social life has not for a long time been considered a major objective of the social sciences. A few years ago, I looked systematically at the literature on development. It had proposed many laws and inspired development policies. Most of them turned out to be fragile.[2] Still, Bunge is right to recall that. there are social laws. Otherwise, societies would be entirely unpredictable, while in fact they are obviously partially and conditionally predictable. Sociologists have probably become overpessimistic in this respect.

Useful above all is Bunge's warning that, in sociology as in other scientific disciplines, one should learn to distinguish a valid theory from an invalid one. This warning is crucial. If the validity dimension of a theory is neglected, sociology can only become bad literature. Bunge goes even further and sees much charlatanism in academic social sciences in many places. Many people wonder effectively with him what "phenomenology" and many other sociological movements have taught us exactly and even whether they have taught us or explained anything.

Though severe, Bunge is right. Thus, one of the sociological theories much quoted and referred to some years ago, the "labeling theory" teaches us that a person is less highly regarded when he or she comes out from jail than when he or she has won a Nobel Prize. Such a "theory" is not a theory in the usual scientific sense. While Descartes' refraction theory, say, explains why a stick appears as broken when immersed in water—a phenomenon the explanation of which is far from evident—the "labeling theory" merely puts a name on a familiar social phenomenon with which any child in any society would normally be familiar. Such a "theory" is socially useful, because it draws the attention of the public to a phenomenon which makes more difficult the social reintegration of former delinquents. But it does not explain anything we would not know before, Many other "theories" produced by the academic social sciences not only fail to explain anything; they are not even useful, as Bunge points out.

To clarify the question as to what makes a sociological theory valid, the simplest method is to consider theories which are generally perceived as illuminating and have after many years never been seriously revised. There are many.

Thus, to draw my examples exclusively from classical sociology, Tocqueville asked why French agriculture remained stagnant at the end of the eighteenth century, at a time when British agriculture modernized rapidly, or why the idea of "reason" was much more popular in France than in Britain at the same time, or why Americans remained religious in spite of modernization while Frenchmen or Englishmen became irreligious; Weber asked why Mithraïsm penetrated into the Roman Empire essentially through the channel of civil servants, as did freemasonry in Prussia; Durkheim asked why all religions introduce, with one name or another, the notion of "soul," why in all societies magical beliefs—beliefs in ungrounded causal relations—can be observed, or why suicide rates decrease in times of political crisis.

These very classical examples belong to the genuine achievements of sociology. They suggest a number of conclusions.

First of all, it can readily be determined that all the above questions are genuine questions: the answer is no more evident than is the question as to the causes of refraction.

Secondly, while one of the above questions deals with a "law," namely Durkheim's law that suicide rates decrease in periods of political crises, the others deal rather with *singularities,* for example, American religious exceptionalism—a phenomenon already observed and analyzed by Adam Smith, then by Tocqueville, by Weber, and by modern sociologists[3]—or with *differences*, such as the difference between France and England with respect to the modernization of agriculture or the popularity of the notion of reason, still others with a *universal phenomenon* rather than a law, such as the observation that all religions include the notion of soul. So, stating and explaining "laws" is merely one objective of sociology among many others.

Thirdly, the answers respectively given by Tocqueville, Weber, and Durkheim to the above questions are generally perceived as valid because the explanation they proposed is in all cases made up of a more or less complex set of statements all of which are acceptable, either because they are trivial psychological statements or valid empirical statements.

I cannot examine in detail all the above examples in this respect. So, I will briefly consider the simplest one. Tocqueville explains that the stagnation of French agriculture in the eighteenth century is due to the fact that landlord absenteeism is much greater in France than Britain. Why? Because being a higher-level civil servant is both easier and more attractive in France than in Britain: as an effect of French centralization, higher civil servants are much more numerous in France; moreover, being a civil servant brings more prestige, power and influence in France, since this amounts to being a part of a powerful central state. So, rich French landlords prefer to buy a *charge royale* rather than to exploit their land as in England. For this reason, the notion of "gentleman-farmer" has no equivalent in France.

To my knowledge, Tocqueville's analysis has never been disqualified by further research. It has rather been continued and refined, notably by Root, who in an illuminating book[4] recognizes his debt to Tocqueville.

Finally, it can be noted that, in his analysis, Tocqueville uses what was later to be called by Weber and Schumpeter "methodological individualism": the ultimate causes of the macrophenomenon to be explained (the stagnation of French agriculture) are individual decisions. These decisions are "understandable" (*verständlich*): their causes lie in the reasons why the actors prefer to buy a *charge royale* to exploiting their land. Obviously, these decisions are taken in a concrete social context, and the decisions of the French landowners are on the average different from the decisions of their British counterparts because the context is different here and then, notably as regards centralization.

The same remark would be true of all the examples I have mentioned above: all use, explicitly or implicitly, the methodologically individualistic approach.

To make clear that "methodological individualism" does not entail any atomistic ontology, some authors have proposed to qualify it as "structural" (Wippler), "institutional" (Bourricaud) or "contextual" (Boudon).

As far as I can see, Bunge's "systemism" is another name for my "contextual methodological individualism" or for Weber's "methodological individualism."

Raymond Boudon
Université de Paris–Sorbonne

Notes

1. Popper, K., *The Poverty of Historicism,* London, Routledge and Kegan Paul, 1957.
2. Boudon, R., "Why the theories of social change fail. Some methodological thoughts", 5th Lazarsfeld Lecture, Columbia University, *Public Opinion Quarterly,* XLVII, 1983, 143–160. *Theories of social change: a critical appraisal,* London, Basil Blackwell/Polity Press, 1986.
3. Chaves, M. and D. Cann, "Regulation, Pluralism and Religious Market Structure: Explaining Religious Vitality, *Rationality and Society,* 4, 3, July 1992, p. 272–290.
4. Root, H.L., *The fountain of privilege: political foundations of economic markets in Old Regime France and England,* Berkeley: University of California Press, 1994.

Preface

The title says it all: I claim that sociology and philosophy are connected. Moreover, I hold that all the sciences—natural, biosocial, and social—intersect with philosophy. That is, the positivist thesis that science and philosophy are disjoint, is false. Example: the concept of society is philosophical as well as sociological, because it occurs in all the social sciences. However, according to methodological individualism, that concept is problematic or even dispensable, whereas holists regard it as unanalyzable. Is there an alternative? Another idea that lies at the sociology-philosophy intersection is that society has emergent or supra-individual properties, such as that of having a structure. But the very concept of emergence, certainly a philosophical one, is still suspect to most. Likewise, the problem of characterizing social indicators is philosophical as well as sociological. Indeed, indicators are observable variables assumed to map unobservable ones, in some cases because they measure overt effects of hidden causes. Notice the philosophical terms in the foregoing sentence: "observable," "hidden causes," and "assumed." Any diligent student of the sociology-philosophy connection will easily detect many other such hybrids upon examining the sociological literature.

My thesis would not have shocked John Stuart Mill or Karl Marx, Emile Durkheim or Max Weber, John Maynard Keynes or Fernand Braudel, Paul Lazarsfeld or James Coleman, let alone Ernest Gellner. It is also unlikely to surprise Raymond Boudon, Robert K. Merton, Albert O. Hirschman, Arthur Stinchcombe, Charles Tilly, Marvin Harris, Nathan Keyfitz, Irving Louis Horowitz, Amartya Sen, or Bruce Trigger. However, the thesis has got to be refined and exemplified again and again, because it is alien to both mainstream sociology and the dominant philosophies. Indeed, sociology students are not taught philosophy, and philosophers rarely read social science. I am grinding the ax because it is as blunt as it is important. And I feel emboldened to do so for having done some sociology.

In sum, philosophy is relevant to sociology. Correction: only some philosophies are, namely, those that tackle the philosophical problematics that arise in social research. Others, like linguistic philosophy, are barren academic games. Still others, like deconstructionism, hinder research and, indeed, rational debate. A fertile philosophy of science will unearth critical presuppositions, analyze key concepts, refine effective research strategies, craft coherent and realistic syntheses, or even identify and help discuss important new problems. It will ask unsettling questions and suggest reassuring though not final answers. In short, it will offer constructive criticism and profound insight.

Consider, for instance, the so-called Thomas "theorem"—actually a postulate. It states that people react to the way they perceive facts rather than to the facts themselves. In other words, social actions involve mental processes, and social relations pass through the heads of people. This thesis is true because people, unlike stars and bacteria, act on the strength of their information, beliefs, and interests. But it raises the philosophical question of whether it supports idealism or else is consistent with realism. At first sight, the "theorem" contradicts Durkheim's thesis that social facts are just as real as physical facts, and it seems to support instead the constructivist-relativist contention that everything social is a product of the observer's (or theorist's) mind. How can social facts be at the same time real and the outcome of actions steered at least in part by subjective experiences?

I submit that the way to ascertain which is the correct interpretation of the "theorem" is to observe, or at least imagine, the manner the average scientific observer will go about testing it. Presumably, he will treat his subjects as real, ask them what they think about a given social fact, contrast their answers with the facts themselves, check whether they behave on their beliefs, and will try not to put words in their mouths. Moreover, presumably the investigator believes in the possibility of giving an objectively true account of his subjects's beliefs and behavior. In short, he behaves as a scientific realist, not as either a constructivist-relativist or a rational choice theorist—neither of whom bothers about empirical tests.

Realists hold that social facts are objective—even when they consist in social inventions—but they also admit that facts may be perceived differently by different individuals. They also hold that all ideas are constructed rather than being found ready-made: they are psychological and epistemological constructivists, though not ontological constructivists. In short, there need be no contradiction between the Thomas "theorem" and Durkheim's realism. But the former does contradict Durkheim's holistic thesis that social facts occur above the social actors: that we are mere pawns in some High Chess Board. People construct society as well as the conceptual tools they employ to act and understand. So there: philosophical discussion can shed light on some scientific problems—particularly those that are also philosophical.

I thank Irving Louis Horowitz for encouraging me to put this book together, and Laurence Mintz for his superb editorial job.

1

The Relevance of Philosophy to Sociology

Two centuries ago, no scholar seemed to have felt the need to prove the relevance of philosophy to social studies nor, indeed, to any other field of inquiry. At that time philosophy and the sciences were still one. But they had already began to become estranged: the sciences were becoming increasingly specialized and rigorous, whereas many influential philosophers began to wallow in Romantic mud.

By the mid-nineteenth century, philosophy had lost its grip on social studies, psychology, and linguistics, and had moved far away from natural science and mathematics. True, Comte founded a whole philosophy—but he did not engage in social research. By contrast, Mill was a social scientist, but he kept too close to Comte's system to count as an original philosopher. As for Marx and Engels, as well as Menger and Weber, they were at the same time social scientists and amateur philosophers. But, because of their attachment to their heroes—Hegel and Kant respectively—they made no novel technical contributions to philosophy.

The situation had not improved one century later, when the eminent sociologist Paul Lazarsfeld (1962: 463) could rightly complain that "[p]hilosophers of science do not pay attention to the empirical work in social research which is actualy going on today." He could have quoted Popper's (1945) eccentric thesis of the autonomy of sociology, or Winch's (1958) extravagant claim that sociology is a branch of the theory of knowledge.

Things have not changed much since Lazarsfeld's scolding. For example, in his book on the logic of the social sciences, Habermas (1988) does not quote a single contemporary social study. Likewise, in their books on the subject, neither Hilary Putnam (1978) nor John Searle (1995), two top American philosophers, quotes a single paper or book in the social sciences. They write about social science much as Kant wrote about geography, namely without ever having left home.

1

However, deep down the "positive" sciences never gained the total independence from philosophy proclaimed by Comte and his heirs. Moreover, it can be shown that such autonomy is not just undesirable but impossible. First, because all the social sciences make use of philosophical concepts such as those of thing, property of a thing, process, knowledge, datum, hypothesis, evidence, truth, argument, and society. Second, because all the sciences presuppose some extremely general principles, such as the logical principle of noncontradiction, the ontological principle of the reality of the external world, and the epistemological principle of the knowability of the world. Third, because the philosophers of science are bound to make some contribution, positive or negative, to the way sociologists tackle the study of social facts and the analysis of social theory. Suffice it to recall the strong influence exerted by positivism, historical materialism, neo-Kantianism, pragmatism, phenomenology, and analytic philosophy.

In short, whereas Comte's problem was to cut the umbilical cord that had joined science to philosophy, ours is to exhibit the vast and deep overlap between the two. However, not all philosophy has been beneficial to science, particularly to social science. For instance, Kant and his followers decreed that the sciences of man cannot be objective; Hegel and the Marxists were mired in the mysteries of dialectics; the positivists have a healthy respect for facts but a sickly fear of theory; the utilitarians and the hyper-rationalists overlook the social constraints on individual agency; and the postmoderns would have us ignore facts and jettison rationality altogether. So, we have still to solve the problem of how best to join philosophy and science, in particular sociology. To indulge in metaphor, the problem is to transform a rowdy and barren common-law union into an orderly and fertile marriage.

Not every bride will do: only a science-oriented philosophy will be able to interact fruitfully with science and, in particular, sociology. Such philosophy can contribute to the advancement of sociology by identifying problems, analyzing and refining approaches, elucidating general concepts, unearthing presuppositions, analyzing and organizing theories, evaluating tests, encouraging interdisciplinary connections, and debunking pseudoscientific and antiscientific tendencies. Let us peek at these various tasks.

1.1. Problems

Philosophers are supposed to have a knack for seeing problems where others don't. Hence, they may help social scientists identify new problems, cast doubts on accepted solutions, or even suggest approaching in new ways old but unsolved problems. This is because authentic philosophers, far from being narrow specialists, have a world view that may serve as a general orientation or road map. We can dispense with a road map only if we do not know where we want to get to—as the Cheshire Cat would have told Alice.

A world view may help us spot holes in our background knowledge. And gaps in the extant knowledge is precisely what problems are. Which is a reminder that problems do not come out of the blue but from examining what is known. In other words, every problem presupposes some body of knowledge, however poor. This is why the more we know, the more new problems we can pose.

Although philosophers do not have a special expertise in posing particular scientific problems, their interest in generalities and their methodological skepticism may prompt them to ask some questions of interest to the sociologist. Here is a random sample of innocent-looking questions. What makes people join in voluntary associations? Given that all social systems, even revolutionary parties, resist change in their midst, how can such inertia be quantitated? How can the concept of social order be defined? Does inequality spur or hinder personal and social development? Is all utopian social thinking useless or worse? What, if any, is the use of counterfactual speculation?

Once an interesting, significant, and presumably soluble problem has been spotted, philosophers may help handle it in some phases of research. In fact, they may do the following.

1. Help clarify the statement of the problem in the light of their general vision and with the help of their logical tools.
2. Help list the conceptual and empirical means required to tackle the problem concerned—means that may have to be crafted if not available.
3. Help recognize whether the proposed solution is such or just a jumble of opaque sentences couched in the jargon of a particular school.
4. Help notice the logical consequences of accepting or rejecting the proposed solution.
5. Help identify the empirical evidence relevant to the checking of the proposed solution.

In principle, philosophers who have no interesting scientific questions to ask, nor can be of any help in solving any scientific problems, should not be noticed by scientists.

1.2. Approaches

Whatever is seen has been looked upon from some viewpoint or other: there is no vision from nowhere. For example, social wholes can be looked upon either as indecomposable totalities (holism), as aggregates of autonomous individuals (individualism), or as systems of interrelated individuals (systemism). A fourth approach is excluded. However, pure holism and pure individualism are hard to implement, because wholes do not hover above their components, and these are never fully free to do what they want because they are now constrained, now stimulated, by their relations with other people.

For instance, everyone knows that Durkheim was a holist and Weber an individualist. So they were—up to a point. For example, Durkheim postulated the existence of a collective conscience and a collective memory, which makes him a holist. But, like Weber (and Marx before him), Durkheim (1988 [1895]: 81–2) admitted that individuals are "the only active elements" of society. And he stated that, whenever individuals of any kind combine, they form things possessing new (emergent) properties. These two theses taken together are typical of systemism rather than holism. In short, Durkheim—like Marx—wavered between holism and systemism.

Nor was Weber a consistent individualist: he wavered between individualism and systemism. For example, he held that rationality, an individual trait, coevolved with the economy and the polity. He explained the decline of slavery in the Roman empire as a result of the end of the wars of conquest—which had been the main suppliers to the slave market—rather than of calculated decisions of the slaveholders. His thesis on the link between Protestantism and the "spirit of capitalism" links individual beliefs and feelings with capitalism, which is a socioeconomic order, not just the aggregate of capitalists. And the very title of his main work is composed of two words banned from his murky philosophical credo: "economy" and "society." In short, Weber's scientific work does not conform to the social philosophy he learned from Dilthey via his friend Rickert.

There is, then, a third ontology of social matter in addition to holism and individualism, namely systemism. This is the view that every thing is either a system or a component of some system—where a system is of course a complex object whose parts are held together by bonds of one or more kinds (see Bunge 1979). In particular, all features of society—economic, cultural and political—are of a piece. Though distinguishable, they are undetachable. Clearly, systemism encompasses both individualism—since it takes composition into account—and holism—since it emphasizes structure or organization.

Systemism is often mistaken for holism, in particular with Talcott Parson's (1951) fuzzy concept of action systems. His holistic and idealistic version of the concept of a system, as well as his opaque prose, have brought discredit upon the very word "system" among the students of society. Something similar applies to Niklas Luhmann (1990), Parsons's last follower.

But the concept of a system, if not the word, is just as alive in social science as it is in mathematics, natural science, and technology. The reason is that every science and every technology deals with systems of some kind or other, whether conceptual or material: number systems, families of functions, manifolds, or hypothetico-deductive systems (theories); physical systems such as atoms, or chemical ones such as electric batteries; cells, multicellular organisms, cardiovascular systems, nervous systems, or ecosystems; machines or communication networks; and social systems such as business firms, schools, religious congregations, armies, governments, or NGOs. Hence, trying to avoid the word "system" just because of its association with Parsons or Luhmann is like boycotting the word "nation" only because it is abused by nationalists.

The concept of a system is central to sociology because every person is part of several "circles" (systems), and behaves somewhat differently when acting in different systems. The latter, in turn, are affected by their components. In short, no agency outside some system, and no system without agency—whence change. Hence, to define an individual as a node in a self-existing social network—the way Marx did—is just as mistaken as to characterize the individual as a passive toy of higher-level entities. No networks without persons, and no person outside all networks.

True, a particular individual may be identified as the item that is a member of every one of a certain family of classes. But in turn every class is defined as the set of individuals with certain common properties. Although for analytic purposes we may focus either on individuals or on wholes, in reality every individual is part of a whole, and every whole exists and changes by virtue of the actions of its components. Hence individualism and holism may be regarded as components or projections of systemism. The former emphasizes composition and overloooks structure, whereas holism minimizes both—and the two ignore the natural and social environment, as well as the mechanisms that make a system tick. Only systemists analyze a social system into its composition, environment, structure, and mechanism. Whoever does this is a systemist even if he does not call himself such.

I submit that systemism is the natural approach to take for anyone interested in social structure and, particularly, in the mechanisms that maintain or alter that structure. The reason is simply that every structure is the structure of some system or other: there are no structures in themselves, any more than there are the structureless systems. More on this anon.

1.3. General Concepts

Philosophers, like mathematicians, specialize in general ideas. In particular, they deal in hypergeneral concepts, such as those of thing and property, system and component, space and time, change and stability, causation and chance, meaning and truth, data and hypothesis, confirmation and refutation, value and norm. All of these philosophical concepts and many more occur in sociology. Hence their clarification should be of interest and value to sociologists, all the more so since they are as tricky as they are central.

Take, for instance, the concept of social structure. Though central to sociology and, indeed, to all of the social sciences, few if any sociologists have defined it in clear terms. Here is where philosophers can help. They may start by noting that "social structure" is just a specification of "structure," whence it it convenient to begin by elucidating the latter. Let us do it.

In mathematics and other advanced sciences, structures are predicated of complex objects, such as sets and systems, namely thus. The structure of a complex object X equals the set of all the relations among the components of X. Actually this is what may be called the *endostructure* of X. If X happens to be embedded in an environment, the relations between the components of X and its environment may be called the *exostructure* of X. And the union of the two sets constitutes the *total structure* of X.

If X happens to be a social system, then the *social structure* of X is just the total structure of X. For example, the social structure of a business firm equals the set of work relations among its components, plus the business relations among the firm and its customers, suppliers, lawyers, and out-of-house consultants.

However, this is not the end of the story, because there are two kinds of relation: those that make a difference to the relata and those that don't. The former may be called *bonds* or *ties*. For example, marriage, employment, trading, education, and political allegiance are bonds. By contrast, the spatio-temporal relations do not affect the relata: at most they may make bonds possible or impossible. Hence the structure of a social system can be split into two mutually complementary sets: those composed by bonds or ties, and those composed of nonbonding relations, such as those of being older than or richer than, or of being interposed between two given individuals.

If the previous definitions are accepted, then such expressions as "age structure" and "income structure" turn out to be incorrect. Since they consist of families of classes of equivalent age or income, they should be called "age equivalence classes" and "income equivalence classes" respectively.

Obviously, the concept of social structure is only one of the many key sociological concepts that raise philosophical problems. Others in the pile are those of agency, function, rationality, power, social class, and social progress. For example, is every action individual, or is it legitimate to speak of social action, and if so in what sense? Shall we dispense with the concept of social function just because of the flaws of functionalism, or do we tacitly use it whenever we describe what a particular social system does? Is "rationality" an unambiguous term, or does it designate many different concepts? What are influence and power: things or relations; and if the latter, in what sense can one speak of power sources? In what sense, if any, are social classes more (or less) real than biological species? And how is the concept of social progress to be defined: as identical to economic growth, technological advancement, political enfranchisement, decrease in social inequality, or enhancement of the quality of life? Every one of these questions is not only scientifico-philosophical: it is also ideological. Which is a reminder that even a rigorously scientific social study can be an ideological minefield—a good reason for keeping philosophically alert.

1.4. General Presuppositions

All research, whether empirical or theoretical, proceeds in the light of a number of logical, ontological, and epistemological presuppositions or tacit asumptions. For example, the need for clarity and logical consistency are usually taken for granted—except of course by the postmoderns, who take pride in "weak thinking." Besides, most social scientists admit the existence of irreducibly social facts—that is, facts that, though produced by organisms, are not biological like eating or feeling pain. This presupposition is far from obvious, and in fact it is rejected by the sociobiologists, who attempt to reduce social science to biology. But these can explain neither social inventions, such as the corporation, the university, or the sports club, nor the large variety of social orders. Nor can they explain social revolutions, such as the introduction of agriculture, the emergence of the state, the industrial revolution, mass literacy, democracy, the abolition of slavery, land reform, or the information revolution that has just started. After all, none of these processes can be traced to changes in the genome.

Another important philosophical presupposition is that there are social totalities (systems) characterized by emergent properties, such as social mobility, economic growth, and political stability, that cannot be attributed to persons. True, radical individualists reject the emergence hypothesis, but they do so at a high price: that of failing to understand why one and the same individual is likely to act differently when enacting different roles, either in different social systems or in the same system upon promotion or demotion.

Moreover, the very notion of social role or function makes no sense except with reference to other people in the same system. Think, for example, of the roles of office boy, apprentice, clerk, foreman, salesman, or manager. Every job description prescribes the task that the job holder is expected to perform in relation to other members of the system. Example: "Individual B is an executive in company C if, and only if, some members of C, other than B, report to B, and B is empowered to give them instructions likely to improve their performance." Thus, the actions of any member of the system only "make sense" (are functional) in relation to those of other members of the system.

A further philosophical presupposition of scientific sociology is that society exists independently of sociologists. This is the ontological component of scientific realism. Its epistemological partner is the thesis that social facts can be known at least in outline—or, equivalently, that there are objective sociological truths, albeit partial ones in most cases.

These theses contradict subjectivism, in particular constructivism (which will be met in chap. 9). But of course they are inherent in any scientific research. Indeed, if there were no social facts it would be impossible to study them, and if we do not hope to learn anything from their study, we won't bother.

But, as argued in the preface, realism is consistent with the so-called

Thomas "theorem," according to which whatever is regarded as real, will treated as if it were real. In other words, people, unlike most other animals, react not to real facts but rather to the way they see them. In particular, social relations, unlike physical relations, pass through the heads of people. For example, the relation between political boss and political client is not simply that of leader to voter. Indeed, the boss expects loyalty from his constituent in exchange for favors that he can do by using or abusing his power; and the client sees a possible benefactor in someone who may actually be a public malefactor for misusing a public good. Acknowledging the truth of the Thomas "theorem" involves no concession to subjectivism: it only adds subjective experience to the domain of facts to be studied objectively.

1.5. General Hypotheses

The opponents of the scientific approach to the study of social matter deny the existence of social laws: they hold that the social studies are necessarily idiographic or particularizing, not nomothetic or generalizing. Yet we do know a few social laws. Here is a random sample:

1. Birth rates are directly correlated with infant mortality and inversely correlated with the standard of living.
2. Social change is more frequent in heterogeneous than in homogeneous societies, and it is the deeper, the more pronounced the stratification.
3. The concentration of economic power is accompanied by a concentration of political and cultural power.
4. The cohesiveness of a social system is proportional to the participation of its members in various groups and activities, and decreases with segregation.
5. Modernization tends to replace the extended family with the nuclear family.
6. All organizations decline unless overhauled once in a while.
7. Poverty stunts physiological development.
8. Malnutrition and lack of skills hinder increase in productivity.
9. Pronounced social inequality hinders economic growth.
10. Sustained development is at once economic, political, and cultural.

In addition to these sociological, socioeconomic, and biosociological laws, there are a number of economic laws, such as that of diminishing returns, and politological ones, such as Tocqueville's—people revolt not when oppression is maximal but when it begins to slacken. So, social science is nomothetic as well as idiographic.

Still, it must be admitted that the set of known social laws is tiny by comparison with that of physics and chemistry. There are many reasons for this poverty. One of them is that human affairs are rather messy because they result ultimately from individual actions that are seldom fully rational and are often at cross purposes with one another. Another reason is that regularities are usually sought in the wrong place, namely in collections of data such as statistics and time series. While such data may suggest a few empirical regularities, they are unlikely to point to laws proper. The reason is that one and the same law is consistent with a whole sheaf of alternative trajectories or histories that differ from one another due to differences in initial or boundary conditions.

Authentic law statements are tested by data but not secreted by them. They must first be conjectured, then checked. Parallel: theoretical mechanics was not born until Newton invented his three law statements and checked them against the few kinematical laws known to him, among them Galileo's and Kepler's. He could never have inferred the laws from these low-level generalizations, if only because the latter do not include the two key high-level concepts of mass and acceleration.

In short, even assuming that all social behavior is lawful, it does not follow that these laws can be inferred from the reading of social data, that is, descriptions of the outcomes of social actions. Genuine law statements, unlike empirical generalizations, are theoretical: they are either axioms or theorems in hypothetico-deductive systems such as general equilibrium theory.

However, empirical generalizations and laws are not the only general statements in social science. These include also social norms, that is, rules of behavior adopted with the intention of solving social problems. Unlike laws, norms are social inventions and therefore they can be occasionally broken and eventually discarded.

1.6. Theory

Data hunters and gatherers distrust theories and oppose them to research—as if theoretical research did not exist. This distrust of theory has two roots: Positivism and the failure of "grand theories," such as those of Marx, Spencer, Dilthey, and Parsons. But the failure of a few attempts does not prove the failure of all endeavour to organize social knowledge into a family of theories. The failure in question only suggests starting by crafting what Merton (1957a) called "theories of the middle range." These are theories of a degree of generality lying between the all-purpose "grand theory" and the theoretical model that applies to a narrow range of facts.

Philosophers, as such, are not equipped to build social theories. However, their experience in analyzing existing and defunct theories in various fields should allow them to suggest the following rules for constructing theories.

1. Start by identifying a kind of social facts—or, what amounts to the same, a type of social systems, such as families, gangs, business concerns, or political parties.

2. Select a few features (properties) of the referents, namely those that look salient and are likely to be related to other features.

3. Represent every feature by a precise concept , such as a set or a function.

4. Guess relations among the resulting concepts—such as "Set A is included in set B," "Function f maps set A into set B," "The rate of change of function f is proportional to f itself," or "The frequency of the transition (mobility) of individuals from group A to group B is inversely proportional to the distance or dissimilarity between A and B (where this distance equals the numerosity of the difference A \ B)."

5. Conjoin these hypotheses with the relevant social indicators, to obtain propositions that can be confronted with the relevant empirical data. That is, operationalize the hypotheses.

6. Confront the operationalized hypotheses with the pertinent empirical data.

7. Evaluate the discrepancy between theory and evidence: check whether or not it is significant and, if it is, estimate the error.

8. Perform the corrections required by the disagreements with the data or other theories.

9. Apply the theory or model to a problem other than the one(s) that gave rise to it.

10. Generalize the theory or model either to include more variables or to apply to a wider kind of systems.

In short, philosophers of social science may contribute to restoring the balance between empirical and theoretical research, thus helping to avoid mindless data-gathering as well as wild speculation.

1.7. Theory-Data Bridges: Indicators

All social scientists are agreed on the importance of social indicators. But there is still no consensus as to what an indicator is. The reason for this deficit may be that the problem is not technical but philosophical. Indeed, an indicator is an observable variable that is assumed to manifest a latent or unobservable property or process. Shorter: an indicator is a symptom of an unobservable feature. For example, longevity indicates quality of life, GDP economic activity, voter turnout political participation, and number of citations intellectual influence.

However, it would be naive to believe that indicators raise only epistemological and methodological problems. They also raise the problem of causation, which is an ontological (or metaphysical) one. Indeed, in many cases symptoms are effects of underlying (often unobservable) causes. For example, ill-health may be caused by malnutrition, itself frequently an effect of poverty; technological advancement may reduce employment; political riots are manifestations of economic or political dissatisfaction—and so on. In all these cases changes in the observable variables—morbidity, employment rate, rioting frequency—are used to infer changes in the corresponding unobserved ones—malnutrition, technologiocal innovation, dissatisfaction. However, such causal links are not to be taken for granted, since sometimes, particularly in social matters, one and the same event may be due to different causes. This holds for sickness, unemployment, and violent street demonstrations. Because of such multiple causation, methodological caution is in order when proposing or using social indicators.

Indicators can be qualitative of quantitative. For example, political stability is an ambiguous indicator of either satisfaction or repression. On the other hand, the U.N. human development indicator is quantitative. Another splitting of indicators is into empirical and theoretical. A theoretical indicator is justified by a theory showing that it indicates what it purports to exhibit. So far, most social indicators are empirical. By contrast, some economic indicators are theoretical. For example, price elasticity—defined as the partial derivative of demand with respect to price—is an exact indicator of the willingness of consumers to pay a higher price for a commodity.

Physical and chemical indicators are reliable because they are backed up by theories, in which the observable variable, such as the angle of deviation of a magnetic needle, is a precise function of the electric current intensity. By contrast, most social indicators are problematic because they are not backed up by theories. Consequently, they tend to be either ambiguous or partial. In either case they invite philosophical analysis. Consider, for example, the problem of welfare indicators. The standard welfare indicator is money-income. However, income is an input, not an output. To be sure, the output—welfare—depends upon the input. But the latter is more than money-income: in fact it includes such noneconomic variables as health care, education, work environment (stressful or stimulating), and social status. The output in question is physiological fitness, including a low stress level associated with work satisfaction.

For example, malnutrition and poor health care during childhood lead to stunted growth and high rates of morbidity and mortality, which account for low labor productivity, which in turn helps explain economic underdevelopment. This was, incidentally, the theme of Robert Fogel's (1994) remarkable Nobel lecture on economic growth, population theory, and physiology. In it we learn, among other things, that the graph of the average mortality rate in a population vs. the body-mass index, equal to the weight in kilograms divided by the square of the height in meters, has the U-form and is minimal for 25. Consequently, the optimal average weight equals 25 times the square of the average height. We also learn that the average weight and height of male Frenchmen at the time of the French Revolution were 50 kg and 1.62 m respectively. As a consequence of their stunted growth, which in turn resulted from malnutrition, about 20 percent of the population could do no more than three hours of light work per day—whence the high percentage of beggars at the time (see also Tilly 1998).

This story is of interest to social metatheory on several counts. First, it shows that a well-corroborated causal relation can serve as a robust indicator when the effect is observable. Second, sociologists would be ill-advised to ignore biological and economic features—just as they would be wrong to attempt to reduce sociology to either biology or economics. A division into academic turfs need not map a division into social territories.

1.8. Inter-Theory Bridges

The standard view concerning the various social sciences is that they are mutually independent. Philosophers, who specialize in generalities, are likely to point out that this isolation is artificial and pernicious, because all the social sciences study one and the same thing, namely social facts. This does not entail that rational choice theorists are right in upholding the "economic imperialism" program, according to which all social facts ultimately result from calculated choices, whence all the social studies would be reducible to the study of individual behavior. I shall argue in chapter 5 that this program has fared just as poorly as the attempt of human sociobiology to reduce social science to biology and, in particular, genetics.

The fact that all the social sciences handle differently the same material only suggests that there there must be bridges between them. In fact, there are several such bridges or intersciences, such as social psychology, bioeconomics, socioeconomics, political sociology, and economic history. Besides, at least two social sciences, namely anthropology and archaeology, examine and interrelate all the aspects of the social systems they study, from kinship relations to production to trade to political organization to value and belief systems.

In sum, the social sciences are one, not because they have all been reduced to a more basic science, such as biology or psychology, but rather because, by virtue of the bridges among them, they constitute a conceptual system. In turn, this conceptual systemicity reflects the systemicity of the subject matter, namely society. To be sure we must distinguish the various subsystems of society—the biological, economic, political, and culture—but we should not detach them, for they are strongly bonded to one another. Consequently, some variables that are initially confined to special sciences, end up by being tackled by intersciences. For example, fertility depends on economic status and educational level, and it can be regulated by political measures.

1.9. Values and Morals

Max Weber's injunction to sociologists, to abstain from value judgments, has a philosophical root. This is Hume's emotivist or subjectivist view of values and morals as purely matters of taste. Since emotivism makes no room for the obvious cognitive component of valuation, Weber's rule is suspicious. Moreover, if adhered to it leads to cultural relativism, the view—fashionable among the so-called postmoderns—that all cultures are equivalent, whence there can be no social progress. Indeed, "[t]he price that must be paid for adopting this position is to make it impossible to condemn and suggest alternatives for even the most selfish and socially destructive ideas and behaviour, except on purely subjective grounds. It leaves no basis on which to act for the betterment of all human beings" (Trigger 1998: 5).

To be sure, Weber was no cultural relativist. On the contrary, he emphasized the overall progress brought about by modernization, and he indicted the Junkers for entrenching social backwardness in eastern Germany. Weber's motivation for preaching value-neutrality in sociology was purely methodological: he wished to preserve objectivity, which is indeed an essential component of the scientific approach. Regrettably, Weber confused objectivity with impartiality. Let me make this point with an example.

A sociologist of Hinduism is expected to state that this religion justifies the caste system. This is a well-known fact, and Weber (1920–21, 2 : chap. 1) pointed it out in no uncertain terms. But this need not end here: nothing prevents an objective sociologist from noting the oppression and moral degradation inherent in the caste system, and from asserting the social and moral superiority of rival egalitarian religions, such as Christianity and Islam, as well as of quasi-religions, such as Buddhism and Jainism. Yet Dumont (1966, 52) has claimed that "caste is a state of mind"—overlooking the fact that, until not so long ago, any attempts to climb up the caste system, even from shoemaker to tailor, were punishable by death. In short, scientific objectivity is compatible with ethical and political partiality.

Presumably, Weber did not realize that the ontological and methodological individualism he preached, but hardly practiced, had a moral concomitant, namely, selfishness—just as abject conformism is the moral companion of holism. Another example: Marx's adoption of dialectics, the ontology of conflict, led him to stating that "violence is the midwife of history." Mercifully he was not consistent enough to praise warmongering. But those of his followers who earned their living fighting in the Cold War can be accused of hypocrisy when preaching peaceful international coexistence while teaching a philosophy of war. This attitude was regrettably matched by the support democratic governments gave corrupt anticommunist dictators the world over. Ideologies can mask as well as reveal.

In sum, scientific sociologists cannot ignore values and morals, but should identify and study them objectively. And, to succeed in this enterprise, they cannot help using some value theory and moral philosophy.

1.10. Conclusions

Some of the toughest philosophical problems have been solved by science. Examples: What are matter, life, and mind, space, time, and chance? Likewise, all of the deepest scientific problems involve some philosophy. Examples: What is society: aggregate or system? What is more important in social life: strife or cooperation? How are social facts best studied: scientifically or hermeneutically? Is mathematical modelling necessary, sufficient, or neither to understand social facts? This being so, such problems cannot be handled successfully without a modicum of philosophy.

Because they are professional generalists, philosophers should be naturally curious about the general ideas of social science. And, because they are expected to master certain formal tools, they are also expected to excel at the task of analyzing general ideas. However, these expectations are rarely fulfilled: in fact, most philosophers stay aloof from current social research even while pretending to write about it.

This failure of most philosophers to come to grips with the philosophical problematics of social science has had a bad effect. It has led most social scientists to feel indifference or disdain for philosophy, while tackling some of the philosophical problems they have come across without the benefit of either a general philosophical view or such philosophical tools as formal logic and semantics.

This instant diagnosis of the present state of the sociology/philosophy interface suggests the remedy: Let philosophers familiarize themselves with social research; let sociologists try and contribute to the philosophy of their own discipline; and let people from the two groups hang out together and exchange puzzles, methods, guesses, and findings.

2

Mechanism

If we wish to understand a real thing, be it natural, social, biosocial, or artificial, we must find out how it works. That is, real things and their changes are explained by unveiling their mechanisms: in this respect social science does not differ from natural science. Thus molecular motion explains evaporation, fermentation the transformation of grapes into wine, and cooperation coordination. The following examples should help to make this point.

The way Medicare works for all Canadian residents is this. Whenever you are in need of health care, you present your Medicare card to the doctor or hospital of your choice, and are treated without paying anything directly. The doctor or hospital bills the provincial government, which pays the bill out of tax revenues. These two intertwined processes, involving the patient-caregiver and caregiver-government relations, constitute the mechanism of Canadian Medicare. Like all other social processes, this one occurs on two tiers: the microsocial or individual, and the macrosocial or collective ones.

Second example: How to explain the strong positive correlation between poverty and unemployment? Are people poor for being unemployed, or the other way round? It turns out that both simple causal arrows are simplistic, if only because they omit a crucial factor, namely malnutrition, which decreases a person's productivity (see, e.g., Dasgupta and Ray 1986, Fogel 1994). This suggests that the correlation in question is the outcome of a more complex social process. A possible mechanism is the causal cycle (aka positive feedback loop): Poverty → malnutrition and lack of skills → marginality → uncmployment → poverty.

And yet there are remarkably few studies of social mechanisms. For instance, none of the review articles published by the *Annual Review of Sociology* between 1975 and 1995 deals specifically with social mechanisms. Could this neglect be due, at least in part, to a research strategy informed by the empiricist philosophy of science, according to which the sole aim of science is to gather data and compress them into empirical generalizations, abstaining from conjecturing the hidden mechanisms underlying the perceptible facts and thus explaining the corresponding data? This suspicion motivates the present philosophical inquiry into mechanisms, in particular social mechanisms, and explanation. This inquiry requires the elucidation of a number of key concepts, such as those of system, process, mechanism, and explanation through the unveiling of the mechanisms that drive (or block) processes in natural or social systems.

2.1. The Importance of Mechanism

Let us start by noting that the original concept of a mechanism has been considerably broadened since the seventeenth century, when natural science was dominated by mechanics. (See d'Abro 1939 for the decline of the mechanistic world view in physics itself.) Indeed, whereas a few of the mechanisms studied by contemporary science and technology are mechanical, most are not. Indeed, there are mechanisms of many kinds: electromagnetic, nuclear, chemical, cellular, intercellular, ecological, economic, political, and so on. For example, inclusion and exclusion, conflict and cooperation, participation and segregation, coercion and rebellion, are conspicuous social mechanisms. So are imitation and trade, migration and colonization, technological innovation and the various modes of social control. Likewise the *modi operandi* in formal organizations, such as schools, business firms, or government departments, are social mechanisms.

For instance, Merton (1957b: 111) conjectured the operation of various "social mechanisms [such as status ranking, distribution of power and authority, and creation of a private sphere] which serve to articulate the expectations of those in the role-set [set of roles associated to a status] so that the occupant of a status is confronted with less conflict than would obtain if these mechanisms were not at work." And Tilly (1998) analyzes and inter-relates four mechanisms that cause and maintain social inequality, which he calls exploitation, opportunity hoarding [acquisition of monopoly on a resource], emulation, and adaptation. Note that the mechanisms referred to by both Merton and Tilly are not things but processes, that is, changes of state. This point is central in the definition of the concept of a mechanism to be proposed below.

Any explanation involving reference to a mechanism may be said to be *mechanismic*. This qualifier distinguishes explanation proper from mere subsumption of particulars under universals—as in the standard "covering law model" of scientific explanation proposed by the neopositivists. Regrettably this distinction is drawn only occasionally (e.g., by Bunge 1979 [1959], 1964,1967b,1983; Wallace 1983; and Athearn 1994). Yet it should be obvious. Indeed, stating that a certain fact happens the way it does for being an instance of a generalization is no explanation at all, for it supplies no understanding: it is just identifying the fact in question as a member of the class defined by the given generalization.

For example, it is correct but not very illuminating to reason that someone is bound to die eventually because he or she is human, and it so happens that all humans are mortal. Though logically impeccable, this argument is unilluminating because it does not point to any mechanisms. Some scientists are trying to uncover the senescence and death mechanisms, such as repeated DNA damage and rearrangement, as well as accident and apoptosis (genetically programmed death), to understand why humans must die. Likewise, it is well known that there are two main suicide mechanisms, which are sometimes strongly coupled: clinical depression and social marginality.

Again, the statement that human triads (of equals) tend to be unstable subsumes, but does not explain, why this or that particular business or government triumvirate did not last. What does explain the instability of triads of equals is of course that two members of the triad may gang up against the third: in this particular case the mechanism is coalition. By contrast, in triads of unequals, third parties may divide, exploit, or else consolidate the original dyads, depending on the process they set in motion—such as fueling dissent, arbitration, or bridge-building (Simmel 1950 [1908]: 87–169). In both cases the *tertius* is bound to alter some of the mechanisms operating in the dyad, whether by throwing a spanner into its works or by acting as buffer, lubricant, or even adhesive—to indulge in engineering metaphors.

Mechanismic explanation differs not only from mere subsumption but also from the "comprehensive" or "interpretive" account favored by the hermeneutic or *Verstehen* school. According to this view, to understand a social fact is to "interpret" it, that is, to show (actually guess) the "sense" or "meaning" (actually purpose or goal) it has for the agent(s) in question—much as one interprets a text. The *Verstehen* operation has been variously construed: by Dilthey as empathy, by Weber as attribution of purpose; and by Pareto and Boudon as a reconstruction of the reasons, good or bad, driving the agent. In either version the product is an intuitive and empirically untestable conjecture, not a testable scientific hypothesis. Indeed, social scientists *qua* such—particularly historians— do not have the tools to "get into people's minds"—particularly if, like Durkheim, Pareto and Weber, they decline the help of psychology.

Moreover, an invocation to *Verstehen* makes no reference to any *social* mechanism: it only hints at an inner (mental) source of individual action, whether social or not. For example, stating that I "understand" (*verstehe*) why Private Johnny fled the battlefield, because I would have done the same had I been in his boots, or that he fled because he must have wanted to stay alive, may well be true. But in either case no mechanism proper is being conjectured or discovered: both are descriptions in ordinary language and folk psychology terms. Hence, *pace* the hermeneuticists, *Verstehen* (comprehension or interpretation) cannot replace explanation in social science: at best it may suggest investigation, or supplement explanation proper for heuristic or pedagogical purposes. However, given Dilthey's and Weber's obscurity in methodological and philosophical matters, any hermeneutics of their own hermeneutics is debatable (see von Schelting 1934; Albert 1994; Bunge 1996).

Finally, mechanismic explanation differs also from functional or teleological explanation, as in "Feature A evolved (or was set up) for function B, which is necessary for (biological or social) viability." Indeed, conjecturing that a certain system is driven by such-and-such mechanism(s) involves no reference to adaptation or value, in particular usefulness to the given system or some other system—all the more so since certain features of either organisms or social systems can be maladaptive. The emergence of an interesting new thing or property of a thing should certainly be explained in terms of some mechanism or other, but not necessarily by reference to its value, which may be nil or even negative rather than positive. (For instance, could dollar bills not be blue rather than green? Why are there dysfunctional mechanisms in every society? And why is Academia destructing itself by producing and diffusing "postmodern" gobbledygook?)

To be sure, some human actions are purposive, but indicating their (known or conjectured) purpose, function or usefulness performs only part of the job. We also need to know (or guess) something about the mechanism(s) likely to bring about the desired goal or prevent its attainment. For example, it is not enough to state that strict monetary measures were adopted to curb inflation: we must also know whether such measures were effective—that is, whether the given cause had the expected effect. Besides, if tight credit control proves to be effective to curb inflation in a given case, we also need to know whether it may not have monstrously perverse side effects, such as mass unemployment or even social unrest and the concomitant threat to democratic institutions. And all this requires an adequate macrosocioeconomic theory, one that has so far eluded economists—perhaps because they usually overlook the complex socio-economico-political mechanisms that underlie all large social changes. Unless such mechanisms are known, the corresponding changes remain unexplained. And unless a mechanism is known, if only in outline, it cannot be regulated efficiently. This holds for social systems as well as for brains, cars and things: No mechanism, neither understanding nor efficient control. This is the main thesis to be expounded, discussed and illustrated in the following.

2.2. Mechanisms in General

I stipulate that a *mechanism is a process in a concrete system,* such that it is capable of bringing about or preventing some change in the system as a whole or in some of its subsystems. Shorter: a mechanism is whatever process makes a complex thing work. In other words, a mechanism is the way a process proceeds. For example, the mechanism of flotation (a process) is the resultant of two mutually opposed forces: gravitation and buoyancy. Plants grow (a process) by way of two mechanisms (processes): cell swelling and cell division. The sudden deficits in motor coordination (a process) or in speech (another process) that accompany a stroke result from either of two vascular mechanisms (processes): hemorhage or blocking of circulation in the brain. Biological evolution (a process) proceeds mainly via two mechanisms: genic change and selection. Social systems "work" (a process) through two main mechanisms (processes): cooperation and competition. Scientific teams and communities advance (a process) driven by several mechanisms (processes): observation, hypothesis, calculation, discussion, and so on.

Presumably, an omniscient being would not need the concept of a mechanism, because to him all boxes would be translucent. He could make do with the single concept of a process, for he would conceive of every process as a (simple or composite) mechanism. He would think that only finite beings, who must guess what goes behind appearances, need to resort to the function/mechanism distinction. However, whether or not omniscient, every knower needs to distinguish between essential and inessential processes in a system: those that make the system what it is, and those that can be stopped without changing the nature of the system. Only the former qualify as mechanisms. For instance, trading is the mechanism that keeps a business firm going. Other processes occurring in the firm, such as smooth coordination or infighting, growth or decline, are important but do not define the type of system as much as trading does.

Most of the contributors to the Hedström and Swedberg (1998) collective volume on social mechanisms—the first on the subject—define these as models. By contrast, in my view—which is that prevailing among natural scientists and engineers—mechanisms are not pieces of reasoning but pieces of the furniture of the real world. Only the conceptual models of mechanisms belong in our scientific reasonings about the world. So much so, that usually one and the same mechanism may be modeled in different ways, and that some hypothetical mechanisms, such as Divine Providence and the Invisible Hand, have no real counterparts.

A few examples should illustrate and clarify the proposed definition. A physiological mechanism is a collection of processes inside an organism, and a political mechanism—such as popular mobilization in favor or against a proposed bill—is a collection of processes inside a polity or among polities. Again, in the ideal free market the price mechanism is the process that sends prices up when demand increases, and down when supply is in excess. Banks, insurance companies, the IMF, and OPEC are systems endowed with specific mechanisms to offset or at least cushion the impact of large unexpected changes in income and expenditure, namely saving during bonanzas and spending during hard times.

Far more generic mechanisms are displacement and rotation, oscillation and damping, accretion and attrition, combination and dissociation, feedback and feedforward, fermentation and metabolism, cell division and natural selection. By contrast, concentration and dispersal, just like contagion, birth, and death, are not mechanisms but processes or events resulting from the operation of mechanisms—such as those of cell division and morphogenesis in the case of birth. Likewise economic growth is a process resulting from such mechanisms as technological innovation, the acumulation of capital, and sometimes the looting of colonies as well. And the economic cycles are not mechanisms but processes whose mechanisms are still largely unknown.

The preceding calls for a clarification of the notions of a system and a process in a system. A *concrete system* is a bundle of real things held together by some bonds or forces, behaving as a unit in some respects, and (except for the universe as a whole) embedded in some environment. Atoms, molecules, crystals, stars, cells, multicellular organisms, ecosystems, cohesive social groups—such as families, firms, and entire societies—are concrete systems. So are all material artifacts. By contrast, theories, classifications and codes are conceptual systems; and systems of signs, such as languages, are semiotic ones. On the other hand mere collections of items, even if they are of the same kind, are not systems, for they do not hang together. For example, cohorts, same-income groups and social classes are not social systems but aggregates, best called "human groups."

It may be helpful to distinguish five basic types of system: (a) *natural,* such as a molecule or an organism; (b) *social*, such as a school or a firm; (c) *technical*, such as a machine or a television network; (d) *conceptual*, such as a theory (hypothetico-deductive system) or a legal code; and (d) *semiotic,* such as a language or a blueprint. Every system kind is characterized by properties of its own, and neither kind is reducible to another, even though it may be composed of items of a different type. Thus, organisms are composed of chemical entities but they are not chemical systems; likewise, organizations are composed of persons but they are impersonal.

A caution is in place. Systems are sometimes called "structures," a misnomer because every structure is a property, not a thing. (There are structureless objects, such as photons, but not objectless structures: every structure is the structure of some object.) Whoever conflates the concepts of system and structure risks incurring oxymorons such as "the structure of a structure." As for the notion of a process in a thing, it may be elucidated as a sequence of states of the thing in question, such as the diffusion of a habit, the recovery of an economy, or the democratization of a polity—all three of which are irreducibly social.

A concrete system may be analyzed into its composition (collection of parts), environment, and structure (set of bonds or couplings between system components and things in the environment that influence or are influenced by the former). Obviously, concrete systems come in a huge variety of kinds and sizes. In particular, there is an uncounted number of types of social system, from the childless couple to the informal social network, from the neighborhood supermarket to the transnational corporation, from the village council to the U.N., and so on. (For a semi-formalized and general theory of systems with applications to sociology see Bunge 1979. Incidentally, beware of systems theories purporting to account for everything without the help of empirical investigation, as well as of systems philosophies that are nothing but old reheated holism.)

A further clarification is in order, namely this. Every mechanism is a process, but the converse is false. For example, economic growth is a process resulting from the operation of certain production, trade, and political mechanisms, such as R&D, marketing, and intervention in foreign affairs, together with unforeseen favorable circumstances—aka as good luck.

So much for terminological matters. Let me now stick my neck out and propose a few substantive assumptions. To begin with, I submit that *all concrete systems are endowed with one or more mechanisms that drive or block their transformations.* (The rule is one mechanism-one system, not the converse.) Note the qualifier "concrete": it makes no sense to speak of mechanisms of conceptual objects such as theories. To be sure there are mathematical systems, such as groups, spaces, and their corresponding theories, but not mathematical mechanisms—though of course there are mathematical representations of some mechanisms. Note also the word "system": indivisible things, such as electrons and photons, change without the intervention of any mechanisms. Such simples can only be components of systems. (See Bunge 1979: 282 for both the definition and the assumption.)

Every mechanism is thus a mechanism for either change or control of change. Hence, whereas existence is not to be explained, both coming into existence (emergence) and extinction (submergence) do call for explanation. The change may be quantitative, qualitative, or both at once. For example, displacement and rotation, as well as accretion and attrition, are quantitative changes—although they occasionally result in qualitative leaps. By contrast, alterations in mode of production, trade, or governance are qualitative. The most important of all qualitative changes are alterations in structure, such as the restructuring of a developing organism or a formal organization. Such changes may or may not result from or in changes in either the composition or the environment of the system. For example, a business firm may be reorganized, in order to meet new technological or market challenges, without firing or hiring anyone.

The disclosure of a mechanism starts by analyzing the system in question, that is, by showing (or conjecturing) its composition, structure (relations among the parts), and connections with the environment. And it proceeds by showing (or hypothesizing) what the system components do (specific function) and how they do it (specific mechanism).

For example, one explains the behavior of a weight-driven grandfather clock by revealing its parts and the way they interact, as well as the action of the gravitational field upon the driving weight. Pharmacodynamics explains how drugs work by exhibiting the biochemical reactions they elicit or block, quicken or slow down. Likewise we explain the performance of a business firm by exhibiting its composition, organization, and environment (in particular the market): we show what the firm members do, the way they do it, and the manner in which they interact with one another and with their environment. Should anything go wrong with the firm, one should attempt to locate the fault in the system composition, structure, or environment: this is the practical import of the conceptual analysis of a system. (For more on the composition-environment-structure analysis see Bunge 1979, 1996, 1998.)

Every major social change is likely to be biological, psychological, demographic, economic, political, and cultural—either simultaneously or in succession. (Think of the changes, both micro- and macrosocial, brought about by war, rapid industrialization, mass unemployment; or of such major social inventions as the state, taxation, military draft, the university, insurance, capitalism, large-scale manufacture, the transportation network, federalism, family planning, labor unionization, or social programs in public health or education.) Hence the mechanism of every major social change is likely to be a combination of mechanisms of various kinds coupled together. (For example, modernization comes together with industrialization, urbanization, the strengthening of the state, advances in education and political participation, bureaucratization, and secularization—as well as pollution, the spread of contagious diseases, and social unrest.) Therefore all unifactorial (in particular unicausal) explanations of social change are at best partial.

Let me emphasize a point made a while ago. Because change occurs only in concrete complex things, it makes no sense to talk about mechanisms in pure ideas or abstract objects, such as sets, functions, algorithms, or grammars, for nothing happens in them (when taken in and by themselves). In other words, the concept of a mechanism is alien to logic, mathematics and general linguistics, neither of which knows of time. This is why logic, mathematics, and general linguistics explain nothing by themselves. (Of course, workers in these fields may explain the motivations for some of their actions, but this is part of methodology, psychology, or didactics.)

By the same token, there can be no question of mechanisms operating in the putatively immaterial soul or mind, for nothing happens in it.

(Plato realized that ideal objects, such as mathematical constructs, are unchanging. He was wrong only in assuming that ideas exist by themselves and forever, a double error first corrected by Aristotle, then by the history of ideas, and finally by physiological psychology.)

Therefore, strictly speaking, we must regard the expression "psychological mechanism" as shorthand for the corresponding neurophysiological mechanism. In other words, only physiological psychology can explain the mental processes described by classical (or "empty organism") psychology. Psychology can tell what and when, but only neuropsychology can find out where and how. (Not surprisingly, Karl Lashley's major work, published in 1929, was titled *Brain Mechanisms and Intelligence.*) For example, neuropsychologists are trying to account for decision-making processes (and their impairment) in terms of neural mechanisms, particularly in the frontal lobe (see, e.g., Damasio et al., eds. 1996). (For the explanation of mental processes in terms of biological mechanisms, such as those of cell assembly and cell death, see, e.g., Hebb [1980]; Kosslyn and Koenig 1995; Beaumont, et al., eds. [1996].) Plans, strategies, methods, algorithms, computer programs, and the like are parallel: only their implementation in physical, chemical, biological or social matter are mechanisms.

Resorting to immaterial mechanisms is an indicator of spiritualism or even magical thinking, as exemplified by the psychoanalytic account of forgetfulness in terms of repression. By contrast, it makes good scientific sense to talk about the *brain* mechanisms involved in feeling or thinking, or about the *social* mechanisms that favor or inhibit religious, linguistic, and other cultural changes. For instance, it makes sense to ask why pure mathematics has grown sensationally since the Second World War, whereas mathematical sociology started to decline in the 1970s. Both questions cry out for causal answers, that is, for hypotheses involving causal mechanisms operating in the scientific communities and their host societies during the periods in question, in addition to the purely intellectual processes occurring in some brains—inquiring ones in the former case, and hostile to clarity and rigor in the second.

Mechanisms can be causal, probabilistic, or mixed. Consequently, an explanation can be constructed in terms of causation, randomness, or a combination of both—as with the cases of hit-and-miss processes, the deliberate random shuffling of a pack of cards, and random mating. For example, an explanation of rebellion in terms of relative deprivation is causal. By contrast, an explanation of the heterogeneity of a given collection of items in terms of either random encounters or of random sampling is probabilistic. And the evolutionary explanation of speciation in terms of random mutation, hybridization, symbiosis, geographic isolation, and a few other "forces" is hybrid. So is the contagion mechanism: the pathogen is a causal agent, but many of the contacts between sickness carriers and others are random. The propagation of rumors is parallel. Not so the diffusion of technological inventions: they may be a priori more or less likely to occur, but not more or less probable.

Two types of causal mechanism must be distinguished: Type I, or involving *energy transfer,* as in manual work and combat; and type II, or involving a *triggering signal,* as in giving an order to fire a gun or an employee (Bunge 1996). In the first case the quantity of energy being transferred is critical, whereas in the second a small energy transfer may trigger a process involving a large energy. Hence type I and type II causation may be called strong and weak energy transfer respectively. (Caution: there is no such thing as pure information, that is, information without a physical carrier.) In other words, in Type II processes the effect may be "disproportionate" to the cause: that is, a very small cause may trigger a process ending up in a catastrophic effect—such as the proverbial shout in a canyon, that triggers a landslide. This is particularly the case with unstable systems, such as social systems relying on a strong but, alas, mortal leader, as well as with unpopular governments that rely only on coercion. In these cases the removal of a single very powerful person may cause the breakdown of the whole system—provided the latter was unstable to begin with.

It may be conjectured that causal mechanisms of both types exist on all levels of reality. However, type II mechanisms are particularly conspicuous and important on the biological and social levels. This is because all organisms and all social systems (a) are endowed with communication systems, and (b) are at best in either a steady or a metastable state, at worst in an unstable one. Perhaps all major (that is, structural) social changes involve tangles of causal arrows of both types, enhanced or weakened by "accidents" or interfering circumstances, such as bad weather, the discovery of a new natural resource, the invention of a new idea, or the intervention of the right person at the right place and time.

2.3. Conjecturing and Formalizing

Most mechanisms, whether social or physical, are hidden. Thus, we do not perceive the senescence mechanisms of business firms, such as low reinvestment rate, technological conservatism, job dissatisfaction, and the complacency generated by monopoly, anymore than we perceive the mechanisms of planetary motion, telecommunication, photosynthesis, or metabolic turnover. Now, occult mechanisms cannot be inferred from empirical data: they must be conjectured. For example, astronomers can measure positions and velocities, but they cannot read the law of gravitation off their data: such law had to be invented (and of course checked). Likewise, economists cannot read socioeconomic mechanisms off economic indicators, statistical correlations, or time-series; and political scientists cannot read structural changes off the statistics of mass rallies, riots, or political crimes. The mechanisms underlying such empirical information must be conjectured.

But of course a conjecture has got to be empirically testable if it is to be regarded as scientific. (Ideally a scientific hypothesis, unless it is extremely general, is both confirmable and falsifiable: see Bunge 1967b.) And the conjecture must have been empirically confirmed to be regarded as true to some degree. For example, since the mid-twentieth century it had been known that lung cancer and smoking are strongly correlated. But only laboratory experiments on the action of nicotine and tar upon living tissue succeeded in testing (and confirming) the hypothesis that there is a definite causal link underneath the statistical correlation: we now know definitely that smoking may cause lung cancer. (And we also know of further cancer mechanisms, such as the switching on or off of certain genes.) Likewise, it has been found that obesity—which affects about 20 percent of the American population—is strongly correlated with excessive television watching. The mechanism seems to be this: About half of American television commercials advertise food, particularly junk food, so that television addicts are stimulated to eating in excess while being glued to the screen, on top of which they get no exercise. In short, epidemiology—a biosocial science—is necessary but insufficient: We must try to ferret out the mechanism(s) underlying every epidemiological association. For example, only behavioral epidemiologists have been able to establish that intensive tobacco marketing doubles the risk that adolescents start smoking, which in turn more than doubles their risk of their contracting nicotine-related diseases.

Because most mechanisms are hidden, they must be conjectured before they can actually be discovered. Consequently, no self-respecting empiricist (or positivist) can condone the very idea of a mechanism. In fact, consistent positivists in the Ptolemy-Hume-Comte-Mach-

Kirchhoff-Pearson-Duhem-Ostwald-Watson-Bridgman-Skinner tradition are descriptivists: they reject explanations in terms of hidden mechanisms, in particular causes, for regarding them as metaphysical misfits. They care only for descriptions of observable facts and for associations between directly observable variables such as inputs and outputs. For the same reason they distrust generalizations going much beyond the data base.

Hence, for all their professed love of science, positivists will refuse to explain, say, why biomedical researchers wish to dig below symptoms to track down the disease mechanism in order to alter it so as to restore good health. Nor will positivists attempt to explain why all bureaucracies, whether governmental or private, are conservative. And yet it is worth while to try and explain this trite yet true descriptive statement, by showing what makes bureaucracies tick. A plausible hypothesis is that every bureaucracy is set up or maintained to shore up the establishment or implement given policies, not to rock the boat—and the bureaucracy itself is one of the systems to be preserved in the interest of its members.

Descriptivism not only curtails scientific research: it also encourages collecting disjointed anecdotal material and the blind search for statistical correlations. This strategy may also encourage superstitious beliefs rooted in mere coincidences or "synchronies," whereas a demand for plausible mechanismic explanation would rule them out. And descriptivism enshrines mysteries instead of turning them into research problems. For example, eclipses used to inspire terror until their mechanism (namely, the interposition of either the moon or the sun) was disclosed. Malaria, bubonic plague, tuberculosis, syphilis, epilepsy, and other diseases used to be attributed supernatural origins until the respective causal agents were discovered. There is nothing like the disclosure of mechanism to destroy myths and to empower us to control natural and social processes.

Descriptivism also encourages taking seriously mirages such as immortality and the paranormal. Indeed, if the mortal condition could only be confirmed by mortality statistics, then we could not exclude the possibility that one day an immortal man or woman will turn up. (Incidentally, this hypothesis is empiricaly irrefutable in real time.) Only biologists can prove that all multicellular organisms are bound to die eventually even if they were to suffer no accidents (recall section 2.1). "All men are mortal" has thus ceased to be a mere empirical generalization supported only by observation, to become a biological law. An induction has been explained in mechanismic, hence noninductive, terms.

Likewise, if the only way to evaluate the paranormal were to go on making observations and experiments on individuals who claim to possess paranormal abilities, then parapsychologists would be justified in retaining their faith despite a century and a half of disappointments. But even a modest acquaintance with physiological psychology suffices to realize that there are *can* be no mechanisms underlying telepathy, precognition, telekinesis, and the like, because mental processes are brain processes, and therefore as little transmissible at a distance as digestion. In general, the demand for plausible and empirically testable mechanism is bound to reduce gullibility and spare us wrongheaded research projects.

Although positivism-bashing has become a fashionable sport in the antiscience camp, positivist practice is still rampant even in that camp. Thus, despite their loud condemnations of positivism, the phenomenological sociologists (such as Alfred Schütz), hermeneuticists (like Clifford Geertz), and ethnomethodologists (such as Harold Garfinkel) too reject generalization and mechanism. In fact, their findings concern only banal occurrences in everyday life ("lifeworld"), with no indication of the psychological source or the social context, much less of the mechanisms, of the facts they record. Good novelists and playwrights, such as Cervantes, Shakespeare, Austen, Balzac, Tolstoy, Ibsen, or García Márquez, have handled similar empirical material with far greater psychological and sociological insight—and without pretentious jargon.

In the natural sciences empiricists have systematically favored kinematics over dynamics, and they have denounced atomism and supported stimulus-response (or behaviorist) accounts of animal behavior. And in the field of social studies positivists devote all their energies to data gathering and "data mining," that is, the search for associations (in particular statistical correlations) among variables. (Imagine what would have happened if Newton had abstained from positing unobservables such as mass and gravitation, and from postulating laws, focusing instead on observable properties and events and their statistical correlations. It has been noted that, luckily for science, the very concept of statistical regression was unknown in Newton's time.)

As is well known, positivists since Hume have rejected causal mechanisms. If preferred, they have redefined causation as regular conjunction or succession. This explains their preference for phenomenological law statements such as "In an ideal gas at constant temperature pressure times volume is a constant," and rate equations of the form "The rate of change of X is such and such a function of both X and time." Such equations are strictly descriptive. The former does not tell us that, as volume decreases, the number of molecular impacts on the container wall increases—this being the mechanism of the increase in internal pressure. Nor does a rate equation tell us what might drive or stop the change in question.

Incidentally, although I admire mathematical sociology, I do not share the belief that formalization, particularly when it involves differential equations, compels the investigator to specify the mechanism of a process (Sørensen 1979). In fact, a rate equation may represent a purely kinematical "flux of forms," to employ a medieval expression. Hence it is good only for description and prediction. Fourier's equation for the propagation of heat along a slab is a case in point. As Fourier (1888 [1822], I : 538) himself emphasized, the equation merely describes a diffusion process: it represents no mechanism, although it precludes none. In particular, Fourier's equation is consistent with the hypotheses that heat is a fluid ("caloric"), or random atomic or molecular motion and collision.

Actually some mechanisms can be modeled without the help of differential equations. This point bears some elaboration because mathematical economists have abused this mathematical tool without any effects other than intimidating or seducing sociologists. Consider for instance the following mechanismic (and systemic) explanation of voluntary human migration (Bunge 1969b). Assume that what attracts people to other countries are differences in opportunities, or possibilities of attaining certain basic personal goals, which may range from mere survival to advancement of self or family. (Note the reference to both a micro level and a macro one.) The strength of this drive may be called *migratory pressure*. Let us expand this intuitive hypothesis into a formal model.

Call P_{ij} the migratory pressure from region i to region j, and suppose that it is only a function of the difference $E_j - E_i$, where E_k is the enticement offered by region k—as measured, for instance, by the going median annual disposable income in k. More specifically, assume that the migratory pressure is a linear function of that difference:

$$P_{ij} = a \left[(E_j - E_i)/(E_i + E_j) \right] + b , \qquad [1]$$

where a and b are real numbers to be estimated from data concerning the (i, j) pair. A possible interpretation of these parameters is this:

Whereas a represents the permeability of the border (in the $i \rightarrow j$ direction), b is a global representative of all the remaining enticing variables.

Let us now add a second assumption: namely, that the migratory flux φij between the regions i and j, at any given time t, is proportional to both the migratory pressure P_{ij} and the population density $\delta_i (t)$ of the sender region at that time, relative to the population density δ_j of the receiver region at the same time. In symbols,

$$\varphi_{ij} = P_{ij} \cdot \delta_i (t) / \delta_j (t) \qquad [2]$$

Clearly, the total migratory flux into region j equals the sum of [2] over all the socially (but perhaps not geographically) adjacent regions:

$$\Phi_j = \Sigma_i \varphi_{ij} . \qquad [3]$$

The explicit expression for the total migratory flux into region j is obtained by introducing [1] and [2] into [3]:

$$\Phi_j = \Sigma_i \neq_j a [\delta_i (t) (E_j - E_i) / \delta_j (t) (E_i + E_j)] + b . \qquad [4]$$

Note the following points of methodological interest. First, [1] is a typically mechanismic hypothesis: it tells what drives people from one place to another. Second, whereas the fluxes are sociological variables, the enticing factors are biopsychosociological ones. Thus the social process described by Φ_j is explained by "dipping to the level of the individual," as Coleman (1990) would say—though not all the way, because no reference to brain mechanisms had been made. However, the decision to emigrate depends not only upon personal circumstances but also upon irreducibly social (or systemic) features, such as living standards and border crossing facilities and barriers. Here, as elsewhere, choice and constraint (or agency and structure, individual and system) go hand in hand. Third, the measurable variables are the enticing factors E_k, the population densities δ_i, the partial migratory fluxes φ_{ij}, and the total flux Φ_j. By contrast, the migratory pressures P_{ij} are hypothetical constructs: their values must be inferred from the population densities and the partial migratory fluxes via formula [2]. Fourth, the above model can easily be complicated, and thus rendered more realistic, by including all the known enticing variables. Moreover, the same initial assumption may be couched in probabilistic terms—actually in two alternative ways (see Bunge 1969b). Fifth—and this is the point of the exercise—this model describes the conjectured mechanism of a process without involving any differential equations. Whether the model actually matches the data is beside the point in the present context.

In conclusion, whereas description is indispensable, descriptivism is crippling. This is one more reminder of the pertinence of the maxim: Adopt a shallow philosophy and you'll engage in superficial scientific research.

2.4. Mechanismic Hypotheses and Theories

A description of a process, without any reference to the underlying mechanism(s), may be said to be *kinematical.* Kinematical accounts are devoid of explanatory power. Thus, the statement that the bottom of the valley is the ultimate resting place of a boulder rolling down the slope of a hill, because this is the least energy state, is true but hardly more illuminating than Aristotle's view, that it is the boulder's "natural place." What does have some explanatory power is the statement that the bottom of the valley exerts a reaction that balances the boulder's weight, and thus prevents it from going further down. Likewise, it is true that the spherical configuration of air bubbles, drops of oil in water, and cell membranes corresponds to the lowest energy state, but this does not explain much. What does explain the spherical shape of such things is that they are subject to molecular impacts in all directions, and that their components are held together by certain forces. This is an explanation proper because it points to mechanisms.

Any study of mechanisms of some kind may be said to be *dynamical.* (Regrettably, nearly all of the so-called dynamical models of social change are actually kinematical: see, e.g., Tuma and Hannan 1988.) Exhibiting the (actual or possible) mechanism of a process entails being able to describe it, but the converse is false. In other words, the composition and structure of a concrete system jointly determine its behavior, but not conversely. Again: dynamics entails kinematics, not the other way round. In other words, mechanismic explanation subsumes subsumption, not conversely. Indeed, one and the same kinematics may result from alternative dynamics.

(To put it formally: a kinematical law statement of the form $A \Rightarrow B$ is entailed by the pair of dynamical laws $A \Rightarrow M$, $M \Rightarrow B$. Replacing M with an alternative hypothetical mechanism N will yield the same phenomenological result $A \Rightarrow B$. To a positivist, this only shows that mechanisms are dispensable. To a realist, it shows that mechanismic hypotheses are richer than the corresponding black box ones, but must be checked before being pronounced true.)

For example, the hands of a watch may be driven by either mechanical or electronic works. A computation may be performed either by a brain or by a computer, although the mechanisms operating in the two systems are totally different. Headaches are symptomatic of a variety of alternative physiological processes. Likewise, human population changes may be caused by changes in natural birth and death rates—which in turn depend on changes in standard of living or in lifestyle; or they may result from predation, migration, war, epidemics, or natural catastrophes. And a price hike may be due to either sudden scarcity, a market "force"—such as excess demand—or oligopolistic mark-up.

The methodological consequence is clear: Given (or assuming) the mechanism of a process one may deduce its kinematics; but, given the kinematics, one can only guess at the various possible underlying dynamics. In the general theory of machines there is a theorem stating that, whereas composition and structure determine behavior, knowledge of the latter is insufficient to find composition or structure. The first is a direct problem, the second an inverse one. A direct problem, if soluble, has a single solution, whereas an inverse one has multiple solutions—or none.

For example, inflation (a process) in a given economy (a system) can be accounted for by alternative mechanisms, such as demand-pull, cost-push, excessive consumer spending on credit fueled by publicity, easy credit, or government overspending. Neither economic statistics nor econometrics can tell us which of these mechanisms has brought about a given inflationary process: the mechanism has got to be hypothesized. Another example is this: A Leontief input-output matrix, of the form $O = BI$, relates outputs O to inputs I via a black box denoted by B, which merely summarizes the contributions of every sector of the economy to the other sectors. O is uniquely determined by B and I. But the mechanism behind B cannot read off the data I and O : it must be guessed—and of course the guess must be checked.

This is why the program of "inferring" the "laws of motion" of a social system by inspecting the latter's behavior is logically impossible. (In general, the inductive logic project is doomed: see Popper 1935.) For example, mere demographic data about either an abnormally low birth rate or an anomalous sex ratio in a certain country do not tell which of the various population control mechanisms has been operating: drop in sperm count, contraception, infanticide, or child (in particular girl) neglect. Again, there can be no hope of finding the laws of the market by just analyzing time-series of quantities, prices, earnings, bankruptcies, or what have you. Econometrics can only record economic processes and check economic hypotheses. Likewise epidemiologists can describe an epidemic but are not equipped to explain the contagion mechanism: this requires a deeper study—example, of the way *Salmonella typhosa,* once ingested, acts on the digestive system. However, the concept of conceptual depth is seldom elucidated, whence it requires some discussion.

Three kinds of scientific hypothesis or theory may be distinguished as regards depth, perspicuity, or explanatory power (Bunge 1964, 1967b, 1968, 1983):

(a) *black box, descriptive,* or *phenomenological,* which answer only questions of the "What is it?" type;

(b) *gray box, semiphenomenological,* or *semitranslucent,* which give only sketchy or shallow answers to questions of the "How does it work?" kind; and

(c) *translucent box, mechanismic,* or *dynamical,* which answer in detail questions of the "How does it work?" type.

A black box hypothesis or theory involves and interrelates only external (observable) variables, notably inputs and outputs: it is strictly phenomenalist. A gray box theory, such as automata theory, adds internal states (or "intervening variables") without describing in detail any mechanisms in terms of hypothetical constructs. Only translucent box (or mechanismic) theories describe mechanisms in any detail. Black box models are favored by accountants, whereas innovative managers—and of course scientists and original technologists as well—prefer gray box and translucent box models. And, whereas positivists countenance only black box models, realists go for translucent box ones and regard the gray box paradigm as the lesser evil.

Note that the above classification cuts across the deterministic-probabilistic dichotomy, since there are semi-random mechanisms in addition to causal and stochastic ones. For example, the mechanism of long-distance communication is the propagation of electromagnetic waves passing through more or less "noisy" channels, such as a cable, the atmosphere, or empty space, either of which causes irregular distortions of the original signal. Let us now exhibit a few examples to consolidate what we have learned so far.

Examples of black box hypotheses or theories. Kepler's laws; ray optics (in particular Snell's law and Fermat's minimal optical path principle); classical thermodynamics; electric network theory; the exponential law of radioactive decay; the assertion that catalysts (such as enzymes) make certain chemical reactions possible; classical biological morphology; the applications of catastrophe theory to biology and social science; behaviorist or stimulus-response learning theory; psychology without "hardware"; role theory (role → behavior); any strictly descriptive model of a social process (such as migration); the standard linear production model used by industrial economists; time-series (of, e.g., prices or quantities); path analysis (or structural equation) models; organization charts; box-and-arrow diagrams.

Examples of gray box hypotheses or theories. Newtonian gravitation theory and Ampère-Weber electrodynamics, both of which involve action at a distance; classical chemical kinetics; the assertion that catalysts (such as enzymes) make certain chemical reactions possible by binding with one of the reactants and then leaving it (as in A + B + C → AC + B → AB + C, without accounting for the AC and AB bindings); the account of an organism's development in terms of the switching on ("expression") of certain genes; phenotypic evolutionary biology (as exemplified by the game-theoretic account of evolution), which ignores the genetic and developmental mechanisms underlying phenotypes; neobehaviorist psychology in terms of drives and motivations that are not analyzed in neurophysiological terms; automata theory, in particular the theory of Turing machines, which is substance-neutral and centered on the "<stimulus, current state> ↦ next state" correspondence; statistical information theory; information-processing (or "computational") psychology, which plays on the multiple meanings of the term "information," as well as on metaphorical accounts such as the memory schema: Incoming information → encoding → short-term storage → storage → retrieval; most network models of social systems; social mobility theories; reference group theory.

Examples of translucent box hypotheses or theories. Einstein's gravitational field theory; electrodynamics (in terms of fields generated by and reacting upon electric charges); wave optics (main mechanisms: propagation, interference and diffraction of light waves); the kinetic theory of gases; statistical mechanics; any quantum theory (e.g., that of radioactive decay); Turing's theory of the generation of chemical waves by the combination of two mechanisms: chemical reaction and diffusion; the account of digestion in terms of enzymes (such as ptyalin, found in saliva, and which converts cooked starch into sugar); acquired immunity theory (in terms of antibodies and the selection of adaptive cells); population dynamics (main mechanisms: birth, natural death, predation, parasitism, and dispersal); evolutionary theory (main "forces": genic mutation and recombination, natural selection, and dispersal);

the molecular explanation of the pollution-cancer link (in terms of mutations caused by the combination of carcinogens present in dirty air with DNA); Hebb's learning theory (mechanism: neurons that fire together tend to associate or self-assemble into systems with properties that their components lack); the explanation of creativity in terms of the ability to form new systems of neurons; Merton's conjectures about the social mechanisms involving status and role; Richardson's mathematical theory of an arms race ("The more weapons you accumulate, the more will I"); neoclassical microeconomics (in terms of subjective probabilities and utilities); any game-theoretic model of a social process (in terms of the expected benefits to be derived from either cooperation or defection).

The translucent box/black box distinction appears in mathematical economics in the well-known distinction between *structural* and *reduced* models. The former contain formulas exhibiting the relation of every dependent variable to independent variables on various levels; on the other hand the corresponding reduced model exhibits the net or overall relation between the dependent and the ultimate independent variables. For instance, a structural economic model may boil down to a formula of the form

$$z = f(x, y), \qquad [5a]$$

where in turn

$$x = g(u), \text{ and } y = h(v). \qquad [5b]$$

Substituting [5b] into [5a] yields the corresponding reduced model:

$$z = \varphi(u, v) \qquad [6]$$

Note the following methodological differences between the two models. First, whereas [5b] "explains" (computes) the intermediary variables x and y, which presumably represent salient real features of the system under consideration, [6] does not even contain them. In other words, [6] is shallower and therefore simpler than [5], for skipping one level, that of the properties represented by x and y. Second, [5a] and [5b] jointly imply [6], but the converse does not hold. That is, the task of going from the structural to the reduced model is merely computational (hence deductive) . By contrast, the task of going the other way round, that is, from the reduced or black box model [6] to the structural or translucent box model [5], is an inverse problem—hence one with an indefinite number of solutions. This problem is likely to require more ingenuity than that of inventing the richer model. The moral is obvious: Apply your talent to building structural models, leaving the reduced ones to computer-aided curve fitting.

In mathematics, foundational work—in particular axiomatization—leads to uncovering ever deeper layers, as David Hilbert taught us. By contrast, in factual science the search for depth is a search for mechanism: it consists in uncovering lower or higher layers of organization, not in digging for deeper mathematical foundations. (This is why the increasing mathematical sophistication of economics has seldom resulted in deeper insights into economic systems or processes: it has mostly embellished century-old assumptions.) In other words, in factual science a *deep* theory is one that postulates some mechanism on different levels of organization: it is a *mechanismic multilevel* theory, by contrast to a phenomenological single-level theory. In this regard, some sociological theories may have gone deeper than the most glamorous of factual sciences, namely molecular biology, which has yet to find the precise mechanisms of protein synthesis and even protein folding. (The standard statement that DNA contains "information" and acts as the "template" for protein synthesis, as well as the tiller of development, is at best a soothing metaphor, at worst an obstacle to the search for mechanisms.)

In the vast majority of cases the "works" driving a system are imperceptible. (This holds even for a grandfather clock, since the gravitational field that pulls the weight is invisible.) But, of course, if the theory is scientific, then the mechanism in question must be empirically accessible, however indirectly. Thus, the quantum theory of solids explains successfully the macroproperties of solid bodies in terms of a comparatively rigid system composed of ionized atoms and a swarm of electrons moving among them; and physiological psychology is gradually succeeding in explaining emotion, cognition and overt behavior, both normal and abnormal, in terms of neuronal and interneuronal activities. These assumptions are experimentally testable; moreover, tests have confirmed some of them. By contrast, the fashionable game-theoretic models in sociology, economics, politology, and history are not empirically testable because the corresponding payoff matrices are contrived *ad hoc,* so as to "explain" any facts (Bunge 1996, 1998). Again, the Marx-Engels hypothesis that all historical events have been the result of class struggles is mechanismic— but, alas, not universally true, as shown by the large number of social changes resulting from legislation, technological innovation, and ideological change. Moral: Depth is worthless without truth—just as shallow truth is cheap for being abundant.

The reference to levels of organization in the preceding is intended to suggest that, whenever systems are involved, global or systemic changes (such as modernization, urbanization, income redistribution, and the conversion of military into civilian economy or conversely) are likely to result from internal processes as well as from environmental stimuli. This is what compels one to adopt a multilevel approach—or, in other words, to perform a levels analysis.

For example, electric network theory allows one to calculate the electric current intensity in any metallic circuit. But it does not answer such questions as "What makes the current flow?," and "Why can the resistance in an a.c. circuit be greater than in a d.c. circuit with the same resistors?" Only electrodynamics answers these questions, namely thus. The electric current flows because the electrons in the wire are pulled by the electric field generated by the generator. And the variable current induces a variable magnetic field, which in turn induces a countercurrent, so that the net effect can be described phenomenologically as an increase in resistance. Thus, electrodynamics is a mechanismic theory, whereas electric network theory is merely a kinematical one. Moreover, the former theory subsumes the latter. Again, the Big Bang cosmological model is deficient for involving no mechanisms accounting for the hypothetical initial explosion. Likewise, a theory of a social movement that failed to involve any specific "seeding" and diffusion mechanisms should be regarded as being seriously incomplete.

A deep theory tells us not just (part of) what happens but also what makes it happen, or else what prevents something from happening: it involves some causal, probabilistic, or mixed mechanism. This is why it has explanatory power. For example, a graph-theoretic model of a social network is turned from a gray box into a translucent box if the strengths of the ties linking its members is added—that is, if every edge in the graph is assigned a weight. This is how Granovetter (1983), in a classic paper, explained "the strength of weak ties" in the process of job hunting. Likewise a linear production model can be rendered translucent upon specifying the production mechanism and turning the givens (in particular the goal) into functions of market variables (such as demand).

Moreover, a deep hypothesis or theory may prove to be of practical interest for, if we know how a thing works, we may effectively alter its mechanism to advantage. For example, knowing that the depletion of fish stock is caused mainly by overfishing, a responsible fisheries manager will reduce the allowable harvesting quotas to allow the fish population to regain earlier levels. Likewise, knowing that a rise in disposable income decreases fertility, the demographic planner will recommend rising the standard of living as an effective contraceptive. As well, knowing that, in the absence of unemployment compensation insurance, a 1 percent increase in unemployment is accompanied by about 1 percent increase in criminality, suggests that full employment is a better crime deterrent than law and order. (The mechanism is obvious: the hungry must steal to eat.) Again, knowing that the mechanisms of health care are social as well as biological, encourages the adoption of a combination of environmental, public health and educational preventive measures. This is the crux of social medicine (or normative epidemiology). A last example: The statement "No civilization without taxation" is likely to be a social law. This is so not just because it holds for all known civilizations, but because we can easily surmise what the underlying mechanism is. Indeed, civilization involves the creation or maintenance of expensive public goods (and bads), which can only be funded through tributes of some kind. The practical import is obviously that the fashionable political slogan "No taxes" amounts to "No civilization, please: we want to be barbarians." The corresponding moral teaching is that voter education (rather than persuasion) involves instruction on some of the key social mechanisms. Without it the citizenry is merely electoral fodder. Which shows the social relevance of the search for mechanismic explanation.

Many physical, chemical, and biological mechanisms are driven by forces. But not all of them are. For instance, forces play only a minute role in the propagation of heat along a pipe or in the diffusion of smoke in rarefied air (where molecular collisions are unfrequent). External forces play no role at all in spontaneous radioactivity. Some complex processes, such as the propagation of an electromagnetic wave in vacuum, involve no forces at all: these only emerge when the wave hits an electrically charged body or particle. (True, the electromagnetic field is often called a force, but this is a mistake, because Maxwell's equations for a field in vacuum do not include any forces. The same holds for the gravitational field as described by Einstein's general relativity. Physical fields exert forces but they are things, not forces.) Other familiar stimulus-independent processes are the self-assembly of nucleic acid molecules in a medium containing their precursors; the formation of feelings, images and thoughts "out of the blue"; and the spontaneous emergence of cliques of friends or accomplices.

Let me stress that, though the existence of a force implies that of a mechanism, the converse is not true. For example, voting, public debate and mass mobilization are mechanisms for democratic political change (or stasis), but they are not forces. On the other hand public opinion, coercion, graft, and lobbying for special interest groups are political forces because they alter the mechanisms of a democratic polity. Much the same holds for culture: the cultivation and consumption of science, technology, the humanities and the arts are not forces but mechanisms of cultural change. But, of course, a cultural system, such as a school or a scientific institute, does not exist in a social vacuum but is subject to (sustaining or debilitating) economic and political forces.

In short, wherever there is a force there is a mechanism, but the converse is false: some mechanisms operate without forces. When a force does act upon a system, it may be said to either drive or brake the latter's mechanism(s). For example, the gravitational pull is what drives a grandfather's clock; a light beam activates a photocell by inducing an electric force that knocks off some of the electrons in it; and the actions of a newcomer may either strengthen or wreck a marital relationship.

In other words, to explain social change one need not always invoke social forces or powers—unless these actually exist and are well-defined, which is seldom the case. (I have found no paper on the general concept of a social force in the venerable journal *Social Forces*.) In line with the above, I propose the following rough definition. A *social force* (or *power*) is a social factor, internal or external, that alters the tempo or mode of the mechanism(s) operating in some social system(s). Examples of social force are overpopulation, the difference between supply and demand, and political or cultural intimidation. On the other hand the armed "forces" and the "forces" of law and order are social systems, not forces—though of course they are capable of exerting decisive force. And environmental disasters, such as floods and earthquakes, may be regarded as forces and they may have social effects, but obviously they are not social forces. Which suggests this general hypothesis: *Whereas every social cause has (by definition) a social effect, not every social change results from a social cause.* The methodological consequence is obvious: *Not every correct explanation in social science is of the causal type.* This result goes against the grain of the Aristotelian tradition, and it is at variance with the crossing of Aristotle with Hume proposed by Hicks (1979).

A methodological caution is in order. To ascertain whether a given social force is in fact acting in or upon a system, one must be able to identify and alter the putative force to the point of countering it, and observe (directly or indirectly) the effects of such variation. Otherwise talk of social force or power is just metaphorical or programmatic. For example, we know that capital is indeed a social (in particular economic) force, because it is a factor of modern production—as one finds out by varying investment and watching the corresponding change in output. By contrast, work is more than just a factor of production: it is no less than the central mechanism of any economic organization, regardless of its degree of automation.

The following table may help to understand the differences that have just been drawn.

System	Main mechanism(s)	Main social force(s)
Factory	Production	Capital, demand, supply, profits, wages
Store	Trade	Capital, excess demand, profits, wages
Office	Management, info. processing	Demand, supply, incentives
School	Learning	Social demand, family pressure
Research team	Investigation	Peer recognition, criticism, funding
Hospital	Healing, prevention	Demand, incentives, funding
Army	Combat	National defense, discipline, politics
Government	Management of public goods	Politics, public opinion, special interests

There are many kinds of social force and, whereas a few are generic, most are specific. For example, conflict, cooperation, communication, state regulation, incentivation, coercion, and state regulation are generic social forces: they alter the "works" of social systems of very many kinds in modern society. On the other hand capital, technological expertise and contracts are very special social forces: they only alter or keep in place the mechanisms that operate in modern business—mainly work and trade.

In sum, social forces (or powers)—whether economic, political, or cultural—shape and shake things. They do so by altering the mode or tempo of social mechanisms, or the equilibrum of the corresponding social system. A social force may be so strong as to compel people to set up or dismantle some system. (On the other hand it makes no sense to talk about weak or strong mechanisms.) And, whether weak or strong, a social force alters the structure of the social system in or upon which it acts: that is, it modifies the strength of the bonds that hold the system together, and may thus alter its *modus operandi.*

Needless to say, whereas some forces are convergent (that is, add up), others are mutually opposed—yet not necessarily mutually destructive. For example, the effectiveness of an organization depends on a balance of such forces as standardization and innovation, discipline and initiative, cooperation and competition. When no such balance is achieved, the system may stagnate, decline, or break down. Which leads us to our next topic.

Let us finally say a few words about the linear-nonlinear distinction, which has come to the fore in recent years. The vast majority of scientific theories are linear: they assume that the basic variables are additive, and that a small change in one of them effects a "commensurate" (neither explosive nor implosive) change in some other variable(s). In plain words, more of a cause has more of the same effect. For instance, the total mechanical force acting on a body equals the (vector) sum of all the applied forces, and a small change in the impressed force causes a small change in the acceleration. However, some important theories— such as Einstein's theory of gravitation, fluid dynamics, chemical kinetics, the law of growth of a biopopulation, and the Volterra-Lotka predator-prey theory—are nonlinear. And nonlinear mechanisms are (positive or negative) multipliers: they transform small causes (inputs) into very large (or very small) effects (outputs). Moreover, some nonlinear mechanisms lead systems to unstable states or irregular motions, and others to breakdown.

It is widely suspected that processes in increasing numbers will eventually turn out to be driven by nonlinear mechanisms. This is likely to hold, in particular, for certain hydrodynamic (e.g., atmospheric), biological, ecological and social systems, where states that are initially very close together may end up far apart, or where regular—for example, periodic—changes get transformed into irregular—for example, aperiodic—ones. (See, e.g., Glass and Mackey 1988.)

Due in part to the current popularity of "chaos"-theoretic talk, and partly to the growing interest in disequilibria and instabilities, in the near future we are likely to see a proliferation of nonlinear dynamical models in social science. However, for the time being there is little more than suggestive metaphor and shameless hype about the relevance of chaos theory to social science. Indeed, so far no precise (i.e., mathematical) chaos-theoretic model of any social mechanisms seems to have been both formulated and confirmed with data sets such as time-series. (See, e.g., Baumol and Benhabib 1989; Brock & Dechert 1991.) Hence, for the time being the social sciences will have to make do with nonchaotic causal, stochastic and mixed mechanisms, and the corresponding generalizations and explanations.

To be sure, chaos-theoretic models of social processes do loom in the horizon. Still, there is no cause for either alarm or rejoicing, since knowledge of chaotic dynamics allows one to control it, at least in principle, in the cases of experimental subjects as well as made things such as social systems—whereas randomness is hardly controllable. Indeed, a nonlinear mechanism can be controlled by "turning the knob(s)," that is, by modifying the value(s) of the control (or tuning) parameter(s) in the equation(s) describing the mechanism, and either avoiding or seeking the "dangerous" intervals, according as one wishes to elude or provoke chaos. For example, chaos has recently been induced experimentally by deliberately varying the mortality rate in an insect population (Costantino et al. 1995). Conversely, recent numerical "experiments" (computer simulations) have shown that chaotic behavior can be tamed (rendered regular) by disorder (Braiman et al. 1995). A possible and puzzling consequence of this finding for social science is that, if social systems are indeed potentially chaotic, then they might never go actually chaotic for being, like their human and artificial components, accident-prone. Accident (and chance) might keep them near the edge of chaos-as Kauffman (1993) believes to be the case of organisms. In any event, so far there has been more hype and promise than accomplishment in the exploration of the potential of chaos theory in social science (see, e.g., Kiel and Elliott, eds. 1996).

So much for mechanisms. Let us next explore their relevance to scientific explanation.

3

Explanation

Etymologically, "to explain" means to unpack, or rendering explicit what was tacit. However, not all deductions explain. For example, theorems are deduced, and thus proved, but not explained—except in a pedagogical sense. Strictly speaking, only facts can be explained.

In order to *explain* the emergence of some concrete thing, or any of its changes, we must uncover the mechanism(s) whereby it came to be what it is or the way it changes. Thus, the "birth" of stars is explained in terms of the assembly of atoms pulled together by gravitational attraction, and their "death" in terms of gravitational implosion as a result of the exhaustion of nuclear "fuel." Likewise, changes in a polity are sometimes explained by the changing attitudes of its leaders and citizens in response to (real or imaginary) economic or cultural issues.

Some of the earliest explanations were mythical: they invoked supernatural agents or miraculous events. But others were causal, that is, they explained certain facts (real or imaginary) in terms of more or less plausible causal mechanisms: primitive man did not believe in coincidences and had no inkling of randomness. A causal mechanism is of course one activated by events (causes) of a certain kind. The causes can be external or internal, that is, environmental stimuli or internal events. The environmental causes can be natural, social, or a combination of both, such as a sound wave transmitting a command that, upon being heard, triggers a brain process which in turn triggers and guides an action. And the question whether a given conjectured mechanism is in fact in place, is one for scientific investigation. Still, general philosophical considerations suffice to write off mythical mechanisms without further ado. Thus, no scientist would conduct experiments to check the Aztec myth that human sacrifice keeps the sun going.

Some of the internal causes of overt human behavior are mental events such as decisions motivated in turn by intentions (which are in turn processes in the frontal lobes of primates and perhaps other higher vertebrates as well). In the latter case the causes are usually called "reasons." However, seen from a psychobiological viewpoint, an explanation by reasons is just a particular case of causal explanation. It is only when detaching reasons from the reasoning processes occurring in a living brain that we are justified in emphasizing the peculiarities of explanation by reasons. And this we must do when weighing the epistemic, moral or practical merits of the reasons given for taking any actions.

Nor does purposive or goal-directed action escape ordinary or efficient causation. Indeed, if an individual performs action A in order to achieve goal G, he is being driven to doing A by his current mental representation M of G, not by G itself. Indeed, nonexistents, such as unattained goals, are devoid of causal efficacy. Thus, in purposive action the causal link is not G → A but M → A. In other words, what is traditionally called *final causation* is nothing but efficient causation with an effect (goal) in view. "Rational causation" might be a better name, were it not for the fact that we often choose foolish goals or wrong means. What holds for such mechanisms also holds, *mutatis mutandis,* for the corresponding explanations. That is, explanations in terms of purposes, intentions or functions are, in the last analysis, causal explanations.

However, functional explanations, though important in social science, are insufficient. It is just as important to discover the underlying mechanism(s), all the more so since any given function can be discharged by different mechanisms. For example, one can earn a living, communicate, or teach in various ways, that is, through different mechanisms. The fact that the relation between the set of functions and the set of mechanisms is not one-to-one exhibits the severe limitations of functionalism, whether in biology, psychology, or social science. It is not that functionalism is false: it is just shallow. Functionalism is also practically barren, for we can alter the course of things only by tampering with their mechanisms. Thus it is essential for a mechanic called to repair an aircraft engine to know whether the defective mechanism is a propeller engine or a jet propulsion one. Likewise the macroeconomist called to help a nation recover from a recession must begin by finding out what caused it, so as to remove the cause(s). For example, knowing that the zero-inflation policy pursued in recent times in the U.K., Canada, Argentina, and elsewhere has caused severe and protracted depression—by eliminating jobs and cutting social expenditures on a large scale—a socially responsible macroeconomist will suggest altering that policy, proposing instead that the speed of inflation reduction be reduced and made compatible with social welfare.

3.1. Conditions on Mechanismic Explanation

The only conditions for a mechanismic hypothesis or theory to be taken seriously in modern science or technology is that the mechanism in question be *concrete* (rather than immaterial), *lawful* (rather than miraculous), and *scrutable* (rather than occult). The first two conditions disqualify algorithms as possible mechanisms, for algorithms are formal devices. (By contrast, "embodied" algorithms, such as discs guiding computer-aided calculation or design, do qualify as mechanisms. But of course they are artifacts, not natural items.)

Now, concrete, lawful, and scrutable mechanisms are specific or, if preferred, substance-dependent. Hence there can be no universal explanations of the mechanismic kind. Thus, explanations in physics are unlikely to be of any use in sociology. Even within a given broad field, such as physics or sociology, universal questions, which beg for universal answers, should be eyed just as suspiciously as "grand" theories such as the Romantic philosophy of nature, Marxism, Parsonianism, rational choice theory, critical theory, and the popular versions of information theory and systems theory.

Yet economists and management scientists still debate such broad questions as "Why do firms borrow?" This question presupposes that all firms are roughly the same—which of course is not true. One firm borrows because it wants to expand; another because it needs retooling in order to adopt a new technology; a third because interest payments are tax-deductible; a fourth because it gambles on inflation; a fifth because it is being hounded by its creditors—and so on. Unless one has an inkling of the particular mechanisms and forces at play, together with the circumstances, one cannot give a correct answer to the original question. And as soon as one obtains the requisite knowledge, one should restrict the scope of the original question, to a narrower and therefore more manageable one, of the form "Why do firms of type A, in situation of kind B, find it convenient to borrow up to C percent of their assets?" Different kinds of system, with different mechanisms, and under different forces, call for different explanations. In sum, mechanismic explanations are just as system-specific as mechanisms.

Reductive explanation may be regarded as an important particular case of mechanismic explanation. An explanation will be said to be *reductive* if and only if at least one of the premises occurring in it is a reductive proposition. For example, an explanation of the formation of a concrete system, such as an informal social network, in terms of the self-assembly of individuals with common interests, is of the *microreductive* (or bottom-up) kind. By contrast, the explanation of the behavior of a system component in terms of the place it holds or the role it performs in the system, is *macroreductive* (or top-down). The research strategy that favors microreduction may be called *microreductionist*. Likewise, the research strategy centered in macroreduction may be called *macroreductionism*. In the social sciences these strategies are known as methodological *individualism* and *holism (or collectivism)* respectively. I shall argue that neither is sufficient, though each of them contains a nugget.

Consider for instance Schelling's (1978: 139) highly acclaimed bottom-up or microreductive explanation of social segregation and congregation, as in the formation of all-white and all-black comunities in the U.S. It all would depend primarily on individual choice guided by preference: "To choose a neighborhood is to choose neighbors. To pick a neighborhood with good schools, for example, is to pick a neighborhood of *people* who want good schools." No time is spent clarifying that most people cannot afford to choose good schools, whence have no access to "good" neigborhoods and are thus forced to live in ghettoes. The consistent individualist overlooks the fact that individual intentions and expectations, hence choices, are largely shaped by social circumstances: that few individuals are free to choose the social rank they wish to belong to. Such oversight of the social context of agency is bound to lead to utterly false models of social facts, as well as to immoral social policies, that penalize people for not rationally choosing their circumstances.

To be sure, research on the origin of life, or on the emergence of private organizations, calls for bottom-up explanations—yet even in these cases the environment has got to be reckoned with. By contrast, the car mechanic and the social psychologist of a sociological bent typically resort to top-down explanations. However, I suggest that the most adequate reductive explanations are *combinations* of the two basic types—as when a political event is explained as the outcome of the concerted actions of a number of individuals in response to an irreducibly social issue, such as high unemployment, inflation, or political oppression. The combination of microreduction with macroreduction is characteristic of the *systemic* (or systems-theoretic) approach. According to systemism, to explain how a system works—that is, to unveil its mechanism—one must not only take it to bits (microreduction), but also show how the bits fit together giving rise to emergent features (macroreduction).

The following diagram summarizes the preceding.

Individualism	*Holism*	*Systemism*
Microreductionist	*Macroreductionist*	*Micro cum macroreductionist*
or bottom-up	*or top-down*	*or bottom-up cum topdown*
Macrolevel	Macrolevel	Macrolevel
↑	↓	⇅
Microlevel	Microlevel	Microlevel

If an explanation is found incorrect or shallow, it is the scientist's tacit faith that it can be improved on by conjecturing a different mechanism. Moreover, if no plausible mechanism is found to account for controversial data, such as those about miracles, telepathy, faith healing, collective hallucination, and crowd psychology, the scientist may question the very data: he may suspend his judgment or even doubt that the data describe any objective facts. Moreover, he may demand further investigation—or its termination, as was the case with the U.S. office for the investigation of UFOs. A scientifically plausible mechanism is one that, no matter how counter-intuitive, satisfies known laws or at least quasi-laws.

3.2. Mechanismic Explanation Subsumes Subsumption

The mechanismic view of explanation differs from, but is consistent with, the so-called *covering law model* of scientific explanation. This was first proposed by Mill (1952 [1872]: 305), adopted by Popper (1935), and formalized by Hempel and Oppenheim (see Hempel 1965). As will be recalled, according to this "model," to propose a scientific explanation of a fact consists in deducing the latter from the law(s) and circumstance(s) of the case—such as equations of motion (or field equations) together with initial (or else boundary) conditions and constraints. Schematically: Law(s) & Circumstance(s) ∴ Explanandum (proposition describing the fact to be explained).

In my view this operation is not exactly an explanation but rather the *subsumption* of particulars under generalities. Indeed, it overlooks the ontological side of explanation proper, illuminating only its logical side—the "unpacking" of premises (Bunge 1979 [1959], 1967, 1983). For instance, knowing that the salary in a given job category is 25 percent lower for women than for men "explains" why Mary earns $375/week, whereas her colleague Peter makes $500/week. But does this argument really count as an explanation, or do we want to know the mechanism underneath this unequal treatment?

Whereas the social statistician may take salary differentials and other social inequalities for granted, they pose a problem to the sociologist: he wants to know the mechanism that produces and maintains them. And the social policymaker must obtain such knowledge if he is to devise effective social equalization policies and programs. This is why Tilly (1998) tackles the politics of inequality only after having devoted six chapters to the various kinds of mechanisms of durable inequality. For the same reason, the car mechanic called to repair a gearbox starts by finding out whether it is standard or automatic.

Consider the ecological problem whether interspecific competition is for real. This question did not even arise until recently; competition was taken for granted, and so was the assumption that it is exhaustively accounted for by the famous Lotka-Volterra equations. However, an analysis of more than 150 field experiments designed to test the hypothesis failed to corroborate it: nearly half of the species studied did not exhibit competition. Tilman (1987) attributes this failure to the fact that the experiments determined the total effect of one species upon another, not the mechanisms of interaction. In turn, these mechanisms, which are bound to be species-specific rather than universal, were overlooked under the influence of the standard phenomenological theory, centered in the Lotka-Volterra equations. Only a study of the physiology, morphology, and behavior of organisms belonging to individual species can supply the relevant mechanisms and thus the wanted explanations. Might not something similar be needed in social science, particularly in economics, which has so long been under the spell of the dominant theory of general equilibrium, that points to no specific mechanisms, as a consequence of which it cannot recommend any effective measures to restore lost market equilibria?

Dissatisfaction with the "covering law model" has led some scholars, notably Elster (1989), to advocate replacing laws with mechanisms. But this would condone fantasies about miraculous or paranormal "mechanisms," such as divine intervention, extrasensory perception, and the sheer power of charisma. A similar dissatisfaction has induced

Athearn (1994) to propose that the standard "model" be replaced with a "narrative causal explanation" independent of any laws. But if we did this we would obtain nonscientific and furthermore *ad hoc* explanations—that is, more or less plausible stories—rather than *general scientific* explanations. The right research strategy is not to substitute either mechanisms or causal narratives for laws, but to prefer law statements that incorporate mechanisms of some sort—causal, stochastic, hybrid, or other.

Unlike a mere subsumption, a scientific explanation makes explicit reference to a known or conjectured mechanism of some kind: causal, stochastic, or mixed; and it may be natural, biosocial, social, or artificial. That is, the structure of an authentic scientific explanation is this: *Testable mechanismic hypothesis or theory & Circumstance(s) ∴ Explanandum.*

I submit that any correct explanation of a social fact fits basically the same schema, with the difference that the explanans set may contain, in addition, value judgments and norms of some kind—technical, legal, or moral. (Remember that, unlike laws, norms are made; and that they are either conventional, like those of etiquette, or based on laws, such as those of technology.) For example, Merton (1957a:134) explained anomie or normlessness as an effect of a mismatch between social norm (or aspiration) and opportunity: a discrepancy between what is socially acceptable and desirable, and what the individual can actually achieve by socially sanctioned means. This norm-fact dissociation would be the mechanism of deviant behavior.

Because of the importance of social norms, the logical structure of most social science explanations is likely to be slightly more complicated than that of explanation in natural science, namely this:

Testable mechanismic hypothesis or theory and Value judgment(s) and Norm(s) and Circumstance(s) ∴ Explanandum.

Example 1. How did social stratification emerge? Possible explanation:

Generalization: Unless a society is held together by strong links of reciprocal altruism, and includes effective equalization or compensation mechanisms (such as consensus and potlatch), some individuals are bound to acquire more biological, economic, political or cultural power than others, and are thus likely to constitute a ruling class.

Datum: The solidarity links and equalization mechanisms in society X were weakened by natural calamities, war, or tyranny.

Value judgment: Survival and advancement of self and kin is the foremost imperative.

Norm: Do whatever is convenient unless explicitly prohibited.

Example 2. Why was the welfare state instituted? Possible explanation:

Generalization: Poverty is a source of both personal unhappiness and social unrest.

Datum: There are some poor people in our society.

Value judgment: Poverty is undesirable, for being painful and degrading to the poor, and dangerous to the rich.

Norm: To avoid the consequences of social unrest, raise the basic standard of living by redistributing the social wealth through taxes paying for social programs.

In short, the so-called covering law model of scientific explanation is correct but incomplete, for it only covers the logical structure of the same. In compliance with the antimetaphysical stance of positivism, this account of scientific explanation overlooks its ontological nucleus. Aristotle had emphasized the latter in his theory of the four causes. In modern times it was stressed by Descartes, who championed mechanistic explanation—the earliest if limited form of genuinely scientific explanation. The fact that most of the particular mechanisms proposed by Aristotle (e.g., goal-seeking) and Descartes (e.g., vortices) were imaginary is beside the point in the present context. What matters most is that both Aristotle and Descartes, despite their huge differences in outlook, underlined the need to conjecture the mechanisms that may operate underneath appearances. So did Whewell (1847, P. I: 652), who wrote: "No sound theory without Aethiology." (See Meyerson 1921 for a history of the concept of explanation in natural science.)

Where does the preceding leave the so-called *explanation of variables* sought by many social scientists and statisticians? Strictly speaking, there is simply no such thing. Indeed, saying that variable(s) such and such "explain(s)" a given variable is an incorrect way of stating that the latter is a computable function of the former, as in "$y = f(x)$." In other words, there is no explanation of variables: there is only either an analysis of variables or a mechanism describable by certain functionally related variables.

3.3. Biosocial Mechanism and Explanation

Lying between the natural and the social sciences we find what may be called the *socionatural* or *biosocial sciences*, such as demography, geography, anthropology, social psychology, linguistics, epidemiology, and bioeconomics. All these hybrids result from marrying the social with the life sciences. (Incidentally, the mere existence and success of such hybrids is a decisive argument against the dichotomy between the natural sciences and the *Geisteswissenschaften* [spiritual sciences] invented by the hermeneutic, interpretive, or *verstehende* school in its effort to keep social studies in the humanistic fold and prevent them from taking the scientific road: see Bunge 1998a.)

Insofar as they succeed in explaining anything, the socionatural sciences do so by discovering or conjecturing what may be called *biosocial* (or *biopsychosocial) mechanisms*. These bridge individual and society. They explain what makes people behave as they do in given social circumstances: what their drives, interests, and intentions are; how they cope with social constraints, stresses, and opportunities; and how these shape (inhibit, stimulate, or deflect) individual action. (The first question is investigated by psychological social psychology, whereas the second is studied by sociological social psychology.)

To put it metaphorically, biopsychosocial mechanisms are links or flows between the micro and the macro levels—some bottom-up, others top-down, and still others in both directions. Thus, whatever may make "birds of a feather flock together," is a biopsychosocial mechanism of the bottom-up type. By contrast, the hierarchical organization that keeps the young male baboon in the savanna away from the females of his troop is a biopsychosocial mechanism of the top-down type. And of course mechanisms of both types can combine, as in the following classical explanation of delinquency: Social structure → individual deprivation and restraint → frustration → exasperation → criminal action → social impact.

Let me list a few other examples. A courtship ritual, whether among people, penguins, or fruit flies, is a biosocial mechanism for mating. Infanticide and contraception are biosocial mechanisms of population control. Cooperation is a psychosocial mechanism for coordination. Torture and "ethnic cleansing" are biosocial (more precisely, biopolitical) mechanisms of social control. The dissatisfied spouse, customer, student, or citizen can use two mechanisms: "exit" (desertion) and "voice" (protest or action), either alternatively or in combination (Hirschman 1970). The changes in the size of any social system are due to either or both of the following mechanisms: accretion (e.g., by joining) and attrition (e.g., by withdrawing). Likewise, the processes of giving and receiving, of bartering and trading goods or services in face-to-face situations are biopsychosocial mechanisms. So are those of helping and attacking, as well as those of teaching and learning in a formal school setting.

These are biosocial mechanisms because they are individual actions within some social system. That is, such events occur in the individual/society interface: they involve interactions between individuals embedded in a social whole and constrained or stimulated by the latter's structure. (Needless to say, such events need not be accounted for in terms of the mysterious power of mind over matter, or of the no less mysterious ability of society to generate ideas. No plausible mechanisms for such events are known or even plausible.) Hence such events cannot be explained in either purely individualistic or purely holistic terms: they call for a systemic approach (Bunge 1979, 1996).

Only such an approach links the microlevel to the macrolevel instead of attempting to reduce either to the other. For example, a low level of work capacity in a predominantrly agrarian society is hard to explain as a result of either rational choice or structural features alone. But the fact may be explained as a result of malnutrition deriving from a skewed distribution of the low national food production, which in turn is largely due to the low level of work capacity caused by the severely stunted development of the ill-nourished laborers. Thus, in France at the time of the French Revolution "the bottom 10 percent of the labor force lacked the energy for regular work, and the next 10 percent had enough energy for less than three hours of light work daily" (Fogel 1994: 373). The infernal macro-micro-macro cycle is clear: Low national food production $\rightarrow$ Malnutrition $\rightarrow$ Low level of work capacity $\rightarrow$ Low national food production $\rightarrow$ ...

Thus, assuming *either* the Agency $\rightarrow$ Structure direction of social causation or its dual, Structure $\rightarrow$ Agency, is false for two reasons. First, all individual actions, whether prosocial or antisocial, are conditioned, and sometimes motivated, by irreducibly social circumstances, such as scarcity and social conflict. Second, all social actions are aimed at changing other people's behavior, or even the entire group structure in some respect or other. Think of the businessman who takes a product to a preexisting market or who opens a new market; of the soldier who is drafted and confronts or flees the enemy; of the church or party that shapes the personality of its members; or of the state that collects taxes and imposes fines. None of these processes remains on a single level, whether microsocial or macrosocial. Instead, all of them occur between levels (more precisely, between entities belonging to different levels).

Consider, for example, the following hypothesis: "Human conflict has two main possible sources: interest in the same scarce resource, and diverging goals within the same social system." The decision to either cooperate or defect may be regarded as a brain process, but it is one at least partially induced by something outside the individual brain, such as a beckoning resource or a protective or threatening social system. Incidentally, the above hypothesis goes against the grain of the dialectical (in particular Marxist) account of conflict, namely that it occurs only between "opposites," particularly between different social classes. Two dogs will fight over the same bone precisely because they have similar needs for certain scarce resources. Equals may compete just as fiercely as unequals. So much for the dialectical "law" that the "struggle of opposites" is the source of all change.

Explanations invoking biosocial mechanisms are not exclusive to the socionatural sciences. Some of them are also suitable in the social sciences, such as anthropology, sociology, economics, politology, history, and their various combinations. The reasons for such pervasiveness should be obvious. One is that all persons have the same basic needs: this is why the notion of human nature makes sense. Another reason is that the agents in any social event or process are socially bonded (as well as conflicting) individuals acting within a social matrix. These two factors underlie such cross-cultural generalizations as "Social change is more frequent in heterogeneous societies than in homogeneous ones"; "Democracies are more peaceful, prosperous, and long-lived than dictatorships, because they tap a far greater diversity of human resources, leave more room for individual initiative, use mechanisms of peaceful conflict resolution, and benefit a larger section of society"; and "States are ruined when they fail to modify their institutions to suit the changes of the times"—as Machiavelli wrote in his *Discourses*.

3.4. Social Mechanism and Sociological Explanation

The concept of a social mechanism is somewhat vague because it has been insufficiently analyzed and theorized. To get an intuitive grasp of it let us start by listing a few examples.

Empirical finding	*Hypothetical mechanism(s)*
1. Cooperation and conflict are present in all social systems.	Every social system emerges through cooperation, but its members compete for scarce resources.
2. All social systems decline unless overhauled	Decreased benefits, intensification of internal conflicts, unresponsiveness to environmental changes.
3. The larger a social system the slower it changes.	All social change is ultimately initiated by a few individuals against the habits and reactions of others.
4. The Green Revolution has impoverished most peasants.	High-yield grain is expensive and requires a large capital to pay for high-yield seeds, irrigation, and fertilizers.
5. Social inequality has increased in the U.S. since 1969.	Shrinking of the manufacturing sector, decreased demand for unskilled workers, tax breaks for the rich.
6. Technological advances are accompanied by unemployment.	Increased productivity reduces production times and eliminates jobs.
7. Social democracy is losing ground nearly everywhere.	The welfare state has satisfied many socialist demands; no new socialist ideas; consumerism; television-addiction.
8. The Soviet Union crumbled in 1991.	Greater freedom of dissent, economic stagnation, ethnic conflicts, lack of mechanisms to implement *perestroika*.
9. So far, only financial capital has been globalized.	Many of the hurdles to free trade and the free movement of people and ideas are still in place.
10. The conversion of military into civilian industry is hard and slow.	The managers of military oligopolies have neither mental flexibility nor marketing skills

We are now ready for a formal definition. We define a *social mechanism* as a mechanism in a social system. Since every mechanism is a process in some system, a social mechanism is a *process* involving at least two agents engaged in forming, maintaining, transforming, or dismantling a social system. There are many types of social system: think, for example, of childless couples and extended families, streetcorner gangs and informal social networks, schools and churches, factories and supermarkets, economies and polities, local governments and multinational blocs. Correspondingly there is a large variety of social mechanisms.

Note that our definition presupposes a distinction between system and mechanism: the latter is a process in a system. This distinction is familiar in natural science, where one is not expected to mistake, say, the cardiovascular system for the circulation of the blood, or the brain with mental processes. But it is unusual in social studies, where one finds such expressions as "The family is the main mechanism of child socialization," "The market is a resource allocation mechanism," "Organized charity is a social control mechanism," and "Democracy is a mechanism for combining cleavage with cohesion." In light of the proposed definition one should say, rather, that family *life* is the main mechanism of child socialization; that market *transactions* constitute a resource allocation activity; that organized charitable *work* constitutes a social control mechanism; and that the various strands of the democratic *process,* such as public debating, voting, and the managing of public goods, are mechanisms that balance conflict with cooperation.

Our definition both highlights and avoids the following critical problem with rational choice theories. These hold both that (a) individual action is the only source of everything social, and (b) all actors are identical in all relevant respects—in particular, they have the same and moreover unchanging utility function (see, e. g., Stigler and Becker 1977). However, the conjunction of these two hypotheses entails the conclusion that only environmental factors (the social "situation") account for differences in individual action—a typically externalist and holistic thesis that renders individuals passive or even expendable. (Aristotle, Ibn Khaldûn, Hegel, Comte, and Marx nod, as does Tolstoy in *War and Peace.* All of them held that the individual is merely a pawn of society or a tool of History.)

This inconsistency does not occur in the systemic view, according to which agency is both constrained and motivated by structure, and in turn the latter is maintained or altered by individual action. In other words, social mechanisms reside neither in persons nor in their environment—they are a part of the processes that unfold in or among social systems. Hence, by tampering with a social mechanism one can modify some features of the system and thus indirectly alter individual behavior in some regards. For example, a radical reform of the criminal code is bound to affect crime, though perhaps less so than a radical economic change ensuing in a significant increase or drop in employment, schooling, and marginality. Another example is this: the fertility rate of a society can be either varied or held constant through the planned control of two mutually antagonistic mechanisms: increase (or decrease) in the birth and death rates.

The system/mechanism distinction may seem subtle and is somewhat obscure in the field of social studies, but it is quite clear in natural science and technology. Thus one refers to photosynthesis as the mechanism of production of chlorophyll in a plant cell; to circulation of the blood as the mechanism of oxygen distribution and waste elimination in the body; and to a feedback process as the mechanism of a control system. Mechanism is to system as motion is to body, combination (or dissociation) to chemical compound, and thinking to brain.

As noted earlier, corresponding to the large number of types of social system there is a large variety of social mechanisms. There are mechanisms of economic development (e.g., technological innovation) and others of economic stagnation or decline (e.g., collusion); of cultural progress (e.g., free inquiry), as well as of cultural stagnation or decline (e.g., censorship); of political progress (e.g., popular participation) and of political regress (e.g., militarization); of international rivalry and of international cooperation—and so on and so forth. I submit that there is at least one mechanism for every type of social change, and proceed to exhibiting a few examples that the reader may wish to use to test this assumption.

Examples of social mechanism. (1) The abnormal percentage of single women in postwar periods is a result of male war casualties. (2) The anomalous sex ratio in some Asian countries is caused by female infanticide, which in turn is caused by poverty and the economic and cultural undervaluing of females in male-dominated societies. (3) The black American family is currently disintegrating as a result of segregation, chronic poverty, ignorance, lack of community organization, and welfare-dependency. (4) The rapid growth of shanty towns around Third World cities is caused by (a) the decline in traditional agriculture, in turn caused by the growth of market-oriented agriculture, the concentration of land holdings, the expansion of cattle ranches; (b) industrialization; and sometimes also (c) civil war in the countryside. (5) Technological progress causes unemployment because it increases productivity while decreasing the demand for unskilled labor. (6) In the industrialized countries, unemployment is caused by industrial obsolescence, increasing productivity, job export to developing countries, or political change. (7) Keynesian policies work well up to a point because transfer payments and (some) government expenditures add to the national income and stimulate demand, and thus production. (8) The belief that the standard of living, the quality of life, and particularly survival, are at risk moves people to organize themselves—hence the proliferation of mutual societies, unions, lobbies, etc., as well as the mobilization of organizations—notably churches and trade unions—that had originally been created for entirely different purposes. (9) People rebel not when oppression is at its worst but when it begins to slacken, for only then can they complain openly, debate among themselves, and mobilize (Tocqueville). (10) The current reawakening and bellicosity of Islam results from a combination of oil wealth with traditionalism and hatred for the West nurtured by colonialism and religious fundamentalism.

Caution: Not every account that looks mechanismic is actually so. For instance, the statement that technology evolves (or else diffuses) along "the line of least resistance" is tautological for, if the resistance is large, then technology stops evolving (or diffusing, as the case may be). Likewise, to say that a certain economic development aborted because it encountered a "bottleneck" just raises the question of the cause of such obstruction: was it poor planning, insufficient financing, red tape, deficient transportation, shortage of skilled labor, or something else?

All mechanisms are *system-specific*: there is no such thing as a universal or substrate-neutral mechanism. For example, different governments are likely to manage their revenues and expenditures in different ways. Thus, the mechanism that resulted in the current astronomical American fiscal deficit was a combination of tax cuts with tripling the military expenditures between 1970 and 1990. The mechanisms underlying the fiscal deficits in other countries have been different. For instance, Third World countries owe their fiscal deficits to a combination of deficient tax collection with inept administration, Pharaonic projects, corruption, excessive military expenditures, and sustained fall or stagnation in the international prices of their main exports since about 1960.

Although all mechanisms are specific (or substrate-dependent), it is possible and desirable to group them into large classes on the strength of their similarities. For example, selection and diffusion are—to write in a Platonic vein—"instantiated" in all kinds of matter: physical, chemical, biological, and social. Again, the spontaneous aggregation of people and business firms resembles superficially the self-assembly of molecules and cells. Social changes are like chemical reactions in that the mechanisms operating in both cases consist in the making or breaking of bonds or ties. And the competition between two firms for a given item resembles the competition between two chemical reactants for a third, as well as the competition of two biopopulations for a given resource. Moreover, competition can combine with cooperation. For example, although birds compete for seeds with rodents and ants, the latter unwittingly facilitate bird foraging by favorably modifying both soil and vegetation (Thompson et al. 1991). Managed or regulated competition is a social example of such composite mechanism.

The occurrence of mechanisms of this hybrid kind in both nature and society suggests crafting general models of competitive cooperation or cooperative competition (see Bunge 1976). It also suggests the general concept of a dual (or mutually complementary) mechanism: one of which tends to undo what its dual does. In turn, this concept suggests a somewhat wild but possibly interesting speculation: that every mechanism has or generates at least one dual. For example, self-organization is countered by scrambling mechanisms; division of labor elicits coordination; competition calls for regulation; and the formation of any pro-X organization is countered by the assembly of anti-X people. (Caution: These conjectures bear only a superficial resemblance to dialectics, whose central principle is that everything is a "unity of opposites"—a "law" that has as many counterexamples as instances.)

To be sure, all of the above are just formal and therefore superficial, if bold, generalities garnered by gutting and collecting particular cases. Consequently, hypergeneral hypotheses or theories of growth, decline, selection, diffusion, self-organization, competition, cooperation, or any other generic mechanisms, can explain no particular facts—let alone predict them. But those general (or structural) hypotheses or theories that happen to capture salient and pervasive features of real mechanisms may have some heuristic power in modeling specific mechanisms. For instance, the Lagrangian and Hamiltonian formalisms, though born in theoretical mechanics, can guide theoretical research in almost any field, from thermodynamics and field physics to economics and management science. (For synergetics, that is, the study of self-organization in general, see, e.g., Haken 1989.)

There are of course similarities as well as differences between social mechanisms and mechanisms of other types. The commonality is that, by definition, all mechanisms bring about or stop changes. The specificities derive from the particular kind of matter (physical, chemical, biological, or social) the system is composed of, and therefore the peculiar forces acting in or upon it. Thus, one of the peculiarities of social mechanisms, by contrast to natural mechanisms, is that, though constrained by laws of nature, they are driven by actions that follow conventional (though not necessarily arbitrary) rules—some explicit, others tacit. (Habit and know-how may be thought of as fitting tacit rules that might be made to surface through painstaking psychological research.) Think, for instance, of the operation of a soccer team, an orchestra, a school, a factory, a government department, or a political party. Every one of these social systems operates in accordance with a set of specific norms believed—rightly or wrongly—to bring about optimal efficiency. In other words, in such cases the mechanism is identical with the implementation of one or more norms and strategies.

Whereas some social systems and their corresponding mechanisms emerge more or less spontaneously, others are designed. Examples of the former are families, circles of friends, informal social networks, streetcorner gangs, local markets, most towns, and even entire economic regions (see, e.g., Krugman 1996) . Designed systems and their corresponding mechanisms are usually called "organizations." An example of an organization is the law-enforcement system, a social control mechanism and, in particular, one aimed at protecting rights or privileges as well as enforcing obligations. Another such designed mechanism is the European Monetary System, devised to contain currency fluctuations. A third is any program of massive vaccination—a mechanism designed to prevent the outbreak of epidemics by boosting immune systems. In general, all social inventions are or involve mechanisms for attaining or maintaining certain desiderata. Just think of advertising as a mechanism for boosting sales, of education as a mechanism for learning, or of academic tenure as a mechanism for securing academic freedom.

Assuming that every society is made up of three artificial systems— the economy, the polity, and the culture—leads to distinguishing the corresponding types of social mechanism. Thus producing and trading are economic mechanisms, voting and mobilizing are political, and learning and teaching are cultural ones. But of course distinction need not entail detachment: the operation of a mechanism of any of the three kinds is likely to affect the operation of mechanisms of the other two types. Thus, a sharp increase in productivity is likely to cause unemployment, which in turn may produce cultural deprivation and political unrest. And an improvement in public education is unlikely to have lasting effects unless accompanied by a rise in the standard of living, which in turn can be attained and defended only through mass participation in the democratic process. Thus the social mechanisms of all three kinds—economic, political, and cultural—are coupled.

But the strong coupling among social mechanisms of several kinds calls for, rather than impedes, their analysis. All social mechanisms should be broken down into levels and their mutual actions. (Caution: since levels of organization are collections, not things, the expression "interaction between levels" must be understood as short for "interaction between individuals belonging to different levels.") One reason that such analysis is necessary is that social relations pass through the heads of people. That is, any given social fact is ultimately a result of individual actions; consequently, it may be "perceived" or "interpreted" differently by different individuals, who may then react differently. (Incidentally, I submit that this is the true component of ontological and methodological individualism—a virtue shared by the systemic view that follows.) Another rationale of systems analysis is that all social relations hold within or among social systems; and, wherever there are systems, at least two levels must be kept in mind. These are the microlevel, or level of the system components (such as persons and social subsystems), and the system (or supersystem) level. (Any number of intermediate levels may of course have to be interpolated. For example, some national corporations are in the economic mesolevel, whereas most transnational companies are in the economic megalevel.)

Consider for example the macrosocial process: Rise in income→ decline in fertility. This is a purely kinematical same-level description. At first sight it is also puzzling, for no mechanism is apparent. Moreover, being confined to the macrolevel it may satisfy holists like Durkheim but not individualists like Weber. Only reference to the microlevel can explain the given correlation. A possible mechanism is this:

Macrolevel	Income increase	→	Fertility decrease
	↓		↑
Microlevel	Old age security & improved education	→	Family planning

A second example is the mechanism whereby "reengineering" (or "lean production") and "downsizing," currently in vogue, are affecting income distribution:

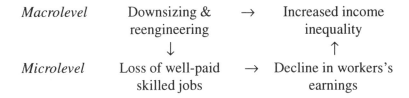

Macrolevel	Downsizing & reengineering	$\rightarrow$	Increased income inequality
	$\downarrow$		$\uparrow$
Microlevel	Loss of well-paid skilled jobs	$\rightarrow$	Decline in workers's earnings

Our third and last example will be taken from political science. According to some social psychologists and political scientists (e.g., Gurr 1970; Di Tella 1986; Moaddel 1994; Muller 1995), the well-known inverse statistical correlation between extreme income inequality and political democracy in modern societies is explained by a somewhat more complex mechanism:

Macrolevel	Income inequality			Repression
	$\downarrow$			$\uparrow$
Microlevel Expectation $\rightarrow$	Relative deprivation	$\rightarrow$	Frustration $\rightarrow$	Rebellion

I call all of the above *Boudon-Coleman diagrams,* in honor of two eminent sociologists who have used them consistently (Bunge 1996, 1998). I suggest that, despite their professed methodological individualism, both scientists have actually adopted a systemic approach, and have shown how to disclose social mechanisms by analyzing social systems into their components and their mutual relations (Boudon 1979; Coleman 1990). Thus they are closet systemists—as Coleman himself admitted in a letter to the writer.

3.5. Conclusions: Some Methodological Rules for the Study of Mechanisms

In the natural sciences no event or process is regarded as having been satisfactorily understood unless its actual or possible mechanism has been unveiled. For example, the very idea of an allergy used to be scoffed at until the antigen-antibody mechanism was uncovered. And cancer research took the right road only when mechanisms of cell proliferation were first conjectured, and then found, only a few years ago. By contrast, some physicists are dissatisfied with von Neumann's postulate that a measurement act causes the instant collapse of the wave-packet representing the state of a microphysical thing, because it involves no mechanism. One should be able to explain the collapse (or rather gradual if swift reduction) as an effect of the interaction between the measured thing and the measuring instrument. But different kinds of measurement would presumably involve different mechanisms, hence would call for different theories.

Another example is this. Even if an association (e.g., a statistical correlation) is found to hold between two variables, it may not be believed unless a mechanism for it looks plausible for being consistent with the known laws. For instance, Stanley Jevons's hypothesis that the sunspot cycles could explain economic cycles was not taken seriously because no mechanism linking sunspots to economic activity could be imagined. It is only in recent years that sunspots have been shown to influence terrestrial climate and thus agriculture. The reason is that now we know that sunspots are strong hydromagnetic storms that cause a decrease in radiation, hence in the amount of solar energy that our planet gets, which in turn affects agriculture—though not nearly enough to explain business cycles.

An important methodological lesson to be learned from natural science is that statistical regularities (unlike probabilistic laws) have no explanatory power: rather, they call for explanation. This remark suffices to disown the entire philosophical theory of statistical explanation—that is, explanation in terms of alleged statistical "laws" (see, e.g., Hempel 1965: 376 ff). Statistical regularities cannot occur as explanans premises (explainers) because, no matter how important, they merely compress the outcome of a large number of individual processes: they point to no mechanisms.

By contrast, probabilistic laws, such as those of quantum mechanics, genetics, and some social mobility theories, can occur as explanans premises because they describe chance (random) mechanisms, some of which consist in bunches of mutually independent causal lines (see, e.g., Stinchcombe 1968: 67–68). Thus, if the probability that a cause C produces an effect E is 1/4—a theoretical statement—then roughly one-quarter of all the *observed* events of kind C will be followed by events of kind E—a statistical statement. (This difference cannot be appreciated by empiricists, who equate frequency with probability, and thus fail to understand that, whereas a probability measures the propensity of an individual item, a frequency concerns a whole population.) In short, probabilistic laws can explain statistical regularities but not the other way round.

Another important methodological lesson to be learned from the natural sciences is that only a mechanismic explanation affords satisfactory—though possibly just provisional—understanding. Hence the methodological rule: No mechanism, no mechanismic explanation, and therefore no real understanding. To put it schematically,

Mechanism (ontological category)
↓
Explanation (epistemological category)
↓
Understanding (psychological category)

Stated in semi-formal terms, we have the following cascade:
I understand fact f if and only if I know a satisfactory explanation e of f.
e is a satisfactory explanation of f if and only if e involves a well-confirmed or at least plausible mechanism compatible with the known laws (or norms) relevant to f (rather than being fantastic or ad hoc).
∴ I understand fact f if and only if I know a verified or at least plausible mechanism for f.

Take, for instance, the question—investigated by Kondratieff, Schumpeter, Kuznets, Braudel, Rosegger and a few others—whether there are "long waves" (or secular cycles) of economic activity. Supposing that a given econometric analysis of an economic time-series were to confirm the suspicion that there are "long waves," what could their possible underlying mechanism(s) be? So far, most of the studies of this problem have proved inconclusive, for being purely kinematical. By contrast, the study of the American and British economies between 1790 and 1990, conducted by Berry and the Kims (1993), proposes the following mechanismic explanation. To begin with, there would be two types of wave: long (or Kondratieff), which are price cycles lasting for about half a century each; and short (or Kuznets) waves, which are national income (GDP) cycles of about a quarter century each. Second, the short waves would nestle in the long ones, and every such cycle would have the logistic shape both upwards and downwards. Third, the cycle mechanism would be this: Obsolescence of the dominant techno-economic system → new techno-economic system & resulting social changes → market saturation → prices drop. Whether these findings will hold remains to be seen. Be that as it may, they illustrate the methodological rule: *Look for the mechanism(s) underlying every constant association and every change.*

To be sure, two allegedly universal social mechanisms have been touted: the bottom-up (or Agency → Structure) and the top-down (or Society → Individual) ones. However, the former underrates or even overlooks the social constraints and stimuli on individual action, whereas the latter minimizes or even ignores the aggregate effects of individual agency. (For instance, whereas microeconomics overlooks the macroeconomic constraints on households and firms—such as the international situation and the going taxation and interest rates—, macroeconomics ignores the microeconomic source of wealth; and both disregard the political and cultural factors.) In short, neither individualism (or atomism) nor holism succeeds in social science, any more than it does in natural science.

The failure of both individualism and holism suggests that the adequate alternative to both is *systemism* (Bunge 1978, 1979, 1985, 1996, 1998). This is just the view that we shape society and it shapes us. That is, individual action and social environment—or agency and structure—always come together because they generate one another. Hence individual action is best understood when placed in its social matrix, and the latter is best understood when analyzed into its individual components and their mutual actions. This systemic view leads to identifying social systems and social changes on various levels of organization, as well as to disclosing the macro-micro and micro-macro mechanisms. Only these can explain the sometimes bewildering same-level (micro-micro or macro-macro) relations and correlations, such as "The Jones's just bought a new car → The Jones's neighbors are feeling the urge to do the same," and "Rise in employment rate → Drop in the stock market."

Furthermore, a systemic approach, together with multilevel analysis and search for mechanism, helps to identify, diagnose, and repair the malfunctions of a social mechanism. Indeed, if we know what makes a social system tick, we may find out what hinders its regular functioning, the levels(s) on which it acts, and how to correct the malfunction of its mechanism(s). An example of the potency of this approach is the following explanation of the well-known yet puzzling fact that market pioneers do worse than those who follow on their heels (Tellis and Golder, 1996). The items in a new line of products are usually flawed and expensive, hence commercially unsuccessful. The "early starters" learn from this failure, make the required alterations, and come up with far better products that sell well. Consequently their failure rate is minimal, and their average market share is almost thrice that of the pioneers. Another example is this. Modeling a corporation as a multilevel system in which a number of mechanisms are active at the same time, and are thus likely to interfere somewhat with one another, should facilitate the search for whatever flaws there may occur in the functioning of the corporation as a whole.This is a practical spinoff of the theoretical approach adopted in the preceding.

The heuristic and systematizing power, as well as the practical usefulness, provided by the systemic view taken together with the search for both micro-macro links and mechanisms, suggests trying the following general methodological rules:

M1. Place every social fact into its wider context (or system).

M2. Break down every system into its composition, environment, and structure.

M3. Distinguish the various system levels, and exhibit their relations.

M4. Look for the mechanism(s) that keep(s) the system running or lead(s) to its decay or growth.

M5. Make reasonably sure that the proposed mechanism is compatible with the known relevant laws and norms; and, if possible, check the mechanismic hypothesis or theory by wiggling experimentally the variables concerned.

M6. Ceteris paribus, prefer mechanismic (dynamical) to phenomenological (kinematical) hypotheses, theories, and explanations, and in turn prefer such kinematical accounts to both equilibrium models and data summaries.

M7. In case of system malfunction, examine all four possible sources—composition, environment, structure, and mechanism—and attempt to repair the system by altering some or all of them.

4

Quality, Quantity, Pseudoquantity, and Measurement in Social Science

Quantitation and measurement have been regarded as the hallmarks of modern science ever since Galileo enjoined us to measure whatever is measurable. His advice was followed enthusiastically and it has produced an immense crop. Even linguistics and historiography are becoming increasingly quantitative. The prestige enjoyed by both operations is such, that sometimes mathematically ill-defined concepts are taken for genuine quantitative variables, and at other times trivial measurements are preferred to insightful qualitative remarks.

The following examples, taken at random, should underscore the importance of quantitation in social studies and social policymaking.

Example 1: At first sight, Latin Americans fare better than Africans. However, statistics show that Latin America has the highest Gini index (of income inequality) in the world (Deininger and Squire 1996).

Example 2 : Intuitively, foreign investment helps economic growth in the development countries. However, the statistics do not bear out this hypothesis. Rather, they suggest that only the initial effect of foreign investment is beneficial. In the long run it increases unemployment (by introducing labor-saving technologies), income inequality, and social unrest (Dixon and Boswell 1996; Kentor 1998).

Example 3: (Feld and Carter 1998) Assume a school district to be composed of four schools: one inner-city and three suburban schools. The first has 300 white and 100 black students, and the other three have 200 white students each. The school authority decides to improve interracial contact by desegregating the schools: it sends twenty black students to each of the suburban schools, in exchange for sixty white students who are bussed to the inner-city school. Before this reform was undertaken, every one of the 100 black students could build, in principle, 300 ties with white students. Since there were 100 blacks, the total potential number of interracial pairs was 100 x 300 = 30,000. After the desegregation, the numbers of potential interracial pairs is 40 x 360 + 3 x 20 x 180 =14,400 + 10,800 = 25,200. The "desegregation" has actually decreased by 16 percent the number of potential interracial contacts. Moral: innumerate social engineering may backfire.

It behooves philosophers to study the general features of quantitation and measurement. Regrettably, philosophers have seldom made useful contributions to this subject. Worse, some of them have consecrated or even invented some bad errors. Among these are the Romantic bias against quantitation and measurement; the confusion between these two; the belief that there can be a general a priori theory of measurement; and the endorsement of controversial concepts such as those of subjective probability and subjective utility. We shall examine these mistakes and attempt to correct them.

4.1. Quality and Quantity

The Scientific Revolution launched a systematic and comprehensive project of quantitation and measurement. This project was continued by the Enlightenment. Inevitably, the Romantic reaction against science and reason in general involved a revolt against quantitation and measurement. In fact, the earliest explicit denunciation of quantitation and measurement was uttered by the philosophers of the Counter-Enlightenment. The Romantic philosophers—particularly Fichte, Schelling, Hegel, Herder, and Schopenhauer—opposed quality to quantity, claimed that the former is superior to the latter, and asserted that nothing of importance—particularly the mind—is measurable.

These beliefs have recently been revived by the new Romantic wave, in particular by postmodernism. Thus critical theorists, symbolic interactionists, structuralists, ethnomethodologists, phenomenological sociologists, relativist-constructivist sociologists of science, feminist theorists, radical philosophers, radical environmentalists, and their kin revile precision. For example, the leading feminist philosopher has denounced precision—in particular quantitation—objectivity and the concern for empirical testing as "male-stream methodology" (Harding 1986). These enemies of science have been reassured by Paul Feyerabend (1981,vol. 1: ix), of epistemological anarchism fame and a major philosophical mentor of the contemporary antiscience movement, that imprecision is fruitful—presumably just because most fruitful ideas are born imprecise. The moral is clear: Prevent the baby from growing up.

The antiexactness and in particular antiquantitative bias is so mistaken and damaging that we must try and correct it at the source. To begin with, quantity and quality are mutually complementary rather than exclusive. Indeed, every quantity is either the numerosity of a collection of items sharing a certain quality, or the intensity of a quality. Hence, in the process of concept formation, quality precedes quantity. Therefore there can be no opposition between them. Let us clarify this point.

The numerosity or cardinality of a set S of things characterized by a certain quality, such as that of being a firm of a certain type T, is some positive whole number. The quality or property in question occurs in the very construction of the set S, namely thus: $S = \{x|Tx\}$, where T denotes the type of firm in question. In short, questions about numerosity are of the form "How many items of kind T are there?", where T stands for some quality (or for the collection defined by T).

A quantitative property, or magnitude—such as GDP or population density—can be analyzed as a function, namely as follows. To begin with, let us note that every property is a property or feature of some object or other: there are no properties in themselves—except of course in a Platonist metaphysics. Thus, physical properties are properties of physical things, social properties are properties of social systems, and so on.

The simplest case is that of an intrinsic (nonrelational) quantitative property, such as longevity and income. A property of this kind can be conceptualized as a function from a collection A of (actual or possible) things into a set X of numbers, such as the natural numbers or the real line. That is, $P : A \to X$. Examples: population, age, and wage.

Most magnitudes have some dimension or other, such as L^{-2} in the case of population density, and $M. L^{-3}$ in that of mass density. Hence the (conventional) choice of unit must be included in their definition. (By the way, it is distressing to see how often dimensions and units are ignored in social studies and in the so-called measurement theory.) Hence, the preceding formula must often be replaced with $P: A \times U_P \to X$, where U_P stands for the collection of all possible units of P (e.g., days, years, etc., in the case of durations).

If the property in question is relational, as is the case with interactions, the domain of the corresponding function will be at least a set of ordered pairs—for example, of sellers and buyers. In general, the domain of a magnitude will be the Cartesian product of $n+1$ sets, and its codomain some set X of numbers or of numerical intervals. That is, P:

$A \times B \times \ldots \times N \times U_p \to X$. Here too quality, as exemplified by the factors in the domain of the function, precedes (conceptually) quantity.

When failing to construct a magnitude we may have to settle, at least temporarily, for a group of qualitative concepts, such as pass and fail, or small, medium, and large. We use such groups of concepts as a matter of routine when evaluating, for example, the proficiency of a student or the size of a firm. For many purposes—in particular for overall evaluation, comparison, data processing and (nonparametric) statistics—it is often convenient to assign numerals to such concepts—for example, 0, 1/2 and 1 to poor, adequate, and excellent respectively. In such cases one may speak of *semiquantities.*

A semiquantity is not quantity proper because its values are numerals (number names) rather than numbers—so much so that they may be replaced with letters or some other symbols. However, a semiquantity may consort with quantities and it may stimulate the formation of the corresponding magnitude. Not being a quantity proper, a semiquantity is not additive. For example, if we attribute each of two individuals 1/2 for judgment (or efficiency, sense of humour, or self-respect), it would be mistaken to attribute 1 to the judgment (or efficiency, sense of humour, or self-respect) of the two together. However, this may only suggest that the magnitudes which may eventually be born from these intuitive precursors are intensive rather than extensive. This seems to be the case with the utilities that occur in mainstream economics and rational choice theory: they cannot be aggregated, as suggested by Arrow's famous impossibility theorem.

To return to the quality-quantity connection. We have asserted that, when constructing a quantitative concept, we use at least one qualitative feature. However, once a quantitative concept is at hand, it can obviously be used to refine the corresponding qualitative and comparative ones. For example, if every member of a collection of commmodities can be assigned a value, then the items in the collection C can be ordered by the preference relation $\geq$ defined as follows: for any x and y in C, $x \geq y$ if and only if $V(x) \geq V(y)$. The transitivity of the preference relation $\geq$ follows from the transitivity of the greater than or equal to relation $\geq$ for numbers. To generalize: The quantitative concepts are stronger than the corresponding qualitative and comparative ones. Still, as we saw above, quality remains the heuristic and conceptual source of quantity.

What holds in the conceptual realm need not mirror what happens in the external world. In particular, it is not true that in the physical or in the social world quality precedes quantity or the other way round. There quality and quantity come together. Thus, every industrial sector has a definite yearly output; that is, the manufactured goods of a given type "come" in certain quantities—for example, so many automobiles or yards of fabric.

In light of the above, the phrase "transformation of quantity into quality" makes no sense. This phrase, a trademark of dialectics, must be understood as short for "In (all or some) processes of quantitative growth or decline, there are critical points where new qualities emerge, or old ones disappear." The dual of the given phrase, namely "transformation of quality into quantity," is in the same boat. It must be construed as the statement that, once a thing acquires or loses a quality, its mode (rate) of growth or decline alters.

We compress the foregoing into the following principles, the first ontological, the second epistemological.

Principle 1: All factual items are at the same time qualitative and quantitative: All properties of concrete entities, except for existence, belong to some (natural or artificial) kind or other, and they all come in definite degrees.

Principle 2 : In concept formation quality precedes quantity: The construction of any quantitative concept presupposes at least one qualitative concept, both logically and epistemologically.

4.2. A Sample of Genuine Social Quantities

To clarify the nature of genuine quantitative concepts, let me propose a short list of new sociological magnitudes. Let us start with anomie, defined as a mismatch between what may be called wishes and attainments, or desiderata and consummata. Calling D the former and C the latter, the qualitative concept of anomie may be defined as the difference between the two sets: $D \backslash C$. This is the collection of whatever items are in D but not in C. Taking the cardinality or numerosity $|D \backslash C|$ of this difference, and dividing it by the number $|D|$ of desiderata, we get the quantitative degree of anomie: $\alpha = |D \backslash C| / |D|$. If all the desiderata are atttained, i.e., if $D = C$, then $D \backslash C = \varnothing$, and $\alpha = 0$. By contrast, if no desiderata are attained, then $D \backslash C = D$, and $\alpha = 1$.

Our second concept is that of connectivity of a social system such as a social network. It may be defined as the number of actual two-person ties or bonds in the system. A more reasonable measure is the ratio of the number A of actual pairs to the number P of of potential pairs. Since, for a total of n members, $P = (1/2) \, n \cdot (n+1)$, the connectivity turns out to be $\kappa = 2A/n \, (n+1)$. A somewhat finer concept is obtained by splitting the ties into weak and strong, that is, by analyzing A into W+S.

We now introduce the concept of horizontal social distance between two individuals. Two individuals who have exchanged more than one casual handshake may be said to be contiguous. By contrast, if a third person is interposed between them, then their social distance equals one; if the number of interposed individuals is two, the social distance between them equals two, and so on. For example, the social distance between Karl Marx and myself is three, because Marx shook hands with Friedrich Engels, who in turn shook hands with Ferdinand Tönnies, who was the boss of Raymond Klibansky, who is a friend of mine. The general formula for the horizontal distance between two individuals a and b is $\delta \, (a,b) = \{x | Tax \, \& \, Txb \, \& \, a|x|b\}$, where Txa stands for "individuals x and x are tied," and $a|x|b$ for the ternary relation "x interposes between a and b." Needless to say, horizontal social distance differs from vertical social distance, or the difference between social rungs.

Let us now examine the participation of a social group in the activities of another group, such as the political participation of the peasants in an agrarian society. The members of grup G_i who participate in the activities of the host group H are the members of the intersection or partial overlap $G_i \cap H$. Taking the numerosity of this set and normalizing, we obtain the degree of participation of the G_i in the H: $\pi_i = |G_i \cap H|/|G_i|$. In other words, π_i is the percentage of G_is that participate in H. The dual of participation, which is marginality, can be defined as the complement of π_i to unity, or $\mu_i = 1 - \pi_i$. By summing over all the social groups in a society, we obtain the total degree of participation, or of marginality, as the case may be.

So much for our tiny sample of genuine, if so far unused, sociological magnitudes. It will be noted that in all cases we started with a qualitative concept, which we proceeded to quantitate.

Let us finally move from concepts to propositions. Assume Parkinson's law were taken seriously in the sociology of formal organizations—as I think it should. How would one go about formalizing it? We start by stating it in ordinary language: The efficiency of an organization increases with the number of its components until it reaches a maximum; from then on efficiency declines until it vanishes. At this point the size of the organization is b times the optimal size, and from then on the efficiency becomes negative—that is, the organization consumes more than what it produces. The simplest formula capturing this proposition is

$$E = aN (N_o - N/b),$$

where E denotes the efficiency or productivity, a and b designate positive real numbers characteristic of the organization type, N the number of components of the organization, and N_o the optimal size (corresponding to maximal productivity).

To be sure, the preceding is just an untried hypothesis. But it may be one worth testing, particularly at a time when there is so much undecisive controversy over both productivity and the right size of firms. A small investment in formalization and empirical testing might have spared us mountains of inconclusive literature on these socioeconomic topics.

4.3. Can Every Feature be Quantitated?

Can every feature be quantitated, that is, turned into a magnitude? I submit that only one property is, with all certainty, intrinsically qualitative, namely existence. I also submit that in every other case quantitation depends exclusively on our ability and interest, so that in the face of failure to quantitate we should suspend judgment and encourage others to try.

It seems obvious that existence is a quality: There are no degrees of existence—save in certain theologies. (In other words, existence is a dichotomic, or yes-or-no variable.) That existence is a property is less obvious since logicians from Russell to Quine have assured us that the "existential" quantifier exactifies "the" concept of existence. Yet it may be argued that (a) there are at least two quite different modes of existence, namely material and conceptual, and (b) the "existential " quantifier exactifies the notion of someness not that of existence (i.e., "$(\exists x)$ Fx" should be read "Some individuals are Fs," not "There are Fs"). Moreover, it is possible, and indeed highly desirable, to define an exact existence predicate; in fact, this has been accomplished (Bunge 1977). However, this point is hardly of interest here.

What is of interest is the question whether we know of any reasons why not every property other than existence could be quantitated. I submit that we do not know of any such reasons. Moreover, I submit that the history of science exhibits a triumphal march of quantitation in all the sciences. Suffice it to recall the explosion of quantitative history since the 1930s, and the proliferation of social indicators over the past two decades. Every serious contemporary social scientist is familiar with data sets and matrices, histograms and probability distributions, averages and standard deviations, time series and trends, correlation coefficients, and the like. Quantitation and measurement have become so pervasive in social studies that sometimes they hide theoretical destitution.

When failing to quantitate certain intangibles, we attempt to find objective quantitative indicators for them. For example, life span is one of the indicators of social well-being or quality of life; input-output ratios (or more generally matrices) are indicators of the level of technological advancement; productivity is a joint measure of technological level, organizational efficiency, and incentive to work; and the percentage of work hours lost due to absenteeism or strikes is an indicator of work dissatisfaction.

Granted, most social, economic, and political indicators in current use are empirical, that is, they are not related to concepts occurring in well-confirmed theories. Hence they are anything but infallible; consequently it is best to have whole batteries of such. Still, they do go a long way toward satisfying the need for both precision and contact with reality. (An empirically accessible variable is a reliable indicator or operationalization of a theoretical concept only if there is a theory containing a functional relation between the two.)

However, it is notorious that numerous attempts at constructing magnitudes and quantitative indicators have failed. Think of the notions of pleasure, pain, beauty, tastiness, desirability, simplicity, product quality, user-friendliness, degree of belief (or certainty), gullibility, responsibility, initiative, loyalty, or chutzpah. We can order items of a certain type with respect to their beauty or their desirability, but so far we have not succeeded in assigning numbers to such degrees. True, some scholars claim that some such properties are reducible to probability (or else to improbability), and that others are reducible to utility. However, the probabilities and utilities in question are subjective and therefore unmeasurable and hardly scientific. (More on this in Section 3.)

But note that all of the above examples of resistance to quantitation are also examples of secondary or subjective properties, that is, properties that only exist in the eye of the beholder. And it may well happen that some of these properties will eventually prove to be accessible to physiological psychology. Thus, one may speculate that the intensity of a pleasant feeling equals the intensity of the activity of the neurons in the pleasure center located deep in the brain. In turn, as is usual in physiological psychology, we may assume that the firing frequency is an adequate objective indicator of that intensity. Moreover, one can imagine that some day someone will be able to implant electrodes in the human pleasure center in order to measure that firing frequency, and consequently the intensity of the pleasure felt by the subject. That day the quantitative science of physiological aesthetics will have been born. We may suppose that other secondary properties are likely to follow suit. True, this is a piece of *Zukunftmusik*. But unless we work on that optimistic assumption this music will never be heard.

We compress the foregoing into the following principles.

Programmatic principle 1: Every property of a concrete thing, other than existence, can in principle be quantitated.

Programmatic principle 2: Given any property of a concrete entity, other than existence, at least one objective indicator and one measurement technique for it can be designed.

At first sight, sex is a counterexample to the first principle. Indeed, sex looks as a prime example of a dichotomic variable: M or F. But it is not. Firstly, there are the cases of intersex and hermaphroditism. Secondly, zoologists have found it necessary to distinguish many more than two sexes in certain species. Thirdly, it is conceivable that, even among humans, it may become possible to define degrees of masculinity and femininity in anatomical, physiological, hormonal, and behavioral terms.

What about value-theoretical and ethical concepts such as those of goodness and virtue? The intuitionist philosophers, such as G. E. Moore, have held that they are nonnatural qualities and moreover unanalyzable, undefinable, and inherently quantitative ones. But they have offered no plausible reasons for this thesis. Moreover, the thesis turns out to be false if it be admitted that needs and wants are the ultimate source of values. Indeed, one may stipulate that an object or process *a* is good for an individual *b* if and only if *a* contributes to meeting a need or a desire of *b*, where *b* is not necessarily different from *a*. Likewise one may stipulate that an action is virtuous if it is disinterested and helps someone meet a need or a legitimate desire. These and other axiological and ethical predicates are then definable and therefore analyzable. (For a systematic investigation of this problem see Bunge 1989.)

Moreover, some value-theoretical and ethical predicates can be rendered quantitative or at least comparative. For example, if a need or want can be assigned a quantitative value, for example, a quantity or a price, then this number quantitates the corresponding goodness. Likewise, if an action can be attributed a measure, for example, in hours or in dollars, then its virtue (or wickedness) is quantitated. After all, legislators, judges, teachers, priests, and parents perform such weighings all the time.

Note that the above principles are restricted to properties of concrete (or material) objects, such as bodies, fields, persons, families, and formal organizations. It does not extend to all constructs. For example, the logical concepts of negation, conjunction, entailment, and consistency are inherently qualitative. The same holds for the basic set-theoretic, algebraic, and topological concepts, such as those of membership, concatenation, and connectivity. Even the concept of a numerical function includes an irreducibly qualitative component, namely the notion of correspondence between two sets.

Obviously, neither of the above principles can be proved. Nor can they be disproved, because any failures to implement them can be blamed on our lack of ability or means. They are no more and no less than heuristic guides and components of a science-oriented philosophy.

4.4. Pseudoquantitation in Social Science

In the field of social studies quantitation was born centuries ago, mainly from the need to solve practical problems in taxation and insurance. But social statistics did not expand and become a branch of scholarship till about 1830, thanks mainly to Adolphe Quetelet. From then on it grew exponentially and became so influential that it contributed to the emergence of statistical physics (see Porter 1986).

Regrettably, the phenomenal growth of social statistics had for a long time only a marginal impact on social theory. In effect, it took nearly half a century to influence economics, and more than a century to influence the other social sciences. For example, most of the classics had little use for magnitudes. Even today, entire schools of economics—such as the neo-Austrian, the institutionalist, and the constitutionalist—are essentially nonquantitative.

Worse, many an attempt at quantitation has been aborted. Let me explain. Like any other intellectual activity, quantitation can be genuine or bogus—and faking may be deliberate or unwitting. By combining imagination with love of precision and a nose for relevant variables, one may endeavor to exactify and even quantitate some of the most slippery notions. A good example is provided by the recent work of the social historian Jack Goldstone (1991). He proposes mathematically precise and empirically accessible indicators of such socio-economico-political variables as fiscal distress (or scarce public treasury), elite mobility, and mass-mobilization potential (or propensity to take to the streets, not to be confused with the level of actual social violence). Given enough data, every one of these functions can be evaluated and graphed vs. time. (For instance, the mass mobilization potential is defined on page 139 as a simple function of wages, the rate or urban growth, and the age structure.) Moreover Goldstone submits (op. cit.: 142) that the product of these three variables equals the political stress indicator, which he uses to analyze several historical cases. As with nearly all social indicators, one may wonder whether this one is adequate, and whether sufficient data for any given historical period before the present are available. However, there is nothing formally phony about this indicator.

In their haste to raise the social studies to the rank of hard sciences, or to make it appear that their own studies are respectable, some students of society have committed the sin of *pseudoquantitation*. That is, they have used symbols that look like numerical functions but actually are no such things because they are not mathematically well-defined (see Sorokin [1956, chaps. 7 and 8] for an early and vehement denunciation of this vice in social science, which he called "quantophrenia"). They have aped the style of science but not its substance, thus incurring what Hayek called "scientism," and I prefer to call "pseudoscience."

The simplest way to fall into this error is to state a definition or a conjecture in ordinary language, and then abbreviate words with letters or other symbols, hoping that, by some miracle, these symbols will turn into numerical functions. For example, we may suppose that happiness (H) is the greater, the more needs (N) and wants (W) are met, and the less pain (P) is experienced in the process. A simple formula that seems to express this idea is: $H = N \times W/P$.

The trouble with this formula is, of course, that the independent "variables" are not defined: they are just letters not concepts. Indeed, we do not even know what their dimensions, let alone their units, may be. Consequently there is no guarantee that the two sides of the "equation" have the same dimensions. In short, the formula is not well-formed. Hence the formula has no precise meaning and therefore it is not empirically testable. We shall say, in short, that the above is a case of *pseudoquantitation*. Unfortunately the social studies literature teems with similar cases of pseudoquantitation. Let us examine a sample—one which, mercifully, is far from being random.

Example 1: Vilfredo Pareto, no doubt an original, insightful, and erudite student of society, and moreover one conversant with mathematics, passes for being one of the founders of mathematical sociology just because he used some symbols other than words. Thus, in his famous *Trattato di sociologia generale* (1916, Sect. 2087), Pareto listed a number of "residues" or "forces," among them sentiments, abilities, dispositions, and myths. He assumed tacitly that the "residues" take on numerical values. But, since he failed to define them, the symbols he used are mere abbreviations for intuitive notions. Unaware of this confusion between arbitrary symbols and mathematical concepts, he wrote about the composition of such "forces" (e.g., Sect. 2148). Further down (p. 1781) he introduced the "equation": $q = A/B$, where A stands for "the force of class I residues," and B for "the force of class II residues" in a given social group or nation. Roughly, q would be the ratio of progressivism to conservatism. Since Pareto made no attempt to define any of these "magnitudes," he had no right to divide them, or to assert that they increased or decreased quantitatively over time in any group or nation. Nevertheless, earlier in the same work (p. 509) he had warned that "Residues correspond to certain instincts in human beings, and for that reason they are usually wanting in definiteness, in exact delimitation." And even earlier in the same work (chap. V) he had devoted an entire chapter to characterizing pseudoscientific theories.

Example 2: Professor Samuel Huntington (1968: 55), the well-known Harvard political scientist, proposed the following "equations" concerning the impact of modernization in developing nations:

Social mobilization/ Economic development = Social frustration,
Social frustration/ Mobility opportunities = Political participation,
Political participation/ Political institutionalization = Political instability.

Huntington does not define any of these "variables," he does not explain how numerical values could be assigned to them, and he does not even bother to tell us the units they come with . Obviously, he is unaware that he is dividing words, not numerical values of honest functions. This was pointed out in 1981 by the mathematician Neal Koblitz (1988) in a paper titled "Mathematics as propaganda," which led Yale mathematician Serge Lang to campaigning successfully against the nomination of Professor Huntington to the National Academy of Sciences. Regrettably, many political scientists and sociologists defended Huntington, thereby exhibiting their mathematical illiteracy (Lang 1981).

Example 3: Professor Gary Becker, of the University of Chicago, is famous for his economic approach to the study of human behavior, which earned him a Nobel Prize. Unfortunately, he peppers his papers with symbols that do not always represent concepts. For example, a key formula of his theory of social interactions (Becker 1976: 257) reads thus: $R = D_i + h$. Here i labels an arbitrary individual, and R is supposed to stand for "the opinion of i held by other persons in the same occupation" ; and "h measures the effect of i's efforts, and D_i the level of R when i makes no effort; that is, D_i measures i's "social environment"." These "functions" are christened but not specified. Consequently words, not functions, are being added. We are not even told what the dimensions and units of these pseudomagnitudes are. Therefore, we would not know how to measure the corresponding properties, and so test for the adequacy of the formula.

Example 4: When confronted with a random process, or one that looks like one, one attempts to build a probabilistic model that could be tested against empirical data. As Poincaré pointed out long ago, talk of probability involves some knowledge: it is no substitute for ignorance. This is not how the Bayesians view the matter: When confronted with ignorance or uncertainty they use probability—or rather their own version of it. This allows them to assign prior probabilities in an arbitrary manner—which is a way of passing off mere intuition, hunch, or guess for scientific hypothesis. In other words, in the Bayesian perspective there is no question of objective randomness, randomization, random sample, statistical test, or even testability: it is all a game of belief and credence. This approach contrasts with science, where credences and gut feelings may be spoken of during coffee breaks but are not included in scientific discourse, whereas (genuine) probabilities are measured (directly or indirectly), and probabilistic models are checked experimentally. This is not to write off the study of belief and credence. Such study is important, but it belongs in experimental psychology and sociology, and it should be conducted scientifically. There is no reason to believe that probability theory, a chapter of pure mathematics, could be the ready-made empirical theory of belief. In fact, there is reason to believe that credences fail to satisfy the calculus of probability, if only because we seldom know all the branches of any given decision tree. (See, e.g., Kahneman, Slovic, and Tversky, eds. 1982; and Bunge 1998.)

Example 5: What holds for subjective probability holds a fortiori for subjective value or utility. Actually the latter is in an even worse predicament because, whereas probability functions are at least mathematically well defined, the utility "functions" occurring in most of economics and sociology are not—as Henri Poincaré (1901) pointed out to Léon Walras (see also Blatt 1983). In effect, the only conditions required of them is that they be twice differentiable, the first derivative being positive and the second negative. Obviously, infinitely many functions satisfy this couple of mild requirements. In the hard sciences one is more demanding: here one only uses functions that are defined explicitly (e.g., by infinite series or products) or implicitly (e.g., by differential equations together with initial or boundary conditions). This greater precision makes for more exacting testability and more rigorous measurement. Finally, experimental studies have shown that preferences and subjective estimates of utility and risk do not satisfy the assumptions of expected utility theory (Allais 1979, Tversky 1975, Herrnstein 1990). In short, the use of utility functions is usually mathematically sloppy and empirically unwarranted.

Example 6: James N. Rosenau (1990), a well-known politologist, has claimed that political instability and turbulence are similar to the instabilities and vortices of fluids, and moreover that they satisfy chaos theory. However, he did not write, let alone solve, any nonlinear differential or finite difference equation for political processes: all he did was some hand waving. Another politologist, Courtney Brown (1994), did write some equations, but they happen to involve two key variables—levels of public concern and environmental damage—that he fails to define, so that the equations are strictly ornamental.

All of the above mentioned examples are exercises in shorthand, not in genuine mathematical social science. What we have here is some of the accoutrements of science without its substance: that is, we are in the presence of pseudoscience.

The seductive power of symbolism should not be underestimated. It can lead even mathematics students to error or paradox. Let the following example suffice. It can easily be "proved" that 1 is the largest integer, namely as follows. Let N be the largest integer. There are only two possibilities: either $N = 1$ or $N > 1$. The second option is false because N^2, which is an integer, is larger than N, allegedly the largest integer. Hence the first option must hold, that is, $N = 1$. But this is absurd. The root of the error is the tacit assumption that there *is* a largest integer. This assumption was made when giving this pseudonumber a name, namely N. Moral: Watch christening ceremonies, because they may consecrate nonexistents.

There is some pseudoquantitation even in that paragon of mathematical sophistication, quantum theory. A clear though unrecognized example of it is Schrödinger's famous cat paradox. Place a live cat inside a steel cage together with a small amount of a radioactive substance and a phial containing a powerful poison that will be released if struck by a product of the distintegration of the radioactive material. According to the standard or Copenhagen version of quantum mechanics, while locked up, the cat is assumed to be neither alive nor dead, but in a superposition of these two states. In symbols, $\Psi = a\Psi_L + b\Psi_D$, where the squares of the absolute values of the weights a and b add up to unity. When opening the lid of the cage, the superposition Y collapses either onto Ψ_L or onto Y_D. That is, the omnipotent Observer giveth life or taketh it. So far, the standard version of the cat story.

But the above formula is meaningless, because the cat's states Ψ_L (live) and Ψ_D (dead) are not specified in quantum-theoretical terms. Indeed, quantum mechanics knows nothing about cats, which are describable only in macrophysical and biological terms. (In other words, we do not know how to set up, let alone solve, the Schrödinger equation for a cat, or even for a bacterium. Actually, even the water molecule still poses a serious challenge to quantum chemistry.) However, such is the power of symbol, particularly when wielded by authority, that even Schrödinger fell into his own trap, and hundreds of able physicists and philosophers followed him like lemmings.

Inevitably, pseudoquantitation invites pseudomeasurement. The most common kind of measurement is "eyeballing" or intuitive estimation. This is done when asking subjects to pin numbers down on pains, pleasures, utilities, probabilities, or rational expectations. The most we can expect from such a request is an "ordinal measurement," that is, an ordering—which of course is no measurement at all. The procedure is similar to asking people to estimate the pull of gravity without a pendulum, or an oven temperature without a thermometer. Not that such estimates are out of place in science: they belong in experimental psychology. But they happen not to be measurements proper. However, measurement deserves a separate section.

4.5. Confusing Quantitation with Measurement

Quantitation, or the construction of measures, is a purely conceptual procedure even when prompted by empirical problems: recall sections 4.1 and 4.2. On the other hand, measurement is an empirical operation—even though it presupposes reasonably clear ideas about what is to be measured and how.

One starts by constructing a concept representing a quantivative property—such as a magnitude—and then proceeds to observing or handling real things in order to find out how many they are, or how much of a property they possess. That is, once one has formed a reasonably clear concept of a measure one may proceed to determining empirically its numerical value for a concrete thing, such as a population or a crop, either by counting or by manipulating measuring instruments such as rulers or scales.

Although measure and measurement are radically different from one another, they are sometimes mixed up in languages which, like French and Italian, denote them with the same word. And they are systematically confused in what has come to be known as "measurement theory" in the behavioral sciences (see, e.g., Suppes and Zinnes 1963.) This theory was once so popular among psychologists and sociologists, that it was the subject of compulsory courses, and it earned an entry in the fifteenth edition of the *Encyclopædia Britannica* .

The origin of this confusion, and of the entire theory resting on it, seems to be a mere translation error. "In fact, when Hölder's 1901 postulates for *Mass* (measure)—not *Messung* (measurement)—crossed the Atlantic, they were rechristened "axioms for measurement." And so the illusion was born that a purely mathematical, hence *a priori* theory, could account for measurement—of anything and apart from both substantive theories and the praxis of measurement. An illusion, needless to say, in the purest tradition of philosophical idealism" (Bunge 1973 : 120–121).

Actually this "measurement theory" deals only with extensive magnitudes, such as length, which it sometimes mistakes for dimensions. Even so, this theory is incomplete for ignoring dimensions (e.g., $L.T^{-1}$) and units (e.g., cm and sec)—which would be unforgivable in any hard science. Furthermore, it ignores subadditive magnitudes, such as mass and entropy, as well as magnitudes which are not even remotely additive, such as the electric resistances of elements connected in parallel. Worse, the theory overlooks all intensive magnitudes, such as densities, on the mistaken assumption that they are definable in terms of extensive magnitudes, while in fact the converse holds in theoretical science. For example, the integral of a mass density over a volume defines the mass of the body occupying that volume. On the other hand, any given total mass can conceivably be distributed in infinitely many ways. In general, extensive quantities are definable in terms of intensive ones but not the other way round.

However, the main philosophical point is that measurement is a laboratory or field operation, not a purely conceptual one like quantitation.

There can be no general theory of measurement proper because the design of a measurement depends both on the mensurandum and on the measurement technique—so much so, that measurements of one and the same magnitude performed with different measuring instruments may require different theories and are likely to yield different results. Moreover, many measurements are indirect, that is, they involve indicators, and these depend on both the mensurandum and our body of theoretical and empirical knowledge about it. No amount of mathematical sophistication can make up for empirical research—just as no pile of data can replace theory.

Do social scientists perform measurements? I submit that most of them hardly ever measure anything, at least personally. When they do use numbers at all, they rely almost exclusively on figures supplied by nonscientists, such as census takers, accountants, and government inspectors. Moreover, many such figures—such as costs, prices, and profits—are read or calculated rather than measured. Others, such as transaction and opportunity costs, as well as shadow prices, are at best guessed.

One reason that social scientists do not measure much, is that most of them rarely if ever meet the objects they study. (Management experts do sometimes perform measurements proper, but then they are technologists rather than scientists.) None of them designs or operates measuring instruments, and most of their data are either soft or second-hand—which is not to imply that they are unimportant.

For example, to find out the intensity with which people subscribe to a norm in a given society, a sociologist is likely to circulate questionnaires, asking the respondents to rank such intensity on some arbitrary scale or other (see, e.g., Jasso and Opp 1997). But this scale is ordinal: it is not an ordered set of quantities, but of what I called semiquantities in section 4.1. The corresponding findings may be revealing, but they satisfy no mathematical laws. On the other hand, the finding that the average number of children per adult Italian women is only 1.2, is precise, and it is strong evidence that those persons do not practice the received Catholic norm about contraception.

In short, measurement plays a much more modest role in social science than in natural science. Which is one more reason not to confuse measurement with quantitation.

4.6. Conclusions

We must counteract the Romantic bias against exactness, and particularly quantity, because it numbs the brain and blocks the exploration and control of reality. But we must beware of pseudoquantitation, for it is part of pseudoscience. We must also refrain from mistaking quantitation for measurement. The former precedes the latter but is no substitute for it.

In all studies, whether of nature or of society, it is well to remember Solomon's words to his Lord: "Thou hast ordered all things by measure and number and weight" (*The Wisdom of Solomon* , chap. xi: xx). But it is also wise to keep in mind that we are still very far from having quantitated all interesting properties. The quest for quantitation is never-ending. So should be its methodological control.

5

The Lure and Disappointment
of Rational Choice Theory

Rational choice theory is about valuation, intention, decision, choice, and action—in particular, exchange or trade. It is based on two simple and attractive ideas. The first is the Rationality Postulate, according to which people know what is best for them and act accordingly. The second master idea is the postulate of Methodological Individualism. According to it, all we need to know in order to account for any social fact anywhere and at any time are the beliefs, decisions, and actions of the individuals involved in it.

Though simple, these two ideas are at first sight very potent. Indeed, if true they would allow us to explain, predict, and plan all human actions in any society. For instance, they would explain why some people commit crimes and others don't, as well as why some "wars on crime" are deemed to succeed while others don't. Furthermore, those master ideas would unify all of the social sciences and social technologies under the aegis of neoclassical microeconomics, the way Gary Becker (1976) and his fellow crusaders for "economic imperialism" claim. The problem is whether the basic ideas of rational choice theory are in fact clear and true, as well as an efficient tool for social engineering.

Actually, rational choice theory is not a single theory but a large and growing family of theoretical models. These are found in psychology, sociology, economics, political science, and social policy studies, and they are making significant inroads into anthropology, history and even ethics, social philosophy, and theology. The justification for referring to that family of theories in the singular is that they all have a common core of concepts, mainly those of utility and probability, as well as of principles: the postulates of utility maximization (or economic rationality) and methodological individualism.

Rational choice theory is often regarded as the vanguard of social theory, and it has become increasingly fashionable in recent times. It attracts naturally all those who believe that social studies should be rational, quantitative, and even scientific. Moreover, many social scientists hold it to be the only viable alternative to the Romantic or "humanistic" approach to the study of society associated with existentialism, phenomenology, hermeneutics, and other opaque and antiscientific philosophies.

Not surprisingly, rational choice theory has raised much controversy. Regrettably, these debates have not always been quite rational, and this for three reasons. One is ideological: Rational choice theory is often perceived or even offered as a blanket endorsement of classical capitalism, hence as an adjunct of political conservatism. (Ironically, the rigid central planning inherent in the now defunct command economies involves a similar faith in the rationality and predictability of human behavior.) A second reason is methodological: Scholars in the so-called humanist camp tend to reject rational choice theory out of hand because of its appeal to reason and its frequent use of symbols and logical arguments. (But they do not offer alternative models.) A third reason for the hostility is philosophical: The theory would appear to countenance a naive and crass utilitarian view of human nature. This is true. But any model of human behavior that ignores the interests and expectations that motivate people is bound to be just as false as any theory that ignores emotions and natural constraints, or social inventions, such as institutions and norms.

I propose to analyze the central ideas of rational choice models. These ideas will be identified and checked for clarity, cogency, testability, truth, and relevance, as well as for compatibility with the ideals of science and their matching with social reality. This analysis is offered as a contribution to the metatheory of social science.

5.1. Individualism

Rational choice theory deals with the deliberations that precede action. It refers to individuals, not to social systems. Moreover, its individuals are not embedded in social networks or organizations of any kind. This is why their actions are deemed to be rational rather than being determined by a combination of social standing and initial endowment with cost-benefit estimate, custom and power, committment and norm, passion, and superstition. In short, the ontology of rational choice theory is the individualistic thesis that society is nothing but a collection of free individuals who differ only in talent.

The mehodological corollary is that the study of social facts is reducible to the study of individuals. This is of course an instance of radical reductionism, or the methodological principle according to which every whole is nothing but the collection of its parts. But this view is mistaken. An army is not just a bunch of soldiers: it is a social system held together and organized by relations of command and cooperation. A disorganized mob of soldiers is not called an army but a ragtag of ex-soldiers.

No doubt, individualism holds for such nonsocial actions as scratching one's head in private. It also works for such trivial social actions as the choice of breakfast cereal. But nontrivial social actions, such as working, attending school, voting, or even greeting one's next-door neighbor, are an entirely different matter: every one of them is embedded in some informal social network or formal organization. There is no social action in a social vacuum.

Only economists continue to focus on exchange relations in a social vacuum. Sociologists have guessed that many economic transactions occur within preexisting social networks. In short, markets are socially embedded (Granovetter 1985). This hypothesis has finally been confirmed with data taken from a national American sample (DiMaggio and Louch 1998).

Certainly, individual actions sustain or undermine social networks and formal organizations. But they can do so only provided the individual recognizes the existence of such supra-individual entities and adapts to them at least to some extent. Even someone intent on undermining an organization must start by admitting its existence, particularly if he intends to fight it from within. In so doing he jettisons whatever individualist philosophy he may uphold in theory. He confirms the view that there is no agency without structure and conversely: agency and structure are just two sides of the same coin.

We make choices all the time, but sometimes other people make them for us. For example, we do not choose the family, social category, or neighborhood we are born into. To be sure, as we grow up we may adopt a different family and move to another social category or a different neighborhood. But such mobility is usually very limited, particularly if we keep the stigmata of low birth. For example, the physical and mental growth of a child of a destitute family is likely to be stunted. As a consequence, when reaching adulthood—if he is lucky enough to survive the deprivations—this person is unlikely to get a good job. The reader can easily complete this, the story of the vast majority of people in the Third World.

Racists and sociobiologists, who are ontological and methodological individualists, hold the reductionist dogma that "biology is destiny." By contrast, holists believe that "sociology is destiny." Neither thesis is true: there is no such thing as destiny. We are the products of our genes, our environment, and our own actions. However, during childhood there is little we can do to craft our own life histories: during that period we are at the mercy of family and society. A poor initial endowment is bound to make for stunted biological and mental growth. Individualists cannot account for this tragedy, which is that of roughly two billion children. In particular, since rationality has little bearing on it, rational choice theorists have nothing useful to say about it.

Robert W. Fogel's (1994) Nobel Prize lecture is an entire treatise on the often tragic interrelations between economic growth, demography, welfare, and physiology. In it we learn, for instance, that at the time of the French Revolution the average height and weight of French adult males were 163 cm and 50 kg respectively. This was a result of malnutrition, which in turn caused low productivity. In fact, 20 percent of the population were so weak that they were reduced to begging. The corresponding figures for England were only marginally better. No wonder that morbidity and mortality were appallingly high. Significant improvements in nutrition and productivity, as well as in morbidity and mortality, started only after mid-19th century.

What do rational choice theorists have to say about this European tragedy of old, which is nowadays that of the entire Third World, where four-fifths of the people happen to live? Nothing. The same applies to other macrosocial issues, particularly those of environmental degradation, overpopulation, sex discrimination, racism, and class distinctions. Those theorists are not interested in these issues, hence they won't lift a finger to alleviate them.

Rational choice theorists are not even interested in the problem of the partition of society into different social categories. Yet every one of us belongs to a number of such categories, only some of which coincide with social classes. Whereas joining some of these categories— such as those of sports fan, religious believer, and political sympathizer—is a matter of choice, it is not so in other cases, such as belonging to the fair sex or to the caste of untouchables. Nor is the very formation of all such categories the result of deliberate choices. Even those who benefit from social inequalities "rarely set out to produce them. More than anything else, they seek to secure rewards from sequestered resources" (Tilly 1998: 11). But these people rarely if ever attempt to calculate the maximal expected utility to be derived from their actions. They have no use for, or even knowledge of, rational choice theory. They live in the real world—something rational choice theorists do not bother to investigate empirically.

True, there have been rational choice models of such important real-life facts as international conflicts, in particular of the nuclear confrontation and the American intervention in Vietnam. I do not know whether any of them has ever been used by the people in charge. What we do know is that no such model predicted the outcome of any of the conflicts in question. Which is not surprising, because they assume naively that all people are rational, whereas in fact we often behave as fools blinded by passion, superstition, or a combination of the two—particularly when blinded by the lust for power. Another reason for the failure of such models is that they involve unknown utilities and probabilities—of which more in the next section.

In sum, rational choice theory cannot be expected to model social reality in a realistic manner, if only because it deals with individuals, not with social systems. And these are characterized by irreducibly social properties—as Arrow (1994), a lifelong methodological individualist, finally admitted.

5.2. Subjective Probability

A main reason for either liking or disliking rational choice theory is that it is chock-full of formulae, such as payoff matrices. It looks exact and ready to be empiricaly tested. Hence it appeals to the scientifically minded as much as it repells the innumerate. I shall contend that neither attitude is justifiable, because most of the formulae in question are phony, whence they cannot put to rigorous empirical tests.

The key concepts of rational choice theory as those of probability and utility of the outcome of a deliberate action, such as marrying or divorcing, buying or selling, cooperating or defecting, attacking or retreating, joining or free-riding, and so on. In the simplest case, an action is assumed to have two possible outcomes: O_1 and O_2, with probabilities p_1 and p_2 and utilities u_1 and u_2 respectively. The expected utilities are weighted by their respective probabilities, so that improbability is balanced by high payoff, whereas high probability is compensated by low payoff. The rational agent is then expected to compare these weighted utilities, that is, the products p_1u_1 and p_2u_2, and choose the course of action O_1 just in case $p_1u_1 > p_2u_2$.

Now, the probabilities and utilities that occur in the vast majority of rational choice models are subjective, not objective. That is, they are assigned a priori and intuitively, not as a result of either calculation or observation. They are in sharp contrast to the objective probabilities and utilities used by gamblers, quantum theorists, and geneticists.

While there is nothing wrong about the mathematical concept of probability, subjective probabilities and utilities are indefensible except as preliminary guesses or estimates. Even so, any guess of a probability value is only justified if the event in question is a chance event—which is the exception in social life. Indeed, society is not a casino: if the agents are in command of the situation, they use causal hypotheses to choose their courses of action. To be sure, in life there are accidents all the time. But only a large collection of unrelated accidents, such as fires and automobile crashes, can be regarded as having probabilistic properties. And yet decision theory and all the other rational choice models deal with individual actions, not with collections of such.

There is more. Any serious application of the concept of probability requires knowledge of all the possible alternatives, because the sum of the probabilities of such alternatives must equal unity. But in real life we seldom know in advance all the possible outcomes of any given action. In particular, we ignore the perverse effects. For instance, we may well assume that an action has only two possible outcomes O_1 and O_2, but it may turn out that the number of alternatives is one or three, in which cases the equality "$p_1 + p_2 = 1$" will be violated, and so the probability estimates will be doubly arbitrary.

5.3. Subjective Utility

The rationality postulate comes in two versions: plain and sophisticated. The former states that the rational agent chooses the course of action more likely to maximize the resulting gain (see, e.g., Boudon 1998: 264). This decision rule is clear and practical, and it is actually adopted much of the time in all walks of life. For example, businessmen make cost-benefit forecasts, and their accountants check for them after the event. Even if inaccurate, such forecasts and checkings are objective: they are expected to rely on hard data. Moreover, in complicated cases the forecasts can be refined with the help of mathematical models crafted by operations research experts.

The plain version of the postulate is plausible if taken as a norm rather than a description of actual behavior, and as long as it is made clear who or what the beneficiaries and victims of the action concerned are likely to be. After all, since every agent is embedded in at least one social network, whatever he does is bound to affect other members of his network, some of whom may be hurt by him, and thus have reason to try and counteract his actions.

In any event, rational choice theory contains the sophisticated, not the plain rationality postulate. The former is taken to be descriptive rather than normative, and it states that all agents act so as to maximize their expected utilities in the technical sense of this expression. The expected utility of an action is the product of the subjective probability by the subjective utility of the outcome of the action. Having examined the first factor of this product in the preceding section, let us proceed to inspect the second.

According to rational choice theory, every agent has a utility function u that depends exclusively on the quantity q of good concerned: $u = f(q)$. But the precise form of the functional dependence f of u upon q is seldom specified. When it is, the function is chosen for computational convenience rather than empirical adequacy. In the former case nothing definite is being asserted, whereas in the latter empirically groundless assertions are made. In either case no science is being done. Let us take a closer look.

The only conditions imposed on the utility u are that it be an increasing but decelerated function of q. This is of course the law of diminishing returns. For instance, when building up wealth, the first few dollars are more useful and pleasant than the last dollar earned or stolen. (This assumption seems to match the experience of everyone except for [a] extremely ambitious tycoons or conquerors, whose desire increases exponentially with their assets; and [b] scientists and research technologists, who know that knowledge increases exponentially with the input.)

But there is a problem: the two conditions in question are insufficient to define the utility function, for they are satisfied by infinitely many functions. Three of the favorites in the literature are $u_1 = \log q$, $u_2 = aq^{1/2} + b$, and $u_3 = aq - bq^2$, with a, b > 0. These functions are very different from one another. Indeed, the changes in utility corresponding to a change Δq in the amount of goods are $\Delta u_1 = \Delta q/q$, $\Delta u_2 = a\,\Delta q/2q^{1/2}$, $\Delta u_3 = (a - 2bq)\,\Delta q$.

How to choose among these or other functions satisfying the same general conditions? Rational choice theory does not help here, because every choice must be assumed to maximize the theorist's utility, which ought to be irrelevant in a scientific study. Only the scientific method should be resorted to: one should choose the function that best fits the empirical data. But these are hard to come by: indeed, there are very few recent empirical investigations on this subject, and the older findings are unreliable and not mutually consistent anyway. So, the choice has become a matter of computational convenience. Worse, most of the rational choice theorists who adopt a precise form for the utility function assume that it is the same for everyone. But this contradicts the initial assumption that persons are individuated by their preferences.

So, the rational choice theorists face the following dilemma: Either they specify the utility functions of the people, or they don't. If they do, they must justify their choice by reference to empirical research; but, since this is elusive, their choice is arbitrary. And if they don't specify the form of the utility functions, then their talk is empty. In short: exactness is unaccompanied by empirical evidence, and inexactness is as good as gibberish. In either case science is being mocked. No wonder then that reality, the referent and test of all scientific theories, is so unpopular among rational choice theorists. No wonder, too, that decision theory and in general rational choice theory have been savaged by psychologists, management scientists and philosophers (see, for instance, Bunge 1996, 1998; Kahneman et al. 1982; March and Shapira 1987; Rapoport 1989).

5.4. Empirical Support

The empirical test of any rational choice model depends on the possibility of measuring the subjective probabilities and utilities concerned. But these are hard to get precisely because they are subjective. Outside the casino, the most we can get are statements of the forms

Subject a regards event b as being more likely to occur than event c.
Subject a prefers outcome b to outcome c.

Neither of these statements is easy to come by, unless the subject concerned can be questioned. Typically, the observer has no access to his subjects, who are anonymous, very distant, or even dead. In these cases all the observer can do is to try and guess the probabilities and utilities his subject assigns to the outcomes of interest. For instance, if the subject attains aim A, it may be guessed that he regards A as being both likely and valuable. However, this guess is uncertain, given that—

as Merton (1957) showed long ago—we rarely accomplish the ends we pursue.

The observer's problem is an inverse one: Given certain effects, guess their causes, which in this case are the subject's actions and the underlying interests, beliefs, constraints, and decisions. Now, mathematicians have known since antiquity that inverse problems have either no solution or multiple solutions. Think, for example, of the problem of finding two digits that add up to 11: it has five solutions.

Hence the rational choice theorist's claim, that he can read individuals's interests and intentions from the outcomes of their actions, is sheer conceit. It resembles the natural theologian's project of reconstructing the Creator's grand plan by treating worldly things as bearing the Creator's fingerprints.

In other words, the hypotheses in any rational choice model are empirically untestable. Take, for instance, a business or political action. If successful, it may be claimed that it was taken in the light of a correct evaluation of probabilities and utilities. If unsuccessful, it may be alleged that the evaluation was mistaken. The theory, like theology, gets it always right: only people can err. In other words, action tests people, not the theory. So, whenever something goes wrong, shoot the person in charge, not the general policy—as Stalin taught.

The only reasons for accepting the postulates of rational choice theory are these. First, they are simple, in overlooking structural constraints. Second, they seem to explain every possible choice: of breakfast cereal or companion, honest occupation or criminal career, peace or war, racial segregation or desegregation, alcoholism or abstention, and so on. This apparent universality reminds one of earlier nostrums: everything that happens is God's will, a product of the spirit of the times, a case of dialectics, a product of evolution, or wired in the brain.

Now, the medieval logicians knew that what is said of everything holds for nothing in particular. For example, the truths of logic, such as "p or not-p," hold come what may, that is, whether or not p is the case: they are not about the real world, whence they escape empirical tests. Likewise, the statement that whatever an agent does results from his rational choice is untestable, since we do not know what the agent regards as rational, or what his preferences really are—let alone the "probabilities" (or rather likelihoods) he assigns to the various possible outcomes.

The postulates of rational choice have been applied to addiction, an obviously irrational behavior pattern. Why do so many people smoke, even knowing that smoking causes cancer and cardiovascular diseases?

Becker and Murphy (1988) speculate that smokers take a calculated risk: they weigh the benefits of pleasure against the pain of sickness, and conclude that the former outweigh the latter. But of course they offer no empirical support for this frivolous fantasy. Social psychologists and epidemiologists know that the answer is far more complex: People smoke because they were hooked during adolescence due to peer pressure, the desire to "belong" to the group and be perceived as adults, and the influence of advertisement. Once hooked, they found it difficult to quit. Addiction is a medical condition strongly linked to social and economic factors.

Why do so many American adolescents take unnecessary risks, such as reckless driving, playing with guns, immoderate drinking, and unprotected sex? Because they calculate the costs and benefits of alternative courses of action? Not so, according to the social psychologists who have studied the matter. First of all, risk-taking is not uniform across cultures. Inner-city black youths take more risks than white suburbanite adolescents. In turn, urbanites and suburbanites take more risks than rural people. Peer-pressure induces risk-aversion in rural societies, whereas it induces risky behavior in urban environments. The goatshepherd has no occasions to engage in joy riding, small store robbery, drug-running, gang war, or even drunkenness.

Rational-choice theorists have tried their hand at marriage, crime, racial segregation, and even religious affiliation. As Smelser (1998:3) says, "*Everything* becomes rational if you push hard enough." Freud did something similar when stating that all dreams have a sexual content, whether overt or latent. How can any such sweeping hypothesis be put to empirical tests? It cannot. And if a hypothesis is untestable, why regard it as scientific, or even worth being discussed except as a piece of fiction?

However, a theory can be even worse than untestable, hence unscientific: it can be irrelevant. I claim that rational choice theory is largely irrelevant to sociology because it is individual-centered and hence overlooks the very kernel of society, namely social structure, or the set of ties that hold people together. This is why the theory cannot tackle successfully such pressing social issues as those of social inequality, marginality, political oppression, and cultural deprivation.

Another reason for the limited power of rational choice theory to tackle important practical issues is that it presupposes that the agents are nearly equal in power. But this is seldom the case with regard to scarce resources: in these cases power is usually more decisive than strategy. And yet power is, along with time, one of the key missing variables in rational choice theory, which assumes that only (instrumental) rationality matters. Witness the cases of slavery, colonialism, dictatorship, and monopoly.

Rational choice theory lets us down even in cases where power is not decisive. In particular, not every competition can be modeled as a game, although game theory is widely regarded as *the* theory of conflict. Indeed, consider the common case of two units (individuals or groups) that compete for a given indivisible resource, such as a bride, a job, a client, a mine, or what have you. This situation resembles the game of musical chairs when played by two children and a single chair: when the music stops, the children stop whatever they were doing and rush to occupy the chair. The game cannot be modeled by game theory, because there is no situation in which the two players can both win or lose. In fact, in this game the only possible outcomes are: <I win, You lose>, <I lose, You win>. The other two elements of the payoff matrix, namely <I win, You win>, and <I lose, You lose> are missing. Hence, no game-theoretic model can be constructed of this simple game.

On the other hand, rational choice theory might be relevant to social psychology, for it deals with one of the sources of social action, namely calculation. For example, it explains in outline why people join interest groups, such as labor unions and professional associations. It also explains why we all plan our actions—though not why plans go awry in such high percentage. But, because it ignores emotion, the theory fails miserably in many important cases. A couple of examples should suffice to bring this point home.

Rational choice theory could explain why inner-city male youngsters adopt a tough macho stance: only the tough can hope to survive in a rough environment. Hence the denial of fear, pain, and shame. But such emotion-denial favors foolhardiness and aggressiveness—which in turn increase the very violence that it is supposed to immunize against. The result is that violence is the most common cause of death among young males in the American ghettos.

The theory also fails to account for protest movements, such as the environmental, civil rights and religious ones, for these are fired by emotion rather than reason. The members of any of these movements do not ask "What's in it for me?": they are genuinely unselfish. And nowadays some protest movements attract more people than any of the traditional movements.

True, emotions are not traded on the stock market. But they help explain why share prices seldom match real (or book) values. In sum, we must reckon with emotion along with calculation. The reason should be obvious: the organ of emotion—the limbic system—is anatomically and physiologically linked to the organ of cognition—the cerebral cortex. This is why radical rationalism is bound to fare just as poorly as radical emotivism.

Should any doubt remain that irrational behavior is at least as frequent as rational conduct, consider the following figures on annual expenditures released by the U.N. Development program. Cosmetics in the U.S.: $8 billion; perfumes in Europe and the U.S.: $12 billion; pet food in Europe and the U.S. : $17 billion; business entertainment in Japan: $35 billion; cigarettes in Europe: $50 billion; alcoholic drinks in Europe: $105 billion; narcotic drugs in the world: $400 billion; world military spending: $780 billion. On the other hand, the additional annual cost to achieve universal access to basic education would be only $6 billion; to water and sanitation, $9 billion; to reproductive health for women, $21 billion; and to basic health and nutrition, $13 billion. Even Dr. Pangloss would be shocked by such huge aggregate irrationality.

In short, whereas economic or "rational" man or woman is a cold calculator, overlooks social connections and status, and ignores propaganda, real man or woman often miscalculates or does not calculate at all, cultivates and uses connections, values high status, and is extremely susceptible to propaganda.

5.5. Applicability

One would expect that a theory ultimately geared to action, such as rational choice theory, would be widely used in business and politics. But this is not the case. For example, management consultants seldom if ever use decision theory to make decisions concerning business policies, plans, or operations. Likewise, political analysts and consultants—unlike political theorists—do not make use of game theory to determine whether any conflicts should be faced or avoided. And rightly so, because any application of the theory requires inaccessible information about the relevant probabilities and utilities. An example will show why this is so.

In one of the papers that earned him the Nobel Prize in economics, John C. Harsanyi (1956) derived a decision rule for any given bargaining party in a conflict of interests situation, to decide whether to make a concession or wait for the opponent to make it. Call S_1 and S_2 the last offers of players 1 and 2 respectively, at some given moment, and let C denote conflict if no agreement is reached. Assuming that each player tries to maximize his own expected utility, it turns out that the greatest probability of a conflict that player 1 would be willing to face, rather than accepting his opponent's last offer S_2, is

$$p_1 = \frac{u_1(S_1) - u_1(S_2)}{u_2(S_1) - u_1(C)}$$

The formula for the greatest risk that player 2 should be willing to face follows from the above upon exchanging the indices 1 and 2. Hence the alleged decision rule: Player 1 should make the next concession if $p_1 < p_2$, and player 2 should make the next concession if $p_1 > p_2$. If on the other hand $p_1 = p_2$, each player should make a concession.

No doubt, this rule is precise. But is it applicable: can the utility functions be assigned precise values? Of course not. For one thing, the rule assumes that the bargaining "game" is a lottery: that every outcome is random and can thus be assigned a probability. But this hypothesis is wildly unrealistic: the whole point of rational action is to minimize the role of chance. It is further assumed each player knows the utilities that his opponent assigns the various outcomes, whence he can calculate the risks involved. But actually there is no way he can obtain this knowledge. In fact, he is unlikely even to know his own utilities. Hence the Harsanyi decision rule is not such. It is one more case of naive faith in the power of pure reason to tackle practical problems.

Consider now a macrosocial issue, such as economic growth. Rational choice theory has nothing to say about national economic planning, because it leaves all economic decisions in the hands of individuals. Nor are mainstream economists well equipped to tackle this problem, because they ignore all noneconomic issues, such as demographic factors, wealth distribution, public health, education, and politics. Yet, it is obvious that all these factors must play a role in economic growth. For example, in a much-discussed paper, Persson and Tabellini (1994) have argued that the relevant statistics suggest that social inequality is an obstacle to economic growth.

A plausible mechanism underlying the inverse correlation between economic growth and inequality is this: (1) poor people are undernourished, in poor health, and unskilled, hence incapable of performing efficiently; (2) low-paid workers are not motivated to increase their productivity; (3) the internal market does not grow as long as the purchasing power of the majority is low. The lesson for socioeconomic planning—a bugbear of individualists—is that one of the keys to economic growth is to favor a more equitable income distribution. But the very concepts of social inequality and income distribution are absent from the vocabulary of rational choice theory, which is strictly individualistic. Hence this theory cannot be used to design social reforms: it is necessarily bound up with conservative politics.

In short, rational choice theory cannot double as an efficient technology because it is not true to begin with. The characteristic of modern or science-based technology, by contrast to magic, is that its rules rest on laws, that is, empirically well-confirmed theoretical generalizations.

5.6. Conclusions

Rational choice theory has been a theoretical and practical flop. What went wrong? The following:

1. *It is not rational enough*, since it pivots around such fuzzy concepts as those of subjective probability and subjective utility, whereas it ignores the key and clear concepts of natural resource and work.

2. *It adopts ontological and methodological individualism* (or atomism), whence it disregards interpersonal bonds—in other words, social structure.

3. *It is far too ambitious*: in attempting to explain everything, it accounts for nothing in particular, and it ignores the peculiarities of social facts of different kinds, which it regards as instances of exchange.

4. *It is triply ahistorical*: (a) it does not contain the concept of time, hence that of change; (b) it is assumed to hold for all people at all times and regardless of social orders; and (c) it ignores Marx's (1986 [1852]: 97) justly famous remark about the limits of choice: "Men make their own history, but they do not make it just as they please; they do not make it under circumstances chosen by themselves, but under circumstances directly encountered, given and transmitted from the past."

5. *Its hypotheses are empirically untestable*, since neither the agents nor the observer can possibly know the probabilities and utilities in question.

Because of these deep flaws, rational choice theory cannot be said to describe correctly human behavior. It might be claimed, though, that the theory is normative, not descriptive. However, this claim is not true, because a normative theory should be effective, just as a descriptive theory should be true. Rational choice theory has not been shown to be an effective guide to action and, precisely for this reason, it is hardly ever used in management or government. This should come as no surprise, because to qualify as a piece of modern technology, a normative theory must be based on a scientific descriptive theory: think of engineering, medicine, or agronomy. And rational choice theory is not scientific because it is fuzzy and empirically untestable. Whereas efficient action may be guided by successful rules of thumb, efficient *rational* action is guided by rules justified by laws.

Having said this, I hasten to acknowledge the important place of rational thought and action in modern society. Suffice it to mention science and technology, social inventions, and planning. Ironically, rational choice theorists have overlooked these activities. Which should come as no surprise, since important new ideas are not prompted by self-interest but by curiosity, and new institutions and social movements may be designed anywhere but on casino tables. If in doubt, try to imagine deliberating on a business merger, or on a new social program, exclusively in terms of subjective probabilities and utilities. Even though the value and the likelihood of success of a research project or a social blueprint are estimated, such estimates are collateral to the main thrust, which is invention or innovation (diffusion of invention).

In conclusion, the spread of rational choice theory is a tragicomic episode. It is tragic because it has seduced some of the most brilliant students of society—and because its failures have discredited scientism. And the diffusion is comic for two reasons. First, because there is little evidence that in human affairs reason is more prevalent than custom, coercion, emotion, or even folly, whereas there is plenty of evidence that "rational"—that is, selfish—individual behavior often leads to collective irrationality (see, e.g., Cross and Guyer 1980, Coleman 1990). Second, because the members of the "humanist" or soft camp reject the theory for believing it to be scientific, while in fact it is not. Indeed, the theory sits squarely in the "humanist" camp, and particularly in the hermeneutic or "interpretive" tradition, since its practitioners purport to have privileged access to the minds of the agents they study, hardly ever describe what goes on outside those minds, and do not bother with empirical testing.

6

Popper's Social Philosophy

I first encountered Popper's *The Open Society and Its Enemies* by accident, exactly forty years ago, when browsing in the library of the Universidad de Chile, where I was lecturing on physics and philosophy. It was love at first sight—as can only happen with half-read books and half-explored persons. Here was, at last, a profound, brilliant, honest and useful criticism of Plato, Hegel, and Marx. I admired the courage it took to plough through their works, and the perceptiveness exhibited in uncovering the intellectual roots of contemporary totalitarianism. And I admired the fairness with which Popper treated Marx, who at that time was regarded either as a demigod or a devil, depending on the side of the Cold War one was on. Upon my return to Buenos Aires I wrote Popper expressing my admiration for that important book. This sparked off a friendship that lasted a quarter of a century. In 1964 I edited the first of the volumes in his honor: *Critical Approaches to Science and Philosophy* (Bunge [1964] 1999). We quarreled only in the early 1980s, though not over social philosophy but over his idealist notion of "world 3" (Popper 1968; Bunge 1981), as well as over psychoneural dualism (Popper and Eccles 1977; Bunge 1980a), both of which I branded as unscientific.

In this paper I intend to identify and examine what I regard as the main pillars of Popper's social philosophy: rationality, individualism, libertarianism, antinomianism, negative utilitarianism, piecemeal social engineering, and a sunken pillar—that of the desirable social order. My conclusions are that the pillars are there all right, but they are shaky and do not support a construction so profound and consistent, as well as ample and detailed, as to deserve being called a substantial social philosophy, let alone one capable of inspiring any social activists or politicians. This may explain why neo-conservatives, classical liberals, and democratic socialists have claimed that Popper is on their side. Thus, ironically, Popper's legacy is no less ambiguous than Hegel's or Marx's.

Which was unavoidable, for any sketch of a complex object, such as a social philosophy, can be completed in an unlimited number of alternative ways.

6.1. Rationality

The good citizen of an open society—that is, a free and progressive one—is a rationalist: he adopts "an attitude of readiness to listen to critical arguments and to learn from experience" (Popper 1945, chap. 24, sect. I). However, as is well known, Popper's rationality is of the negative sort: instead of trying to find reasons for (or justify) any given hypothesis or proposal, he only looks for reasons against it. (More on Popper's negativism at the end.)

According to Popper, the good citizen of an open society behaves basically in the same fashion as the scientific investigator: namely, by trial and error or, more precisely, by conjecture and critical discussion. This attitude is necessary for a reasonably peaceful coexistence with others as well as for learning from others, for bargaining and striking fair deals, for achieving common goals and resolving conflicts without resorting to violence. "[R]eason is the only alternative to violence so far discovered" (Popper 1970a: 256).

By contrast, the loyal subject of a dictatorship must believe blindly what he is told from above, and must obey his superiors without hesitation. (Recall the Italian fascist slogan: *Believe, obey, fight*.) In short, rationality is a necessary condition for freedom and democracy, justice, and progress. No wonder then that dictatorships discourage open rational debate while promoting what Popper (1945, chap. 24) calls "oracular philosophies." By the same token the critique of irrationalism is part of the defense of liberty and, indeed, of modern civilization (Bunge 1944). Those who peddle such moth-eaten irrationalist wares as dialectical logic, phenomenology, existentialism, hermeneutics, or deconstructionism, would benefit from reading Popper on the incompatibility of irrationalism, in particular "oracular philosophy," with democracy.

So much for conceptual or epistemic rationality, which is involved in learning, evaluating knowledge claims, and debating. What about efficient action? Obviously, negative rationality won't help us here. Efficient action calls for practical rationality because we need to know whether a given practical issue does call for action and, if so, which action is to be taken.

But what is practical or instrumental rationality? Popper did not tackle this question in any detail in *The Open Society*. Moreover, Popper (1945, chap. 3, sect. VI) warned emphatically against questions of the form "What is X?" which he dubbed "essentialist," contrary to questions of the form "How does X behave?" which he deemed to be characteristic of "methodological nominalism." But anti-essentialism is an ingredient of the very positivism and linguistic philosophy he wished to overcome. After all, all ontological (metaphysical) questions are of the "What is" type. Witness "What is matter?" "What is life?" "What is mind?" "What is society?" and "What is value?" Moreover, these problems lie in the intersection of science and ontology—an intersection that Popper as well as the positivists decreed empty.

However, two decades later Popper did attempt to answer the question "What is instrumental rationality?" He did so in "The rationality principle" (Popper 1967), a paper that gave rise to a modest but thriving academic industry. The reason for the multiplicity of interpretations of this paper is that it not only fails to distinguish the dozen or so meanings of the term "rationality," but offers an unsatisfactory statement of the principle of instrumental rationality, and an even less satisfactory examination of its methodological status. Let us take a quick look at it.

Popper's version of the principle of (instrumental) rationality is this:

(R) "Agents always act in a manner appropriate to the situation in which they find themselves" (Popper op. cit.: 361).

This statement is so vague that it might be said to hold for an electron in an external field as well as for a human being facing a practical problem: indeed, both act according to their circumstances. Popper (op. cit.) has admitted that R is (a) "almost empty," only to add that (b) it is false—hence nonempty—yet (c) "as a rule sufficiently near the truth," and (d) "an integral part of every, or nearly every, testable social theory," for being the key to the explanation of individual behavior (which would in turn explain social facts).

Since (a) contradicts (b), which in turn contradicts (c) and (d), what is a rational agent to do? Nothing, for contradiction paralyzes. At any rate, R is hardly testable if only because the very concept of "appropriate behavior," on which it hinges, is fuzzy. Not being rigorously testable, R is neither true nor false. Hence, notwithstanding Popper's opinions (c) and (d) above, R should not occur in any scientific social theory. (More on this in Jacobs 1990; Nadeau 1993; Bunge 1996.)

In short, Popper has rightly emphasized that an open society requires, conceptually, rational debate and, instrumentally, rational action. But he has neither analyzed the former nor succeeded in telling us precisely what the latter is, on top of which he has made a mess of its methodological status.

Furthermore, since Popper's rationality principle is empty, so is his situational logic, which he claimed to be able to explain human actions and social facts—even though he never even sketched it. Thus Popper made no lasting contributions to social explanation. Moreover, he could make none for the following reasons. First, agency without social structure is a figment. Second, scientific explanation proper, whether in natural science or in social studies, involves exhibiting or conjecturing some mechanism—that which makes individuals or social systems "work" or "tick"—not allusion to some nondescript "situation."

6.2. Individualism

Most social philosophers of social science are either individualists or holists: they see either the trees or the forest, never both (see Brodbeck, ed. 1968, particularly the Gellner-Watkins exchange, and O'Neill, ed. 1973). Popper adopts the ontological individualism fathered by seventeenth- and eighteenth-century liberal political theorists and utilitarian moral philosophers, and upheld by the neoclassical microeconomists and Max Weber. This is the view that Margaret Thatcher summarized in her famous dictum: "There is no such thing as society: There are only individuals."

In other words, Popper refuses to admit social wholes, such as families, schools, firms, and states, possessing supra-individual features. He even places the social bonds largely in his "world 3" (Popper 1974: 14). (Aristotle would have disapproved of such Platonic detachment of relations from relata—but then Popper did not care much for him.) And he also favors the methodological individualism that should accompany ontological individualism: "the task of social theory is to construct and to analyse our sociological models […] *in terms of individuals*, of their attitudes, expectations, relations, etc.—a postulate which may be called 'methodological individualism' " (Popper [1944–45], Sect. 29, emphasis in the original). That is, like Mill and Weber, and contrary to Marx and Durkheim, Popper teaches that the study of every social fact can and should be reduced to the study of individual actions—though, paradoxically and in agreement with Weber and Pareto, without the help of psychology.

But of course neither Popper nor anybody else could possibly dispense with the very global ("collective") entities or features that he, following Bentham and Mill, as well as Dilthey and Weber, had written off. There are two reasons for this. One is that every human being is part of several social systems—such as families, business firms, schools, clubs, and informal social networks—so that his behavior is unintelligible without reference to them. Another reason is that every social system is characterized by emergent or systemic properties, such as social structure, viability, cohesion, history, progress, decline, and wealth distribution. A third is that the whole point of social psychology is to investigate the individual-social junction in an attempt to account for both individual behavior with the help of sociological considerations, and for the emergence of macroregularities out of the interplay of individual actions.

True, the phenomenally successful and powerful Microsoft corporation advertises the individualist slogan: "A corporation is nothing more than a collection of individuals." But of course the whole point of running a corporation is to make or sell commodities that neither of its individual components could handle, as well as to strike deals with other corporations, such as suppliers and banks, that would not even listen to a private person. Something similar holds for social systems of all other kinds: they have supra-individual features stemming from the division of labor, the cooperation, and the conflicts among their members. (Caution: The systemist thesis, that society is a system of systems, should not be mistaken for holism or collectivism. Whereas the latter is irrationalist, systemism holds that only an analysis of a whole into its components and their interactions can account for it: recall chapter 1 . Hence, it is not touched by Popper's [1944–45] devastating critique of holism.)

Whoever denies the existence of social systems is bound to either smuggle them in or invent surrogates for them. Popper was no exception. Indeed, to explain individual actions Popper invokes institutions and "situations" (or "states of affair"), as other individualists invoke "contexts" and "circumstances." Now, a social situation is nothing but the momentary state of society, for example, a state of war—or of political unrest, economic boom, cultural decline, or what have you. To be sure, there is war only if many people take up arms. But these individuals are organized into battalions, regiments, and divisions, which are supposed to act as units in certain regards. Moreover, the fate of the troops depends not only upon the decisions of their officers but also upon such suprapersonal items as transportation and communication lines, natural and pecuniary resources, logistics, and the international situation. The entire "logic of the situation" resorts then to supra-individual items—on top of which it is anything but a "logic." Popper's social ontology may therefore be characterized as *individholistic* rather than as consistently individualistic. (More on this hybrid in Bunge 1996.)

What holds for social "situations" also holds, *mutatis mutandis*, for institutions, to which Popper rightly attributed great importance, and whose fragility worried him. But, unless one admits the existence of social systems, one cannot form a clear idea of an institution. Indeed an institution, such as marriage, may be analyzed either as a behavior pattern in societies of a certain type, or as the collection of all married couples, every one of which is a social minisystem. Likewise the law may be construed either as the set of legal codes together with the jurisprudence, or as the collection of all the courts of law and law-enforcement systems, every one of which is a subsystem of the political system, which in turn is one of the artificial subsystems of society. Popper, always wary of definitions, does not tell us which of the two construals of "institution" he favors.

Moreover, Popper's (1968) division of reality into his three "worlds" makes no comfortable room for institutions. In fact, these are not physical entities, hence they cannot be "inmates of world 1." Nor are they mental processes, so they do not qualify as inhabitants of "world 2" either. Eventually they land in "world 3," along with problems, ideas, and books (Popper and Eccles 1977: 38). But this "world 3" is an arbitrary grab bag of "embodied" and "nonembodied" items, not a world, structured collection, or system (Bunge 1981). This poses a serious problem for Popper's "worlds" typology as well as for his idea of an institution. And this problem is one more indication that it is impossible to build a philosophy of anything real without a comprehensive and solid ontological framework, one sketching the furniture of the world and the manner in which it is organized.

Why did Popper uncritically adopt the individualist social ontology inherent in traditional liberalism and anarchism? The simplest answer is that he did so in reaction to the holist (or collectivist) conception of society that underlies the thought of Plato, Hegel, Marx, and their heirs. Recall the chilling Nazi slogan *"Du bist nichts, dein Volk ist alles."* ("You are nothing, your people is everything").

Popper cannot be faulted for having failed to transcend the individualism-holism opposition and to adopt a systemic approach for, at the time he wrote *The Open Society* , no explicit systemic philosophy was in existence. But the systemic approach had certainly been practiced in all sciences—natural, social, and biosocial—in a tacit fashion. In particular, social scientists have always studied social systems—such as families, gangs, networks, villages, business firms, political parties, states, and entire regions—though seldom making explicit use of the concept of a system. And they have always situated individual behavior within such systems (or "situations" or "institutions"), though without noticing that, by so doing, they were being unfaithful to both individualism and holism.

And why did Popper fail to sketch an original or even consistent ontology of the social? I conjecture that the reason is that neither he nor his best interlocutors, the members of the Vienna Circle, were interested in metaphysics (or ontology). Moreover, both parties held it to be disjoint from science and epistemology, the foci of their interest. They did not realize that scientific research presupposes a number of ontological hypotheses, such as the autonomy and lawfulness of the external world: that metaphysics is not only a source of science (Agassi 1964) but also an unavoidable component of it. A component that can harm if hidden, help if disclosed and worked out.

6.3. Libertarianism

The individualist is centrally concerned with persons and their freedom to live as they see fit. In particular, a rationalist individualist values above all his freedom to think, speak, and act according to his own beliefs and interests. No wonder then that Popper was a libertarian—though not a radical one like either Bakunin or our right-wing contemporaries, since he realized the need for some social control if only to protect the freedom of the individual.

A libertarian is, by definition, one whose maximal social value is liberty. (Example: the American Civil Liberties Union.) If moderate, the libertarian is a liberal: while defending toleration he admits the need to curtail everyone's freedom to ensure the liberty of everyone else. By contrast, the radical libertarian believes in unfettered personal freedom—particularly in unrestricted free enterprise. He even believes in the right to bear arms, join vigilante groups, and make hate speeches—none of which is permitted in the more civilized countries, all of which restrict personal and civil liberties in order to protect personal freedom and welfare as well as public order. The radical libertarian will be "into freedom" just as much as the hippy of the 1960s, except that the latter claimed to worship equality and fraternity too.

Clearly, Popper was a moderate libertarian, for he favored restricting toleration to the tolerant. Moreover, in harmony with his general negativist philosophy, Popper stressed negative liberty (freedom from) at the expense of positive liberty (freedom to). (See Berlin 1957 for the difference between nonobstruction and self-mastery.) But the good citizen has duties in addition to rights, so he cannot ask to be left alone. As Durkheim (1972 [1898] :150) noted, "political freedom is a means, not an end. It is worth no more than the manner in which it is put to use." Thus Popper's view of liberty is one-sided. Consequently, it is politically ineffective: people do not feel strongly motivated to take part in politics unless they are driven by positive ideals. And, when that happens, apathy and a dangerous political vacuum may develop, into which market worship and ethnic hatred may rush (see Touraine 1994).

Whether moderate or radical, libertarians value liberty far more than either equality or fraternity. Moreover, they believe that there can be freedom along with pronounced social inequality. But this is false. Indeed, wherever there is marked social (in particular economic) inequality, some people wield far more power than others—and power is the ability to alter other people's behavior, and thus infringe on their liberties, to suit one's own perceived interests. In particular, it is well known that the transnational megacorporation, hardly a champion of equality, is nowadays just as strong a source of power—economic, political, and cultural—as the armed forces of a dictatorship.

Since there can be no full freedom among unequals, genuine freedom for all can only be attained together with a good measure of social equality. But of course freedom is needed to protect equality, that is, to prevent the concentration of power (political, economic, or cultural). Consequently, one should refuse to be forced to opt between liberty and equality: one ought to choose equality with freedom instead. As the American legal realist Roscoe Pound (1954: 168) put it, "[m]en's desire to be equal and their desire to be free must be kept in balance. Either carried to the extreme negates the other."

In summary, neither traditional liberalism nor authoritarian socialism is acceptable to anyone caring for either freedom or equality, much less to anyone loving both. Moreover it may be argued that liberty and equality, though necessary for democracy, are vulnerable without a good dose of solidarity. Integral democracy may even be characterized as the old familiar triad: *Liberté, égalité, fraternité.*

6.4. Antinomianism

Holists—such as Ibn Khaldûn, Hegel, Comte, Marx, Engels, Durkheim, and Parsons—are necessitarians: they believe that people are at the mercy of their communities, which in turn would be ruled by iron laws impregnable to individual action. (Popper [1944–45] called this doctrine "historicism"—a deviation from traditional usage which has given rise to much barren controversy.) By contrast, individualists, particularly if libertarian, are voluntarists rather than necessitarians. Consequently they are bound to deny the existence of immutable historical laws: they are antinomianists. Hence they will hold that historiography is an idiographic discipline, that is, one dealing with particulars, not a nomothetic science, that is, one searching for regularities. Popper inherited this view from Kant and the neo-Kantians, in particular Dilthey, Windelband, Rickert, Simmel, and Weber. (Incidentally, the neo-Kantian root of Popper's social philosophy—a skeleton in Popper's closet—has hardly been investigated. Always clever at covering his tracks, Popper left no explicit clues with regard to his philosophical sources: he only told us whom he opposed.)

Antinomianism is in part a reaction against the naturalism that had dominated social thought from Quesnay and Smith to Mill and Marx (see, e.g., Clark 1992). Indeed, antinomianism is inherent in the very idealist (in particular Romantic) philosophy that Popper castigated so effectively in other regards. Antinomianism is also a reaction against fatalism, be it pagan, Moslem, or Calvinist. Thus Popper (1944–45) dedicated his *Poverty of Historicism* "to the memory of the countless men and women of all creeds or nations or races who fell victims to the fascist and communist belief in Inexorable Laws of Historical Destiny."

However, belief in laws, whether natural or social, should not be mistaken for belief in destiny or fate. There might be objective social laws, in particular laws of social change (that is, historical laws), and yet there would be no fatalism about them because, being social, we would be the creators and exterminators of such laws, and would be at least partially in command of them—just as the engineer takes command of physical or chemical processes when triggering, blocking, or steering them in light of his knowledge of both natural law and circumstance.

Even a voluntarist like Alexis de Tocqueville (1985: 300), who in 1853 wrote to the racist Gobineau that "the destiny of man, either as an individual or as a nation, is what he wants to make of it," was not exclusively or even mainly interested in historical details. In fact, as he wrote in 1857, he had sought "the general causes of the occurrence and the movement of the ideas and passions that produced it or sprang from it. After all, only that is absolutely *sure* in history; all that is particular is always more or less doubtful" (1985: 351, his emphasis). Like every other insightful social scientist, Tocqueville rises above details and rejects the particular/general (or idiographic/nomothetic) dichotomy. Likewise Max Weber, who in his methodological works defended the dichotomy in question, made no use of it in his substantive works. In the latter he used idiographic documents and analyses as raw materials to formulate "nomothetic hypotheses about such abstract sociological problems as the relations between institutionalized ideas and social organizations as well as the modes and dynamics of structural interdependence of seemingly unconnected social institutions" (Merton 1987: 15).

True, in *The Poverty of Historicism* Popper (1944–45) had shown that the thinkers whom he misleadingly called "historicist" had failed to exhibit any historical laws: they had only noted some trends. Arnold Toynbee's alleged grand historical laws have been shown to be imaginary. And, after several years' work, the Committee on Historical Analysis of the Social Science Research Council (USA) produced only a meager crop of historical generalizations (Gottschalk, ed. 1963).

However, such failures do not disprove conclusively the existence of historical laws. As a matter of fact, by displacing the focus of research from short and isolated historical events to processes in social systems, some contemporary historians—in particular those of the *Annales* school—have come up with a fair number of nontrivial and plausible historical generalizations, as well as trends, that would have escaped anyone focusing on particulars. (See Braudel 1969 for the shift of focus, from short events seen as caused by outstanding individuals, to large multidimensional social systems seen over a *longue durée*—hence from miniproblems of the type of "Why did Caesar cross the Rubicon?" to macroproblems of the kind of "Why did the Mediterranean world start to decline in mid-seventeenth century?")

For our purposes the following random sample of social quasi-laws should suffice. (1) Any technological innovation that affects the mode of production facilitates social mobility (both upwards and downwards). (2) Rapid population growth → overcultivation and deforestation → erosion and loss of soil fertility → decline in food production → food shortage → political unrest. (3) Social systems deficient in "weak ties" (acquaintanceship relations) tend to be fragmented and incoherent: such is the strength of weak ties (M. Granovetter). (4) All social innovations are introduced by new social groups (E. H. Carr). (5) The depletion of nonrenewable resources eventually kills certain industrial sectors unless substitutes are found for the respective critical raw materials. (6) The institutions of today do not entirely fit the situation of today (T. Veblen). (7) All progress in some regards involves regress in others.

There are then, antinomianism notwithstanding, some plausible candidates for social patterns, in particular historical laws, that is, laws of social change. These have three main sources: (a) we are all immersed in the same biosphere, which "obeys" laws of nature; (b) all humans are animals with the same basic needs, and are willing to do something to meet them; (c) all normal humans are sociable, whence they tend to build or join social systems of various kinds, every one of which has specific functions and thus patterns that inhere in it.

But of course there is disorder—from mere accident to randomness—along with order. (And, as Paul Valéry pointed out, the [social] world is threatened by both order and disorder.) Yet irregularities, or departures from ideal types, are not peculiar to social matter. Think of the impurities at the root of precious gems, and of the accidents in biological development, daily life, and evolution. However, there might be laws underneath some such irregularities. For example, the bad weather caused by a sudden deviation of an oceanic current may result in a poor harvest, which in turn causes a famine, which in turn triggers a wave of political unrest. Bad weather is an accident only from a biological viewpoint, not from a meteorological one. Nor are poor harvests lawless events when caused by bad weather. But political unrest looks as a mere accident if detached from its distal causes.

So, there are social regularities along with accidents. But, admittedly, our knowledge of social regularities is still dismally poor. And it won't be enriched unless the antinomianist bias is superseded by both historiographic research and philosophical analysis.

6.5. Negative Utilitarianism

Popper's moral philosophy occupies all of one footnote (Popper 1945, chap. 5, fn. 6). In fact, it boils down to negative utilitarianism. This is the minimalist doctrine first proposed by Buddha, Epicurus, and Hippocrates of Kos. This view is encapsulated in the maxims "Do no harm," and "Minimize suffering." By implication these principles invite us to treat only symptoms, refraining from removing the sources of evil. Negative utilitarianism has been eloquently defended by arguing that we do not always know what is objectively good; that what is good for one individual may be bad for another; and that the path to hell is paved with good intentions. In short, the advice is: Do not concern yourself over much with others: just refrain from evildoing, and beware of "do-gooders."

Negative utilitarianism is selfishness of the considerate and smart kind: it is the attitude of the individual who is incapable of inflicting unnecessary pain and who realizes that he cannot pursue successfully his own interests unless he respects those of others. The negative utilitarian respects other people but he feels little concern for their welfare. This brings to mind Kenneth Arrow's deep insight: "Concern without respect is at best paternalism and can lead to tyranny. Respect without concern is the cold world of extreme individualism, a denial of the intrinsically social nature of humanity" (Arrow 1992: 45).

The negative utilitarian lets others fend for themselves: he acts more in terms of rights than duties. He ignores that, in a sustainable society, rights imply duties and vice versa (Bunge 1989). Consequently the negative utilitarian makes no contributions to the very social stability he needs to pursue his private interests. He thus jeopardizes his own welfare through neglecting that of others.

The impact of negative utilitarianism upon social policy is laissez-fairism. By advocating planned social engineering, not laissez-fairism, Popper contradicts himself. But, since he has no positive moral philosophy, his advocacy of social engineering is procedural rather than substantive. However, we are trespassing on the next section.

6.6. Piecemeal Social Engineering

Popper knows that every society will have flaws. In particular, he believes that "the injustice and inhumanity of the unrestrained 'capitalist system' described by Marx cannot be questioned" (Popper 1945, chap. 17, sect. III). But, far from being a pessimist like Plato, Vico, Nietzsche, Pareto, Spengler, or his own friend Hayek, Popper believes in the possibility of rational social reform: one based on plans informed by social science. He even chides Marx for denouncing all social planning as utopian and illegitimate (Popper 1945, chap. 13).

In fact Popper—like the social utilitarians, social-democrats, Christian socialists, and "red tories" long before him, as well as the American and Scandinavian schools of legal realism between the two world wars, and the Keynesians after the Great Depression—favors social reform and the corresponding discipline, namely, what used to be called "social engineering" and is now often called "social technology" or "sociotechnology." (See, e.g., Polanyi 1944; Hicks, Misra and Ng 1995.) Indeed, according to Popper (1945, chap. 18, sect. IV), there may be an alternative to capitalism and socialism: "It can be, for instance, the development of a technology for the immediate improvement of the world we live in, the development of a method for piecemeal engineering, for democratic intervention." The result of such social reform has been the transformation of the "unrestrained capitalism" Marx had described into the modern welfare state—which I prefer to call the "relief state." Popper admits the flaws of the welfare state, in particular the bureaucratism it involves. But, far from calling for its dismantling, he favors its improvement (Popper 1959: 246).

Because of his espousal of progressive social engineering, Popper should not be accused of conservatism. The fact that in recent times he has been regarded as "one of the greatest twentieth-century conservative thinkers" (Ranelagh 1991: 194) is another story. This has to do with the dishonesty characteristic of political rhetoric, not with scholarship. Planas (1991: 14) tells us that, as late as in 1991, in front of a large audience at the Universidad Internacional Menéndez y Pelayo in Santander (Spain), Popper denied being a liberal and refused to criticize social democracy. J. S. Mill has been subjected to a similar distortion: the libertarians or neoliberals remember his essay on liberty but find it convenient to keep silent on Mill's loud praise of democratic socialism (in particular cooperative ownership) in his *Principles of Political Economy* as well as in his *Autobiography*. No matter what the famous may actually think, their views will be silenced or distorted by the infamous.

Popper has been accused of inconsistency for being against social revolution but in favor of scientific revolution. His defense was as follows: "If the method of rational critical discussion should establish itself, then this will make the use of violence obsolete: reason is the only alternative to violence so far discovered" (Popper 1970a: 255–56). In other words: Let's all become intellectuals, and every social issue will be resolved through critical discussion. Regrettably this proposal, which would have delighted Leibniz, ignores some well known facts: (a) in all known societies, even the most advanced ones, only a small minority has the chance of getting trained in critical thinking; (b) power (political, economic, or cultural) is often used to mute or even suppress public discussion of social ills and hinder attempts to resolve them by peaceful means; (c) such suppression of the right to critical debate and peaceful social action may invite rebellion.

However, the unfeasibility of Popper's rationalist proposal does not prove his accusers right: One may indeed favor both gradual social reform and radical scientific change. The two are mutually compatible for concerning two different (though admittedly linked) spheres: social order and inquiry. To be sure, permanent social revolution (à la Trotsky or Mao) would impede the growth of knowledge. Worse, it would cause the decline of learning. But social reform is compatible with radical scientific change. Moreover, the two go hand in hand in the less developed countries (Bunge 1980b).

However, one should not call every scientific breakthrough a revolution, the way Popper did following T. S. Kuhn—to the point of warning against the "dangers of normal science" (Popper 1970b). I submit, contra both Kuhn and Popper, that we know of only two total scientific revolutions in history: the birth of science in the fifth century B.C., and its rebirth in the seventeenth century. All the other great scientific changes have been sectoral changes of tempo, upheavals, or breakthroughs, in particular births, splittings, and mergers of special sciences.

There are several reasons for the evolutionary or revisionist (rather than either cumulative or revolutionary) nature of the history of scientific knowledge since the seventeenth-century Scientific Revolution (Bunge 1983: 179–184). First, every scientific novelty is partly built upon what is known; for instance, Marx built upon Smith and Ricardo. Second, every scientific breakthrough is evaluated by comparison with what was known to be true at least to a first approximation. For example, molecular biology was accepted not only for the new insights it supplied into the mechanisms of genic changes but also for being both an outgrowth of biochemistry and compatible with classical genetics. Third, there are certain over-arching philosophical principles that both propel and constrain all scientific inquiries. One of them is the thesis that reality is lawful and knowable. Fourth, all genuine scientific inquiry, whether "normal" or "revolutionary," abides by the *ethos* of science, a set of institutional imperatives first identified by Merton (1942): universalism, epistemic communism, disinterestedness, and organized skepticism. (Popper's own contribution to the ethics of science is minute: see Popper 1970c. And compare it to Einstein's writings and deeds on this matter.) However, this is a side issue: here we are centrally concerned with Popper's social philosophy, not his philosophy of science.

Although he favored planned social reform, Popper never put forth any constructive proposals for it. Moreover, he did not examine in detail any of the social technologies, such as normative macroeconomics, city planning, social medicine, the law, or management science, all of which raise interesting ontological and epistemological problems—such as, for instance, the question of the very nature of plans as different from theories. (Moreover, he was not entirely clear about the distinction between social science and social technology: see Rhees 1969: 52.) Yet Popper has often been quoted in the planning literature over the past three decades (see, e.g., Faludi 1986)—perhaps for the same unreason that Thomas Kuhn is ritually quoted with reference to scientific change.

Popper only asserted that, while history cannot be planned on paper, "*institutions* can be planned; and they are being planned. Only by planning, step by step, for institutions to safeguard freedom, especially freedom from exploitation, can we hope to achieve a better world" (Popper 1945, chap. 18, sect. IV). And he stated that "[*a*] *social technology is needed whose results can be tested by piecemeal social engineering*" (Popper 1945, chap. 23, emphasis in the original).

However, faithful to his antidefinitionist stand, Popper never clarified satisfactorily what he meant by "institution," "social technology," or "piecemeal social engineering." (Other pet expressions of his, such as "situation," "historicism," "indeterminism," and "world 3" are similarly vague—hence a source of unending scholastic controversy.) Still, from the context it is clear that by "piecemeal social engineering" he meant social reform both gradual and peaceful (as opposed to revolutionary), and partial or local (as opposed to global). Its device is "One thing at a time." This is the type of social reform initiated by Bismarck and Disraeli, and carried out massively in Sweden after World War I, in Great Britain and other European countries after World War II, and to a far lesser extent in the United States in the 1960s. These reforms concerned social security, health care, education, civil rights, and crime prevention. And they resulted from a jumble of partial, largely improvised, and never carefully coordinated or even monitored social programs.

As we all know, the Thatcherite conservatives in Britain and the Reagan Republicans and latter-day Democrats in the U.S. have fiercely attacked and curtailed these rather timid essays in social engineering. They have done so for two reasons, one left unsaid and the other stated explicitly. The unstated reason is of course that social expenditures call for progressive taxes, which hurt the rich, who happen to form the core constituency of conservative politicians. The ostensive reason is that, after a few initial successes, those social reforms accomplished little more than to offer relief and—a perverse effect—induce relief-dependency. Indeed, both British and American societies are still being rocked quasi-periodically by more or less severe economic recessions and their sequels, and they remain socially unjust. Worse, inequality is more prominent now in Britain and the U.S. than a quarter of a century ago. For example, it is well known that social inequality has increased steadily and steeply in the U.S. since 1969 (see, e.g., Harrison and Bluestone 1988). Thus 1 percent of Americans own 40 percent of the total wealth. As well, morbidity and early death increased dramatically among the poor in the U.K. under the conservative governments (see, e.g., Wilkinson 1994).

Thus, after several decades, the British and American social reforms have proved not to have been wholly successful. However, it is not enough to find that a social plan has failed: one should try to discover why it failed. I submit that in this case there are two causes for those failures: one local or circumstantial and the other general or principled. The former is that in both the U. K. and the U. S., social expenditures had to compete with the insane arms race, tax cuts for the rich, the support of client governments, and, in the case of the United States, the Vietnam war as well. Social reform was one of the two domestic victims of these political adventures; the other victim, particularly in the U.S., was the balanced fiscal budget. None of the other reformist capitalist countries, particularly West Germany, France, Scandinavia, the Benelux countries, and Italy sacrificed social welfare to the Cold War. In these countries reformed capitalism—what the Germans call "social market"—has succeeded spectacularly in relieving poverty. This is why I call "local or circumstantial" the ultimate failure of the British and American social reforms.

I submit that the general or principled reason for the failure of all known social reforms to secure freedom from exploitation—a goal Popper shared with socialists of all colors—is that they have been piecemeal or sectoral rather than global or systemic. Piecemeal social engineering is bound to produce at best only modest results, because society is not merely a collection or "sum" of individuals, or even an aggregate of mutually independent sectors: it is a system. (A concrete system is a complex thing whose parts or components are held together by strong bonds, the totality of which constitutes the structure of the system.) And a system, be it atom, chemical reactor, organism, ecosystem, family, or society at large, cannot be altered successfully bit by bit, for all its components hang together. George Soros (1998:226), a former student of Popper's who has attained notoriety as a financier and a promoter of the open society, admits that systemic problems cannot be tackled successfully in the piecemeal fashion that his former teacher recommended.

For example, if health care is improved through mass vaccination and sanitation, morbidity and mortality decrease precipitously almost overnight. As a consequence population is likely to increase dramatically, which in turn may lead to food shortages, unemployment, environmental degradation, and political turmoil. Only a combination of health-care programs with educational and economic reforms (such as land reform and the organization of rural cooperatives) can countervail the undesirable side effects of a quick improvement in public health. Another example: education, once believed to be the great equalizer, actually makes the existing social divisions more pronounced. Indeed, only the privileged children and youngsters have access to the best schools and educational tools, such as books, microscopes, and computers. This allows them to outpace all others. In short, by itself education has the unintended perverse effect of widening the social gaps. Only by adopting a systemic or multisectoral approach to social issues can we hope to solve social issues.

In conclusion, in social matters "[w]e can never do merely one thing" (Hardin 1985:58; see also Hirschman 1990). The reason for this is that people always act in and upon some system, whether natural, social, or mixed. Hence, by altering any of its components, one affects several other components, sometimes in unforeseeable ways. To be sure, any part of an automobile can be repaired or replaced independently of the rest—though not while it is in motion. Likewise the anatomist can cut any part of a corpse without disturbing the rest; but the surgeon can only repair a part of a living body provided he immobilizes it and supports the other parts affected by the operation. But society cannot be immobilized. Hence it must be repaired on the go. Hence, analogies with automobiles and corpses won't help the social technologist.

A systemic view of society (as opposed to both the individualist and the holist views) suggests that one can advance gradually provided one does it in all the pertinent sectors at the same time, since they all hang together (Bunge 1980b). In short, the proper device should not be "Piecemeal social engineering" but "Systemic social reform guided by sociotechnology and implemented with the active participation of all the stakeholders." (Paternalist social programs are likely to have lasting perverse effects. Only democratic participation can help detect social dysfunction and overcome political inertia.)

Regrettably, Popper was an individualist, not a systemist: recall section 6.2. Moreover, he was more interested in procedural than in substantive social matters: He told us how we should make things happen—namely one at a time—not what we should do. That is, Popper may be characterized as a *social formalist*, for being far more interested in the rule of law than in the content and purport of the law, and in planning more than in the goals of plans. (Note the parallel with Kant's ethical formalism. And note also that "formalism," as used here, is not to be confused with "formalization," that is, the transformation of an intuitive concept into an exact one. By the way, Popper favored formalization in natural science but not elsewhere. On the whole he, like the neo-Austrian economists, in particular his friend Hayek, was suspicious of quantitation in social studies. True, he did praise neoclassical mathematical economics, but failed to note that its key concepts, namely those of subjective utility and subjective probability, are not well-defined, whence the whole apparatus is purely decorative.)

However, we are encroaching on the next section.

6.7. Social Order: The Broken Pillar

The artificial or nonbiological part of any complex society may be analyzed into three interacting subsystems: its culture, economy, and polity (Bunge 1979). Popper (1945) had much to say about the first and, particularly, about the tradition of free critical inquiry and the need to defend it against irrationalism, dogmatism, and intolerance. On the other hand, he had very little to say about the economy, except to praise the free market and reject out of hand the idea of economic democracy (e.g., Popper 1959). By contrast, Popper espoused a definite political philosophy, namely advanced liberalism, which amounts to legal equality together with political democracy and a modicum of social welfare. Since the latter ingredient was dealt with in the previous section, let us now tackle the first two.

Popper made much of isonomy, or equality before the law. Political theorists hardly discuss this matter nowadays—to the point that there is no entry for it in the authoritative *Blackwell Encyclopaedia of Political Thought* of 1987. There are several reasons for this decline of interest in isonomy: (a) most people seldom sign formal contracts, and the vast majority of people never get to appear before a magistrate; (b) the treatment litigants actually get in a court of law depends crucially upon the legal advice they can buy, or even upon the political strings they can pull; (c) in no civilized country does the law treat children and the incapacitated in the same way as able adults; (d) in most countries corporate persons are exempted from the social responsibility required from ordinary citizens; and (e) legal equality is puny by comparison with economic inequality—an issue that still bedevils all the political democracies, and that has commanded the attention of all serious social philosophers since the time of Thomas More. Recall Anatole France's *bon mot*: "The law, in its infinite wisdom, allows the rich as well as the poor to sleep under the bridges of Paris."

As for political democracy, Popper's reasons for advocating it differs from those of the eighteenth- and nineteenth-centuries liberals, who extolled it for moral and social reasons. Indeed Popper's liberalism, like his moral philosophy, is both negative and free from moral and sentimental elements: it only stems from his horror of tyranny, in particular totalitarianism. In fact, he wrote as follows: "The theory [of democracy] I have in mind is one which does not proceed, as it were, from a doctrine of the intrinsic goodness or righteousness of a majority rule, but rather from the baseness of tyranny; or more precisely, it rests upon the decision, or upon the adoption of the proposal, to avoid and resist tyranny" (Popper 1945, chap. 7, sect. II). Anyone interested in a more comprehensive vision of democracy, in particular one including economic democracy, will have to look elsewhere—for example, in Mill's *Principles of Political Economy* (1871), in Dahl's *A Preface to Economic Democracy* (1985), in Pierson's *Socialism after Communism* (1995), or in my *Social Science under Debate* (1998).

Popper held that the traditional political question "Who should rule?" is ill-conceived, for presupposing that someone must rule. Like most intellectuals, he may have felt some sympathy for anarchism. But he realized that pure anarchism is utopian, not only because any complex society has plenty of public goods that have got to be managed impartially, but also because we need "the protection of that freedom which does not harm other citizens" (Popper 1945, chap. 6, sect. VI). So, Popper replaced the traditional political question of principle with a "thoroughly practical, almost technical, problem" . This is: "how is the state to be constituted so that bad rulers can be got rid of without bloodshed, without violence?" (Popper 1988:20).

In Popper's view the two-party system, as practiced in Britain and in the United States, is the best solution to this problem, for guaranteeing

(a) the rule of law; (b) the bloodless dismissal of bad rulers; and (c) the search for new ideas in case of electoral defeat. He criticized proportional representation for believing that it cushions political downfall and thus fails to motivate self-criticism and the search for new ideas.

Popper's shift of focus from substance to procedure—that is, from matters of political principle to voting mechanics—may not be accidental. It may have resulted from his negative utilitarianism together with his distrust of all ideologies. Hence Popper's prescription: Do not seek the good, let alone the best—just avoid evil; and, should evil occur, cut it short in the least injurious way, namely by plurality vote in political matters. This rule of Popper's parallels his key epistemological injunction, namely "Do not search for truth—just engage in critical discussion in order to uncover falsity and weed it out."

But of course both moral and epistemological negativism are sophistic as well as impractical. Indeed, harm is the opposite of beneficence, just as falsity is the opposite of truth. Hence to assess a course of action as nonharmful amounts to evaluating it as either beneficial or indifferent. (Likewise, to assess a proposition as nonfalse amounts to evaluating it as either true to some degree or nonverified, or else undecidable.) Moreover, the moral person is not content with refraining from doing harm: he wants to help, not just to be a harmless onlooker. Likewise, the scientist does not limit himself to avoiding error: he wishes to make true discoveries or inventions. As Claude Bernard (1865:97) put it, in the search for truth the *contre-épreuve* or attempt at refutation is the necessary complement of the *preuve* (confirmation). Falsificationism holds only for the null hypothesis that two or more variables are not related—but only emerging sciences make use of it. (Moreover, the hypergeneral theories in science and technology, such as general field theory, general evolutionary theory, automata theory, and information theory, are only confirmable: see Bunge 1973, chap. 2.)

Likewise, the responsible citizen cannot derive much satisfaction from punishing politicians by refusing to vote for them when they have misbehaved. He wants to make constructive contributions to society, to participate not only in elections but also between them. At any rate, before every election he is asked to choose among alternative electoral platforms containing promises to do certain things while refraining from doing others. Popper's "new theory of democracy" does not help the voter make up his mind, who asks himself and his friends the very question, "Who should rule?" which Popper dismissed. It is clear then that Popper has no theory of political democracy—not even a definition of it. He does not even address the question of the conflict between the private (or governmental) ownership of the media, on the one hand, and the need for public and uncoerced rational debate of issues and policies, on the other. Popper has dealt only with the question how best to punish the bad political rulers—without however telling us what a good ruler is expected to do besides defending freedom. And this does not help the voter to make a rational and moral choice at the polling station.

Even the technical point Popper makes against proportional representation is flawed. Indeed, Popper (1988: 21) asserts that under this voting scheme "I can no longer choose a person whom I trust to represent me: I can choose only a party." This is not quite true, for in many countries one may replace some of the candidates in the slate of one party with candidates of another. Besides, under a two-party system one always votes for an individual *qua* candidate of one of the parties. True, proportional representation may lead to a coalition government. But this is not necessarily a bad thing, for a coalition may represent the majority of voters and may achieve what neither of the parties would have accomplished separately.

Moreover, the plurality rule, which Popper favors over the majority one, can be grossly unfair to the electorate. First, by disenfranchising all those citizens who agree with neither of the two main parties—as is usually the case with intellectuals. Second, because it may give all the power to a minority. This can happen in at least two ways: (a) if most voters stay home for feeling alienated from two-party politics, a small minority with ample funds for propaganda can win most of the seats— as happened in the 1994 American elections that resulted in the victory of the right wing, which represents only about 20 percent of the electorate; (b) if the electorate is split nearly evenly into three parties, the one that gets 34 percent of the vote may carry the day against the parties that get 33 percent each.

In short, many a conscientious citizen has been alienated by a voting rule allowing a minority to overrule the wishes of the majority. Every political analyst from Condorcet on has known this. Moreover, the general problem of fair representation has been at the center of social choice theory since Arrow's seminal work. Why did Popper, not known for his political participation or even for keeping up to date in political science, let alone in daily political affairs, have to pontificate about these matters? Presumably only to remind us that libertarianism does not entail preference for the rule of the people, that is, straight political democracy. Was this Popper's concession to the neo-conservative wave of the 1980s?

Finally, Popper's rule that one should choose for office a person whom one may trust, rather than a party, is feasible only in small communities, where everyone knows everyone else, so that direct democracy is possible. (Ironically, there is one country where the candidates who run for public office must do so individually rather than as members of a party: present-day Uganda.) But the rule does not work for a large constituency, where the vast majority of voters have only ideologies and programs to go by. Worse, Popper's recommendation to pick candidates rather than parties is an unwitting invitation to overlook issues and support bossism—which is anything but democratic, particularly in the case of charismatic leaders. (Carlos S. Menem won the Argentine presidential election in 1989 with a charming smile and a single slogan: "Trust me, follow me.")

In any event, to a political scientist or philosopher substance should matter far more than procedure and, in particular, electoral mechanics. Any political theory worth its salt focuses on a cluster of social issues and argues for certain social goals, such as survival, security, peace, social justice, public access to culture, environmental protection, and honest administration of the commonwealth. Such goals, together with the means deemed appropriate to secure them, constitute a political ideology. By writing off all ideologies—and moreover without analyzing in any detail the very concept of an ideology—Popper locked himself out of political science and political philosophy.

Furthermore, a social philosophy cannot be restricted to politics (or to the economy, or to culture). It should tell us something about the desirable social order—or "social system," as Popper prefers to call it. But Popper does not tell us explicitly which social order, actual or conceivable, he favors: whether individualist or solidary, divided or classless. Yet this is precisely the most pressing question for any social theorist, and political philosopher, particularly at a time when most people, particularly in the Third World, suffer from a large number of crippling social evils even when they are lucky to enjoy political liberty and political democracy.

What does Popper have to say about overpopulation, environmental degradation, gender and race discrimination, or anomie? Nothing. What about the near-omnipotence of the megacorporations, the North-South inequality, the continuing arms races, the interference of great powers in the internal affairs of other countries, or the appalling standard of living of the vast majority of the people, even in countries which, like India, are said to be politically democratic? Nothing at all. Why did Popper fail to address any of these social issues? I suspect that he just ignored them for living in an ivory tower. (In 1967, when Popper called "third world" Plato's "world" of ideas in themselves, I jokingly remarked to him that this expression was already in use, though with a totally different meaning. He looked puzzled, for he had never heard that expression before, and henceforth changed it to "world 3.")

In short, Popper has had nothing original, let alone constructive, to say about any social order, actual or desirable, beyond that it should be nontyrannical and should involve the protection of the destitute. This pillar of any social philosophy worth the name is thus broken in Popper's case.

6.8. Conclusions

Popper's social philosophy lacks a theory about social order because he has neither an adequate theory of society nor a positive moral philosophy. All Popper's social philosophy does is admonish us to replace the substantive traditional question "Who shall be the rulers?" with the procedural question "How can we tame them?" In other words, Popper's conception and defense of liberty and democracy is limited to law and politics, and even then only to their mechanics. It warns us against despotism but does not help us redesign society to remove the sources of tyranny. Hence Popper's praise of social engineering, though sincere, rings hollow: it enjoins us to plan without specifying any goals other than freedom. The result is a negative, spotty, superficial, formalist, and at places inconsistent social philosophy. It bears no comparison with the social philosophies of Ibn Khaldûn, Machiavelli, Spinoza, Hobbes, Locke, Montesquieu, Rousseau, Mill, Marx, or even Paine, Kropotkin, or Laski. In my opinion it is also inferior to Popper's own contribution to the theory of knowledge, in particular his successful demolition of inductive logic and defense of epistemological realism.

I submit that Popper's social philosophy was flawed because he had only a sketchy and inadequate theory of society, namely ontological individualism (social atomism). This theory is inadequate because it refuses to admit the very existence of social wholes, such as families, schools, and business firms, that possess (emergent) properties their components lack. In turn, this view led him to espouse methodological individualism, a wrong approach to the analysis and evaluation of the social sciences, for these are supposed to study social facts, not individual actions. (See Bunge 1979, 1996, 1998 for a critique of both individualism and holism, and an alternative to them.) This may explain why Popper found just as much merit in neoclassical microeconomics as in Marx's semiclassical macroeconomics: he simply had no criterion, other than that of testability (or rather refutability), for evaluating social theories. This is why he never checked his social views against any empirical social studies, thus failing to comply with his own methodological prescription. And this is why Popper's views have not inspired a single piece of social legislation, let alone any progressive social movement.

An obvious moral to be drawn from Popper's failure to build an original, consistent, comprehensive, profound, and constructive social philosophy compatible with contemporary social research, is this. It is impossible to achieve such a task merely by harping on a single negative, if important, theme, such as the abhorrence of tyranny, social injustice, national dependence, gender discrimination, or superstition. Hamlet, who sees only error and rot, has no torch to show us the right way. A well-rounded social philosophy must include a positive theory of society along with a positive moral philosophy, that is, one positing social goods, however debatable and changeable. Without such a global and positive social philosophy, no clear vision of an open society can emerge. And without such vision people won't be mobilized to build the new society.

What explains the sensational success of *The Open Society and Its Enemies* if, as I have tried to show, it proposes a weak social philosophy? I submit that its success is due to the conjunction of three factors: content, style, and opportunity. *Content*: The book is full of interesting ideas on a large variety of subjects; it has something to say about practically every philosophical orthodoxy; it shows that the ancients can still speak to the moderns; and it proposes and defends the noble if vague ideal of an open society. *Style*: Though a scholarly work, it is clearly and beautifully written; in particular, it is sparing in philosophical jargon and free from Sociologese; last, but not least, it has a catchy title. *Opportunity*: The book pops up unexpectedly in a philosophical desert, and moreover at the moment when the last fruits of Plato's and Hegel's political philosophies lie crushed under the Allied tanks, and when the so-called West unites against its erstwhile allies, Marx's heirs. Consequently *The Open Society* is widely regarded as a scholarly epitaph to totalitarian ideologies and a standard reference work about them.

One must wonder what reception it would have gotten either ten years earlier or fifty years later.

Coda

The bulk of Popper's philosophy is best understood as being signed by negation: Words do not matter; avoid ("like the plague") discussing the meaning of words; belief is unimportant; knowledge does not depend on the knower; never ask "What is" or "How do you know" questions; there are no essential properties; whenever possible refrain from making existential statements (for being "metaphysical"); we never confirm: we can only fail to falsify; never attempt to justify; we may know falsity but not truth; there is no inductive logic; in matters of knowledge the improbable is preferable to the probable; there is no scientific method aside from trial and error; shun normal science; determinism is false; evolutionary biology is not scientific; there are neither social wholes nor social laws; demand only negative liberty (freedom from); all ideology is pernicious; all revolution is bad; there is no *summum bonum* ; do no harm—in particular, don't put philosophy in the service of oppression; do not engage in do-goodism: just refrain from evil-doing—and so on. In short, Popper's philosophy may be dubbed *logical negativism*. In other words, Popper was essentially a skeptic, and certainly the most famous of his century—though, like Bertrand Russell, a passionate one. This is why his philosophy, though extremely interesting, is fragmentary (unsystematic) and rather shallow. It is also more helpful to spot errors and wrongs than to search for truth or fairness.

Popper was undoubtedly right in criticizing school philosophy. He was also right to emphasize the role of rational criticism in the management of social conflicts as well as in the pursuit of knowledge. But surely statements and proposals must be made before they can be subjected to critical examination: creation precedes criticism, just as the tree preexists the log. In any case, all fields of learning are constantly pouring forth abundant justified yeas as well as nays and maybes. Hence no philosophy of science and technology should underrate the former. Moreover, exaggerating the importance of criticism at the expense of creation and analysis, or of observation and experiment, comes dangerously close to both scholasticism and skepticism, as well as to the fashionable view that all research is just discussion. After all, negative truths are more plentiful and thus cheaper than positive ones.

Something similar holds for the realm of action. Constructive action, whether individual or social, calls for positive views and plans in addition to rational discussions of goals and means. In particular, the design, planning, and construction of a better social order requires more than a handful of danger signals to help avoid or fight tyranny: it also calls for a positive social philosophy including a clear vision of the open society—one capable of motivating and mobilizing people. (The warning "Here there be dragons" may be helpful, but it does not point to the right way.) And such a philosophy had better form a system rather than an aggregate of disjoint views, for social issues—like any correct ideas about them—happen to come in bundles, not one at a time. One step at a time, yes; one thing at a time, no.

7

The Enlightenment and Its Enemies

Modernity was born in the seventeenth century and it reached adulthood in the eighteenth. This was the *siècle des lumières* or Enlightenment period. There may always have been enlightened people and obscurantists. But it was only in the eighteenth century that a systematic and concerted effort was made to constitute an enlightened ideology guiding a powerful cultural and political movement that was to achieve a profound and progressive social transformation. That was the century of the American and French Revolutions, of the beginning of secularism and liberalism, and of the deification of reason and the exaltation of science, technology, and industry. It was an age of progress and optimism. It was the second Renaissance. Reaction and pessimism were to come later.

We have come a long way from the Enlightenment. We have made enormous progress, but we cannot take progress for granted any longer: instead, we must work for it and fight its enemies. Moreover, we must admit that much of the progress we have made has had its lead lining. In the face of nuclear arms, overpopulation, environmental degradation, the rapid depletion of nonrenewable natural resources, the persistence of colonial exploitation and racism, the impoverishment of the Third World, the concentration of wealth in a few hands in a few countries, the mass production of cultural junk, and the recent revival of fascism and aggressive nationalism, it would be foolish to believe in absolute progress on all fronts. All progress has its price.

However, it would be even more foolish, and indeed suicidal, to believe that we are condemned to regression and eventual extinction. In particular, it would be foolish and suicidal to despair of our ability to redesign the future and secure the survival of humankind with the help of science, technology, and a humanistic and unselfish morality. Yet in our "postmodern" era it has become fashionable to surrender to such despair and moreover to blame reason, science, and technology—rather than wrong values and our political and business leaders—for our current predicament.

The new Romanticism is fashionable partly because the illusions and promises of my generation have not been fulfilled. Also, because it is the easy thing to believe, because inaction is easier than action, and because irrationalism is favored by the most reactionary forces, which thrive on our ignorance and unwillingness to tackle social issues in a rational and realistic manner. As Isaac Asimov said, it is far easier and less dangerous to reject science and technology than to revolt against the social order: the former only takes ignorance, and it does not put one's life or freedom on the line.

The retreat from the Enlightenment is fashionable but far from original. In fact, the Counter-Enlightenment followed right on the heels of the Enlightenment, it was revived less than a century ago, it triumphed briefly with Nazism, and it is fashionable again under the headings of Counterculture and Postmodernism. Two centuries ago Herder, the Romantic writer and father of cultural nationalism, exclaimed: "I am not here to think, but to be, feel, live." Between 1925 and 1945, the fascists sought to remythologize modern society by replacing the cult of universal reason with that of blood and soil. Nowadays millions of young people listen to Skid Row, one of the heavy-metal "groups," whose motto is "If you think, you stink."

We shall examine the "postmodern" reaction in the field of social studies. However, it will help us understand this reaction if we start by placing it in its historical context.

7.1. Peculiarities of the Enlightenment

The catchwords of the Enlightenment were *nature* and *humankind*, *reason* and *science*, *liberty* and *equality*, *happiness* and *utility*, *work* and *progress*. Reason was placed at the very center of this constellation: if only men were to think and act rationally, the rest would follow. The thinkers of the *siècle des lumières,* who were often called *philosophes*, saw themselves as the bearers of the torch of reason and explorers of the world previously shrouded in the darkness inherited from the Dark Ages.

Suffice it to remember the *Encyclopédie* (begun in 1751), the American Declaration of Independence (1776) , and the *Déclaration des droits de l'homme et du citoyen* (1789), as well as such diverse thinkers as Locke and Hume, Voltaire and Condillac, Montesquieu and Condorcet,

Diderot and d'Alembert, Buffon and Lavoisier, Helvétius and d'Holbach, Quesnay and Smith, Beccaria and Bentham, and Ben Franklin and Tom Paine.

The Enlightenment was a whole new ideology: a world view, a value system and a political agenda. It was the first comprehensive modern ideology, and one wedged between another two comprehensive ideologies: Thomism and Marxism—which in some ways was a continuation of, and in others a reaction against, the Enlightenment. (More on this in section 7.3.)

The Enlightenment ideology may be compressed into the following ten principles:

1. *Trust in reason*—culminating during the French Revolution in the pathetic worship of the goddess Reason.
2. *Rejection of myth*, superstition, and generally groundless belief or dogma.
3. *Free inquiry and secularism*, as well as encouragement of deism (in contrast to theism), agnosticism, or even atheism.
4. *Naturalism* (as opposed to supernaturalism), in particular materialism.
5. *Scientism*: adoption of the scientific approach to the study of society as well as nature.
6. *Utilitarianism* (as against both religious morality and secular deontologism).
7. *Respect for praxis*—craftsmanship and industry—and reverence for the machine.
8. Modernism and progressivism: contempt for the past (except for classical antiquity), criticism of present shortcomings and vices, and trust in the future.
9. *Individualism* together with libertarianism, egalitarianism (to some degree or other), and political democracy—not yet for women or slaves, though.
10. *Universalism* or cosmopolitanism—for example, human rights and education for all "free men."

Some of these principles are part of a world view, others are value judgments, and still others are parts of a program to change society. Although the Enlightenment ideology was a coherent system, some people adopted some of its components while rejecting others. For example, the enlightened European despots and some of the American patricians, both North and South, adopted the philosophical but not the political components of the Enlightenment ideology. In particular, they were against obscurantism but not for social emancipation. On the other hand, the Romantic philosophers and political thinkers rejected all ten principles: they were reactionary all the way.

7.2. The First Counter-Enlightenment

Romanticism, a powerful cultural movement that spanned a quarter of a century on each side of 1800, is usually presented as a reaction against the Enlightenment and the French Revolution, as well as against the Napoleonic invasions. So it was with regard to philosophy and politics. But Romanticism was not just a reaction: there was also Romantic art. And this art was extraordinarily original and rich in literature and music. Furthermore, it was hardly touched by philosophy or politics.

We shall therefore distinguish three strains in Romanticism: the artistic, the philosophical, and the political. Romantic art was philosophically and politically neutral; philosophical Romanticism was obscurantist; and political Romanticism was conservative or worse. A few examples will make this point clear. To begin with, Rousseau—often regarded as the first Romantic—was politically progressive but philosophically obscurantist, for exalting feeling over reason and for holding that science had a pernicious influence on society. On the other hand Heine, Beethoven, and Shelley were artistically romantic but they sided with the world view and the political philosophy of the Enlightenment. Goethe and Blake were politically progressive but anti-intellectualist and in particular they disliked modern science. Closer to us, most of the ideologists of the New Right are rationalists, whereas the New Left (or what is left of it), as well as the feminist and the Green movements, teem with irrationalists—in particular, enemies of science and technology (see Gross and Levitt 1994).

Having drawn a distinction between artistic, intellectual and political Romanticism, we shall henceforth concentrate on the middle strain, for being the one most relevant to our topic. Intellectual romanticism, in contradistinction to artistic romanticism, is a reaction against the philosophy and the value system of the Enlightenment. It is either irrationalist (in particular intuitionist) or idealist; it is antiempiricist (in particular idealist or apriorist), and it is antiscientific and technophobic. In short, intellectual Romanticism is traditionalist or antimodernist—or, if preferred, postmodernist.

The core of intellectual Romanticism was the idealist philosophy of Fichte, Schelling, Hegel, Herder, and Schopenhauer. Though different, all five men were idealists, they opposed the burgeoning science of their time, and attempted to counter the *Entzauberung* or demythologization process that Max Weber, echoing Auguste Comte, saw as the trademark of modernity.

The Romantic philosophers identified ontology with logic, a confusion that gave them leave to speculate freely about reality: they often mistook fiction for fact. They wished to replace natural science with natural philosophy, and social science with social (in particular legal) philosophy. They believed all things to be organic wholes opaque to analysis. And they opposed conceptual and empirical analysis, claiming that all dissection kills.

In the field of ethics and political philosophy, the Romantics proposed replacing bourgeois individualism with holism or collectivism. (By contrast, the Romantic artists were individualists.) Last, but not least, the prose of the Romantic philosophers was remarkably obscure and stuffy. They are the ones who invented the trick of passing off nonsense as profundity. This trick was perfected in our century by the phenomenologists, existentialists, hermeneuticists, and deconstructionists.

As with other intellectual currents, in this case there were a number of border cases. Immanuel Kant was one of them. He was as enlightened as anyone could be in the most backward and isolated of Prussian provinces. He respected mathematics and science although he hardly understood them; and he was a universalist, cosmopolitan, and pacifist. But, because of his idealism and intuitionism, his insistence on the limits of reason, and his dogma that psychology and the study of society could never become sciences, Kant prepared the way for the onset of German Romantic philosophy.

Another case of contamination of the Enlightenment by Romanticism was Marxism. Marx and Engels thought of themselves as the heirs of the Enlightenment and the French Revolution. This they were in some important respects: they were very important social scientists, they pushed liberalism towards the left—with characteristically romantic enthusiasm—they were materialists on the whole, and they thought clearly except about dialectics.

However, Marx and Engels learned from Hegel a few lessons that vitiated their whole system. One of them was dialectical ontology. According to it, every thing is a unity of opposites, and opposition, "contradiction" or conflict is the source of all change—whence the preference for revolution over reform. A second Hegelian legacy was the equation of logic with ontology—which frees ontological speculation from empirical constraints. A third was the belief that, in order to establish the truth of a statement of fact, it suffices to invoke a few favorable examples, without bothering to look for counterexamples (exceptions)—a characteristic of untutored thinking. A fourth Hegelian inheritance was holism or collectivism, that is, the thesis that the whole determines the part—for example, that the individual is at the mercy of social systems and historical forces. A fifth was an ethical consequence of holism, namely that individual rights are as nothing compared with the duty to submit to "historical necessity" and the State or Party that claims to represent it.

I submit that this legacy of Hegel's was definitely obscurantist and it favored the crystallization of Marxism into a dogma disconnected from "bourgeois" philosophy and social science. Notwithstanding these important legacies of Hegelianism, original Marxism was on the whole anti-Romantic. (On the other hand neo-Marxism, in particular Stalinist Marxism, structuralist Marxism, and critical theory, often accentuated the Romantic streaks in Marx and Engels, in particular dialectical mumbo-jumbo and contempt for empirical testing.) So, there is still hope of salvaging some of the ingredients of Marxism—precisely those that harmonize with the Enlightenment. This ambiguity of the Marxist legacy is still to be explored (see Curtis 1997 for a start).

7.3. The Second and Third Romantic Waves

The second Romantic wave came roughly one century after the birth of the first. It was initiated by Friedrich Nietzsche—who was to become the favorite philosopher of Hitler and Heidegger—and Wilhelm Dilthey, the father of philosophical hermeneutics. Other outstanding members of the second wave were Heinrich Rickert (Weber's friend and philosophical mentor), Henri Bergson, Hans Vaihinger, and even the later William James—rightly called a Romantic utilitarian. The neo-Hegelians Croce and Gentile (Mussolini's co-author and minister of education) joined later on.

This was a motley collection: some of them were intuitionists, others idealists, others radical skeptics, and still others pragmatists. But they all shared a mistrust of reason, in particular formal logic and mathematics, and in general a lack of confidence in science. None of them cared for empirical tests, and some of them did not even find use for the concept of truth. Most of them were antidemocratic as well.

The third Romantic wave, which I shall call neo-Romanticism, overlapped partially with the second. It began with Husserl's phenomenology, was followed by Heidegger's existentialism, and culminated in "postmodernism" and the contemporary antiscience and antitechnology movement. Some of the better known names in this movement are

Edmund Husserl and Martin Heidegger, Oswald Spengler and Jacques Ellul, Georg Lukács and Louis Althusser, Albert Camus and Jean-Paul Sartre, Karl Jaspers and Hans-Georg Gadamer, Michel Foucault and Jacques Derrida, Paul Feyerabend and Richard Rorty, Clifford Geertz and Harold Garfinkel, Barry Barnes and Bruno Latour.

Though quite different from one another, these authors share most or all of the following five typically Romantic traits. These are

1. *Mistrust of reason* and, in particular, of logic and science.
2. *Subjectivism*, or the doctrine that the world is our representation.
3. *Relativism*, or the negation of the existence of universal truths.
4. *Obsession with symbol*, myth, metaphor, and rhetoric.
5. *Pessimism*, or the denial of the possibility of progress—particularly in matters of scientific knowledge.

Most of the neo-Romantics write inexact and often impenetrable prose—another Romantic trait. (Remember Nietzsche's contempt for "the offensive simplicity of the style" of John Stuart Mill or, better yet, Heidegger's meaningless and therefore untranslatable strings of words.) Furthermore, they are not interested in moral problems and consequently they have no moral philosophy to offer other than either moral individualism (egoism) or moral collectivism (conformism). Finally, not daring to be thought of as antimodern—that is, reactionary—some of these writers call themselves *postmodern*—an oxymoron, as befits irrationalism (see, e.g., Featherstone, ed. 1988; Harvey 1989).

Up until the 1960s the influence of neo-Romanticism was confined to Germany, France, and their spheres of cultural influence. The major intellectual currents in the Anglo-American world and its sphere of cultural influence had been proscientific, protechnological, and anti-obscurantist. In particular, the academic community worldwide had on the whole been committed to critical thinking and empirical evidence, as well as to liberal politics. The heritage of the Enlightenment was taken for granted. Moreover, we were supposed to have entered the space and computer age. Ours was supposed to be the postindustrial society, run by knowledge rather than by labor. Finally, the continuous economic growth of the industrialized countries between ca. 1950 and 1970 suggested that "we" (that is, one-fith of humankind) had reached the age of plenty and high quality of life.

The combination of affluence and war changed all that in the U.S. Middle-class affluence eroded the work ethic and facilitated hedonism and egoism. The Me Generation was ushered in. However, the Vietnam war, and later on the acceleration of the arms race, gobbled up many of the funds earmarked for liberal social programs. Large sectors of the population became alienated or disaffected. Many students and young academics began to question the received value system and the concomitant ideology—especially when facing either the military draft or unemployment. They became receptive to ideas and lifestyles alternative to the so-called American Way of Life. Among them were drugs and irrationalism—two perfect mates.

From about the mid-1960s on, German and French neo-Romanticism was imported into the Anglo-American academic world. It became influential not just among literary critics and philosophers but also among students of society, particularly anthropologists and sociologists (see, e.g., Fiske and Shweder, eds. 1986, and the journal *Sociological Theory*). The close traditional ties between obscurantism and totalitarian politics were severed or covered up for purposes of consumption in the new market. So much so, that many have mistaken the revolt against reason for a rebellion against the "establishment"—as if logic and basic science were ideologically tainted, when in fact irrationalism is an effective intellectual tool of oppression, for blunting critical thinking and valuation, as Popper (1945) noted long ago.

Let us now examine the influence of neo-Romanticism on social studies in recent times.

7.4. Critical Theory and Phenomenological Sociology

Let us take a quick look at two neo-Romantic schools of social studies: critical theory and phenomenological sociology. Both reject the scientific approach, regard science proper as one more ideology or myth, distrust reason, and are characterized by uncritical thinking and hermetic language.

Critical theory, also called the Frankfurt school, is the variety of "humanistic" (or armchair and innumerate) sociology initially characterized by a critique of capitalism and all known types of social order; the denial of the distinction between science and ideology; the denunciation of science and technology as handmaidens of capitalism; the rejection of positivism, rationalism, and scientism; the claim that rationality abolishes individuality and autonomy: that "the Enlightenment is totalitarian"; repetitive invocations to Hegel, Marx, and Freud; the demand that social science become a tool for social change; and long-winded, heavy, and opaque prose devoid of analysis and argument, of figures and formulas (see, e.g., Adorno and Horkheimer 1972; Arato and Gebhardt, eds., 1978.) Much the same holds for the French structuralists and poststructuralists, in particular Louis Althusser and Michel Foucault.

We shall not touch on the Frankfurt school critique of capitalism, which derives essentially from Marxism—though without whatever empirical support the latter mustered. We shall concentrate instead on some of the philosophical components of critical theory. Firstly, like Marxism, critical theory adopts uncritically Hegelian dialectics: it does not doubt that every thing is a unity of opposites, and that the source of every change is "contradiction" or the struggle of opposites. It does not elucidate the terms "opposite" and "struggle," and it overlooks all the exceptions to the "law" that "contradiction" (opposition) is the engine of change. In particular, it overlooks production, trade, cooperation, demographic change, and technological innovation, none of which can easily be construed as a struggle of opposites—except in the sense that the new sometimes opposes the old.

Secondly, critical theorists reject rationality, believing that it is the supreme tool of the domination of man. Thirdly, they embrace uncritically psychoanalysis, with all of its wild speculations, thus showing that they are gullible and incapable of distinguishing pseudoscience from science. Fourthly, they mistake science for technology, and consequently they are incapable of understanding that basic science cannot be used directly as an agent of social change, and that it is needed not only to understand society but also to redesign it. Fifthly, they reject the distinction between science and ideology. Indeed, the central points of critical theory are that (a) Science = Technology = Capitalist ideology; and (b) sociologists are necessarily committed to either the conservation or the alteration of society—hence the adjective "critical." Moreover, they hold that science is not ethically neutral or even epistemologically objective. They brand as "positivists" those who claim that it possible to gain objective knowledge of social facts. In other words, they equate science and positivism, thus rendering the latter an undeserved service.

Between the two world wars, the Frankfurt school tackled, albeit in a rather literary way, some real social issues: the evils of unregulated capitalism, the crimes of Nazism and Stalinism, and the impotence of liberalism. It performed a useful if modest ideological function, even while mistaking industrialism for capitalism, exaggerating the similarities between liberalism and Nazism, and disparaging the scientific study of society. Since then, critical theorists have continued to criticize capitalism and totalitarianism in imprecise general terms. However, they have turned increasingly to idealistic (in particular neo-Kantian) philosophy, and they have had nothing precise to say about the most pressing social issues in the postwar period, such as overpopulation, environmental degradation, the arms race, the North-South chasm, stagflation, and ethnic conflicts. In particular, Habermas has gradually shifted from an interest in social conflict and oppression to "communicative action"—the type of "action" professors excel at, and first explored by the ethnomethodologists, to be examined in the next section.

By rejecting the scientific approach to social issues, the critical theorists unwittingly block the understanding of such issues, as well as any attempts to tackle them rationally and therefore effectively. In this way, despite its revolutionary rhetoric, critical theory has become a conservative force, a sort of academically respectable safety valve for nonconformists, and one more variety of obscurantism. To top it all, for all their publications over seven decades, critical theorists have neither elucidated any key sociological concepts nor proposed any original and testable hypotheses—much less, theories proper. In sum, critical theory is neither.

Our second example is phenomenological sociology (Schutz 1967, Berger and Luckmann 1967). This is the conservative counterpart of critical theory. It is characterized by spiritualism and subjectivism, as well as by individualism (both ontological and methodological) and conservatism—ethical and political. The first two features are obvious: According to phenomenology, social reality is a construction, not a given, for all facts are "meaningful" and thus are to be "interpreted." Consequently, everything social is spiritual and subjective, or at most intersubjective, rather than material and objective.

The ontological individualism of phenomenology derives from its subjectivism. Because individuals are said to "interpret" themselves and others, without ever facing any brute social facts, the task of the sociologist is to grasp "subjective meaning structures" rather than to construct and test sociological models of social systems. In particular, he must study the *Lebenswelt* (everyday life) of individuals, staying away from large social issues such as gender and race discrimination, social conflict and political oppression, militarism and colonialism. The phenomenologist can capture directly the objects of his study because they are ordinary: they are all in the *Lebenswelt* or daily life. Moreover, he is graced by the "vision of essences," a special insight which allows him instant grasping. Hence he can dispense with tedious fact-finding, meticulous empirical tests, and rigorous arguments. In short, phenomenological sociology is admittedly unscientific.

The ethics and politics of phenomenology are clear: Far from being subjected to social constraints, the individual is autonomous because he constructs social reality. Hence there is no reason to bother about emancipation. The sociologist ought to be interested only in social order, because men crave for "meaning" and order. He ought to shun conflict and, in general, social issues. The social *summum bonum* is stability, with its accompanying rigid order and certainty, not social progress, with the concomitant disorder, risk and uncertainty. In short, phenomenology is ethically and politically conservative. Consequently it is not a guide for any social policy other than "law and order."

7.5. Ethnomethodology and Interpretive Anthropology

Our next example of the neo-Romantic reaction against social science is ethnomethodology, an offspring of the union of phenomenology with symbolic interactionism (see, e.g., Garfinkel 1967). Ethnomethodologists practice what phenomenologist sociologist and critical theorists preach: They observe at first hand trivial events in the *Lebenswelt* or everyday life, focusing on communication and staying clear of any important social activities, such as work, and social issues, such as poverty. They engage in participant observation and shun experiment, which they disapprove of on philosophical grounds.

Lacking theories of their own, most ethnomethodologists adopt the murky pronouncements of phenomenology and even existentialism— two notorious radical enemies of science. Obviously, an antiscientific philosophy could hardly inspire scientific research. Mercifully, the ethnomethodologists make no use of these doctrines in their empirical work. In fact, even while vehemently denouncing positivism, when in the field they behave as common positivists, inasmuch as they spend most of their time collecting data which they cannot assimilate for want of theory.

In fact, the ethnomethodologists audiotape and videotape "the detailed and observable practices which make the incarnate production of ordinary social facts, for example, order of service in a queue, sequential order in a conversation, and the order of skillfully embodied improvised conduct" (Lynch, Livingston & Garfinkel 1983: 206). In plain English: Ethnomethodologists record observable ordinary-life events.

The data thus collected are audible or visible traces left by people who presumably behave purposefully and intelligently. This is the only clue the ethnomethodologists can go by, for, lacking a theory, they cannot explain what makes people tick. The ethnomethodologist's practice does not differ from that of the empiricist and, in particular, the behaviorist. In short, he behaves like a positivist even while engaging in positivism-bashing—which is actually an attack upon the scientific approach.

Only the ethnomethodologists's convoluted lingo suggests intimate contact with their philosophical mentors. Example: Garfinkel (1967: 1) starts his best-known book stating that ethnomethodology "recommends" that "the activities whereby members [?] produce and manage settings [?] of organized everyday affairs are identical with members' procedures for making those settings 'accountable'[?]. The 'reflexive'[?] or 'incarnate'[?] character of accounting [?] practices and accounts makes up the crux of that recommendation." Why such opaque prose to write ordinary accounts of everyday life?

This is not to deny the value of observing everyday life occurrences, such as casual encounters and conversations—the favorite empirical material of ethnomethodologists. The observation of ordinary life, a common practice of anthropologists, yields raw material for the scientist to process in the light of hypotheses and with a view to coming up with new hypotheses. But that material is of limited use unless the subjects are placed in their social networks, for only this may tell us why the actors behave as they do. Indeed, it is well-known that any actor is likely to behave differently in different settings. Yet, ethnomethodologists deliberately overlook the macrosocial context as well as all large-scale social issues. This, combined with the absence of tests of the proposed "interpretations" (hypotheses) and the lack of theory, explains the poverty of findings of ethnomethodology.

Compare this barren individualistic approach to everyday life with that of the institutionalists or "relationists" (i.e., systemists) Chris and Charles Tilly (1998). Their comprehensive study of work under capitalism starts with the following sentence: "Rural French worker Marie-Catherine Gardez, born in 1891 in the Nord region, worked hard for all her long life." The life history of this woman only motivates and illustrates the authors' theses that work in a labor market is just one of many forms of work; that getting and changing jobs occur not within a form-less labor market but within some social network; that wage is not the only work incentive—others being commitment to family or community, and coercion; and that custom, group norm, ideology, and contingency are at least as important as contract. The Tillys work out these and other theses within the institutionalist theory (or rather framework), support them with hard statistical data from a variety of sectors and periods, and show the superiority of this approach over both individualism and Marxism. What a contrast with the parochialism of ethnomethodology!

Let us see now how ethnomethodologists view scientific research (see Lynch, Livingston, and Garfinkel 1983 for a summary). Their findings are essentially two. One is that "something more" is involved in scientific research, than what can be formulated in even the most detailed of instruction manuals. This "something more" is the set of tacit assumptions and of bits and pieces of know-how (procedural knowledge), both of them well known to psychologists, philosophers, and engineers.

The other "finding" is that, no matter how elementary a scientific experiment may be, it cannot be performed without a modicum of theory. This is why a partially paralyzed chemistry student could do his lab exercises with the help of an able-bodied ethnomethodology student, largely ignorant of chemistry, who acted as the former's hand. But did we not know this all along, at least those of us who have had a scientific training and did not fall for the most crass form of empiricism? And if ethnomethodologists understand that there is no genuine science without theory, why do not they produce one?

Interpretive or hermeneutic anthropology, practiced and championed by Clifford Geertz (1973, 1983), is very close to ethnomethodology. In fact, both shun the scientific method, over-emphasize the role of symbols, avoid deep hypotheses, and focus on daily-life minutiae. Interpretive anthropology is thus quite different from Weber's interpretive sociology. Indeed, Weber tackled some important social processes, proposed plenty of hypotheses—and did not allow his declared unscientific philosophy to interfere with his scientific research. It is also different in that, unlike Weber's dull prose, Geertz's can be sparkling and entertaining—which largely accounts for its popularity among undergraduates.

It is amusing to read, for instance, that one and the same trivial episode in Morocco is interpreted differently by a Berber nomad, a Jewish merchant, and a French army captain. But how novel is this finding? And is it science or literature? And how does it compare with the findings of such eminent contemporary non-Marxist materialist anthropologists as Marvin Harris and Bruce Trigger, who strive to understand how people manage to make a living and get along with one another?

Being radical individualists, and focusing on such everyday life practices as conversation, ritual, and entertainment, the ethnomethodologists and interpretive anthropologists openly admit their indifference to the problems of social structure and, indeed, to all social issues—as recommended by Dilthey, Husserl, and Schutz. In concentrating on individuals (or at most pairs of individuals), and in overlooking all important social activities and social systems, they fail to come to grips with social reality. This is why they have made no important social findings. Why should people who only record trivial facts, have no theory to speak of, and disbelieve in objective truth, be counted as scientists? And why should anything but the tally of findings count in ranking scientists?

7.6. Conclusions

The Enlightenment gave us most of the basic values of contemporary civilized life, such as trust in reason, a passion for free inquiry, and egalitarianism. Of course the Enlightenment did not do everything for us: no single social movement can do everything for posterity—there is no end to history. For instance, the thinkers of the Enlightenment did not foresee the abuses of industrialization, they exaggerated individualism, extolled competition at the expense of cooperation, did not go far enough in social reform, and did not care much for women or for the underdeveloped peoples. However, the Enlightenment did perfect, praise, and diffuse the main conceptual and moral tools for advancing beyond itself.

By contrast, the fanatics of the Counter-Enlightenment would have us set the clock back rather than tackle the current issues and try to go forward. They are barbarians intent on destroying modern culture while continuing to enjoy its technological spin-offs. Although they constitute a motley crowd, basically they only differ amongst themselves by the intensity of their hatred of reason and science—which they conveniently dub "positivism." Not surprisingly, they have produced no remarkable findings, not even new interesting errors, the denials of which would constitute valuable truths. However, they have succeeded in attracting a number of academics, such as the self-styled sociologists of science who write about science and society without being familiar with either—as will be argued in the next two chapters.

Ordinary mistakes and scientific errors can be detected and corrected in the light of reason or experience. But when reason and experience are written off, such correction becomes impossible, errors are perpetuated, and cheap nonsense and shallow metaphor replace the laborious search for system and truth. Instead of significant statistics and serious theories, we get stories ("thick descriptions") and frivolous analogies such as "life is a text," "life is a stage," and "life is a game." Worse, when obscurantism is in the ascendancy, freedom and progress are at risk. And when this happens, the so-called eggheads are mobbed by skinheads, whose muddled brains control booted legs anxious to trample on the Enlightenment legacy.

8

Sociology of Science:
From Marx to Merton and Beyond

The sociology of science, once rare and marginal, has become bulky and central. It is being practised by an increasing number of sociologists, as well as by "postmodern" literary critics who, having lost their taste for literary studies, engage in what they call "cultural studies." In addition to a large annual spate of books, there is a quarterly, *Social Studies of Science*, founded in 1970, the *Sociology of the Sciences Yearbook*, launched in 1977, and the biannual *Science in Context*, not to mention numerous pieces in general sociological journals. Besides, the discipline has become a regular feature in the programs of all the major universities. It often comes as the nucleus of the so-called *STS* (Science, Technology, and Society) programs and centers.

Since the 1960s, several new directions have emerged in this field . Although they differ on several points, these new styles share a number of tenets. These are (a) *externalism*, or the thesis that conceptual content is determined by social context; (b) *constructivism* or subjectivism: the idea that the inquiring subject constructs not only his accounts of facts but also the facts themselves, and possibly the entire world; (c) *relativism*, or the thesis that there are no objective and universal truths; (d) *pragmatism*, or emphasis on action and interaction at the expense of ideas, and the equation of science with technology; (e) *ordinarism*, or the thesis that scientific research is pure perspiration and no inspiration, and the refusal to accord science a special status and to distinguish it from ideology, pseudoscience, or even antiscience; (f) adoption of *obsolete psychological doctrines*, such as behaviorism and psychoanalysis; and (g) *substitution of a number of unscientific or even antiscientific philosophies*—such as linguistic philosophy, phenomenology, existentialism, hermeneutics, "critical theory," poststructuralism, deconstructivism, or the French school of semiotics, as the case may be—for positivism, rationalism, and other classical philosophies.

I shall argue that, as a consequence of upholding these seven tenets, the new-style sociologists of science are unable to understand science: They never tell us what makes scientists tick *qua* scientists, which their tacit philosophical assumptions and methodologico-ethical norms are, what distinguishes scientific research from other activities, what is its place in society, and why science has been so successful in understanding reality and in fueling technology—and so unsuccessful in dislodging magic thinking. Worse, they deny that scientists engage in a distinctive cultural activity and that they have an ethos of their own.

This is not to begrudge the few modest accomplishments some of them have attained thanks to their occasional attention to minutiae and despite their flawed philosophy. But their positive contributions to the science of science pale by comparison with the huge regression they have forced on the sociology of science in recent years. This regression is such, that anyone with a scientific background is bound to regard most of the current production in that field as a grotesque cartoon of scientific research.

In this chapter I shall examine what I take to be the fatal flaws of the new directions in the sociology of science. Every one of my criticisms applies to at least one contemporary school in the new sociology of science, and some to all of them. However, before looking into the new directions it will be convenient to take a quick look at the classical sociology of science for, though much maligned by the Young Turks, it contains the embryo of much of what is wrong with the new directions along with much of permanent value.

8.1. Marxist Roots

The sociology of science is of course a branch of the sociology of knowledge, other important branches of which are the sociologies of technology, medicine, art, and religion. Karl Mannheim (1929)—a student of Max Weber's and a Marx scholar strongly influenced by Georg Lukács (1923)—passes for being the father of the sociology of knowledge just because he coined the terms *Wissenssoziologie* (sociology of knowlege) and *Denkstil* (thought style). However, unlike his predecessors Weber and Durkheim, Mannheim did not conduct any specialized research and did not build any detailed theories. Basically he limited himself to stressing the social conditioning of ideas, and therefore the importance of the sociology of knowledge as an adjunct to the history and philosophy of knowledge. And, because he never held that all of the sciences have a social content, he is often scolded by the members of the new sociology of science: They insist that social facts are "constitutive" of science, not just "contingent" factors influencing science from outside.

Actually the modern sociology of knowledge was not launched by Mannheim. It was first sketched by Karl Marx and Friedrich Engels, and cultivated much later in a systematic fashion by Emile Durkheim and Max Weber (both of whom focused on the sociology of religion), Max Scheler, John D. Bernal and his circle, Robert K. Merton and his co-workers and students, and a few others. Because Merton is the last eminent member of the classical school, and because he has stuck to the scientific method and is consequently neither a constructivist nor a relativist, the new-style sociologists of science have turned him into the target of many of their barbs, and like to call themselves "post-Mertonian" and to claim that they have advanced far beyond him.

Marx and Engels are the grandfathers of the new sociology of science in being the first to hold the following well-known theses.

1. "It is not the consciousness of men that determines their being but, on the contrary, *their social being that determines their consciousness* " (Marx 1859, in Marx & Engels 1986: 182, my emphasis).

2. "Upon the different forms of property, upon the social conditions of existence, rises an entire superstructure of distinct and peculiarly formed sentiments, illusions, modes of thought and views of life. *The entire class creates and forms them out of its material foundations and out of the corresponding social relations. The single individual derives them through tradition and upbringing* " (Marx 1852, in Marx & Engels 1986; 118-119, my emphasis).

3. Social science is ideologically committed: it furthers the material interests of some social class or other. In modern times there is bourgeois social science and there is proletarian social science. However, whereas the former is full of error and illusion—for being distorted by ideology—the latter is objectively true because the proletariat represents the interests of mankind as a whole.

These were certainly bold new ideas in the mid-nineteenth century, and each of them holds a grain of truth. In fact

1. Developmental and social psychology have shown that the social environment does *condition* a person's mental make-up—without however determining it fully, for the genome and the nervous system, as well as individual action, which is often upstream, do count a lot to say the least. More on this in section 8.5.

2. Because in a stratified society everyone is born into some social class, the members of which share certain interests, values, beliefs, expectations, and so on, the belonging to a class does influence the *social* scientist's approach—but this does not entail either that he cannot overcome such limits, or that his class does the thinking for him. It is odd for a materialist to hold that a social class, which has no brain, can think. And it is simply false that all ideas, even the mathematical ones, are created out of the economic foundation of society. We shall return to this point in section 8.4.

3. It is true that some branches of economics and political science, particularly those concerned with the management of the economy and with government, are tainted by the interests of the ruling classes. Suffice it to recall the neoliberal economic policies and Leninism. However, ever since the welfare state was instituted, much work in economics and politology has taken it for granted that the state, far from being a tool of the ruling classes, must act as an umpire in the class struggle and must redistribute part of the surplus in an equitable manner. Besides, even at the time of Marx and Engels there were objective social studies, many of which they themselves used to describe and indict capitalism. In short, basic or descriptive social science is very often impartial, whereas prescriptive or normative social studies are often partisan (see Bunge 1998).

It is remarkable that the views of Marx and Engels on the social conditioning of knowledge and the partisanship of social science should have been so influential, for they were sketchy, unsystematic, and none too clear to boot. What exactly does "determine" mean in the sentence "Social being determines consciousness"? Does it mean that society as a whole *causes* mental processes, or that an individual's social position and behavior strongly *influence* the way he thinks? Clearly, the ambiguity inherent in ordinary language lends itself to multiple interpretations.

Moreover, Marx and Engels wavered on these matters. For one thing, while sometimes they held that science and technology belong in the *Unterbau* (infrastructure or economic basis) of society, at other times they placed them in the *Überbau* (superstructure). For another, while sometimes they held that every idea is the creation of a social class and thus distorted by class interests, at other times they maintained that basic natural science and mathematics are class-free, even while being conditioned by social circumstances. Because of such vacillations, sketchiness, and imprecisions, there is considerable variety of opinion and inconclusive controversy on these matters in the Marxist camp.

8.2. Flowering of the Marxist Sociology of Science

The Russian historian and philosopher of science Boris Hessen (1931) wrote "a veritable manifesto of the Marxist form of externalism in the history of science" (Needham 1971: viii). In his paper on "The social and economic roots of Newton's 'Principia,'" Hessen held that Newton's work was a child of his class and time, and that his scientific work was an attempt to solve technological problems posed by the rise of capitalism. Obviously, this thesis has a grain of truth: Newton tackled scientific problems that had not even been posed before the modern era, he did so with the help of thoroughly modern methods, and the sensational success of his work is partly explained by its usefulness to the technology employed by the rapidly expanding capitalist industry—although the Industrial Revolution started only once century after the publication of the *Principia.*

However, this does not prove that Newton's mechanical formulas, let alone his contributions to the infinitesimal calculus, had a social *content*. His mechanics referred to moving bodies, and his mathematics to "fluxions" (time-dependent functions). Besides, how does one explain that Newton happened to be the only "child of his class and time" to produce that monumental work? Why was there only one *Principia* rather than thousands of similar books written by as many contemporaries of Newton's? And why, if Newton was so interested in industry as Hessen claims, did he not design any machines or industrial processes? Why was he a theoretical physicist and mathematician and not an engineer? And why did the same social class produce the atheist Hobbes as well as the deist Newton? Is it not possible that individual brains, as well as social groups, have something to do with original ideas?

Hessen's paper was enormously influential. It helped shape the Western Marxist sociology of science which flourished between the mid-1930s and the mid-1960s. The American quarterly *Science & Society,* which is still going strong, was launched in 1936. The most thorough and influential single book to come from this school was Bernal's *The Social Function of Science* (1939), which the historian of science Derek Price (1964) regarded—mistakenly—as having laid the foundations of the sociology of science. John Desmond Bernal, FRS, was an eminent crystallographer whose work proved to be of crucial importance for the unveiling of the composition and structure of proteins, DNA, and RNA. He was in fact a pioneer in molecular biology, and his colleagues felt that only his communist militancy had prevented him from being awarded a Nobel Prize. (The same may be true of J. B. S. Haldane, one of the architects of the synthetic theory of evolution.) Other scientists who were closely associated with Bernal and contributed to the discipline were the physicists P.M.S. Blackett, FRS (a Nobel laureate) and E. H. S. Burhop, FRS, the biologists J. B. S. Haldane, FRS, J. Needham, FRS, and L. Hogben, FRS, and the mathematician H. Levy. (For a representative sample of their work see Goldsmith and Mackay, eds. 1964. For a lively popularization see Crowther 1941.)

Interestingly enough, Bernal and his friends were *moderate* Marxist sociologists of science and they were mainly interested in science policy rather than in academic sociology of science. They did stress both the social *conditions* of scientific research and the actual and possible social *uses and misuses* of science, but they did not claim that mathematics and natural science have a social *content*. Today they would perhaps be described as internalists, not externalists. They were anxious to have science adequately supported in the universities and properly used in industry, public health, and education, as well as in the defense of Britain against the Nazi onslaught. After World War II they campaigned vigorously against the nuclear bomb.

The overriding interests of the early Marxist sociologists of science were practical, not theoretical. They were mainly concerned with the applications of science, which they wished to see harnessed in the interests of the people, and with the organization of science and technology. None of them had a background in social science; they were all amateurs in this field, were often misled by Marxist dogmas, and they seldom looked for counterexamples to put their hasty generalizations to the test. (Only Needham became eventually a professional historian of science, in fact the leading expert in the history of Chinese science and technology; and Price turned from physics to the sociology and history of science. But neither of them had been an orthodox Marxist.)

However, the "Invisible College" centered around Bernal did produce a number of interesting insights in the sociology of science, because its members had had a rigorous scientific training, had done original research in "hard" sciences, and had participated in the management of science as members of university science departments and, during World War II, in government departments as well. Unlike the proponents of the new sociology of science, who at the most have visited a laboratory, they were distinguished scientists: They knew what they were talking or writing about, even though sometimes they looked at their own work through the optics of dialectical and historical materialism—a rather coarse and outdated philosophy.

At about the same time a number of French scientists and philosophers became interested in the Marxist approach to the sociology, history, and philosophy of science. When the Popular Front came to power in 1935, some of them were given the job of organizing scientific research, which had been severely undermanned and underfunded since World War I. Paul Langevin, the Nobel laureates Jean Perrin, Irène Joliot-Curie, and Fréderic Joliot, as well as other eminent scientists, participated in this task. Others wrote a number of books, many of them published by the leftist publishing house Editions Sociales Internationales—which, to its credit, also published annotated anthologies of a number of French classical philosophers who had been ignored by the philosophical establishment, then as now in the hands of idealists and irrationalists. The main periodical of this group was the monthly *La pensée,* the publication of which was interrupted during the German occupation but which was resurrected after the war and seems now to have entered its terminal phase.

Some of the members of the Frankfurt school too became interested in the sociology of science during their first exile in Paris, but they do not seem to have made their mark. Only Franz Borkenau's big book, *Der Uebergang vom feudalen zum bürgerlichen Weltbild* (1934), is still quoted occasionally. Its basic thesis is very much like Hessen's: the new mode of production engendered the new world view. (It so happens that the new mode of production emerged one and a half centuries after the Scientific Revolution started.)

What is left of all those enthusiastic efforts? Very little, except for the general ideas, by now accepted by nearly every student of science, that science does not work in a social vacuum; that it fulfils an important social function; and that it ought to discharge an even more important function. The main contribution of those students of science was to science policy. As for their proposal to plan all research the way it was done in the Soviet Union, it elicited a backlash. In particular, the distinguished chemist Michael Polanyi (1958) stressed the need for freedom of research and detachment from ideology. Regrettably, at the same time he exaggerated the tacit and irrational aspect of scientific research, claiming that tacit knowledge is superior to explicit knowledge. (For this thesis, and in general the know-how/know-that distinction, see Bunge 1983a.)

8.3. Scientific Beginnings: The Merton School

The main effect of historical materialism on historiography has been indirect: it is a major root of the achievements of the French school of the *Annales*, whose best-known member was Fernand Braudel. The members of that school have conducted important original research into the material (environmental and economic) aspects of a number of societies instead of just repeating Marxist slogans. Likewise, the main effect of Marxism on the sociology of science has been indirect: Marx is one of the three most important influences on the work of Robert K. Merton and his school—the other two being Max Weber and Emile Durkheim. In both cases Marxism had to be watered down and activated (rather than recited) to be of any use. Watered down, that is, stripped of its radical externalist thesis that context determines content; and activated, that is, transformed from rhetoric into research.

Merton, a sociologist and historian of ideas by training and one who has worked in several fields of empirical and theoretical sociology, is the real founding father of the sociology of science as a science and a profession; his predecessors had been amateurs. When Merton started his academic career in the mid-1930s, all the students of science, with the exception of the Marxists, were strict internalists. This applies in particular to George Sarton, Alexandre Koyré, Aldo Mieli, Charles Singer, and Herbert Butterfield. True, Sarton—one of Merton's mentors—did make a few noises about the "social background" of science, but he did not establish links between it and the problematics and the general outlook of science. Moreover, he emphatically rejected any attempt to explain the history of science primarily in social and economic terms. He claimed that "such an explanation would apply only, at best, to the jobholders, hardly to the enthusiasts, the crazy individuals" (Sarton 1952, vol. l: xiii).

Merton's doctoral disertation, submitted in 1935 and published three years later, was titled *Science, Technology and Society in Seventeenth-Century England*. (The first four words of this work designate nowadays an established academic field.) The central general hypothesis of that book is what Merton himself, with uncharacteristic arrogance, was to call "the Copernican revolution in the sociology of science": that "not only error or illusion or unauthenticated belief but also the discovery of truth is socially and historically conditioned." The specific hypothesis was that the Puritan ethic promoted the rise of science in England. (See Cohen, ed. 1990 for an anthology of studies on this thesis.)

A sociologist of the sociology of science might hold that this idea "was in the air," particularly in view of three recent experiences. One was the popularity of Marxism among Western intellectuals in the 1930s, and their enthusiastic reception of the radical externalist theses formulated by the Russian delegates, particularly Boris Hessen, at the International Congress of History of Science and Technology which met in London in 1931 (recall section 8.2). A second fact was the vigorous support of scientific research given by the Soviet government before it embarked on the disastrous road of *partinosty* (partisanship) and scientific witch-hunting—a support all the more remarkable given the Soviet economic underdevelopment and the miserly science budgets in Britain and France at that time. A third event was the rise of the so-called Aryan science (*Rassenkunde*, German physics, etc.) and the persecution of the so-called Jewish science in Nazi Germany, in particular the role played by Nazi intellectuals and officials, such as the university rectors and party hacks Martin Heidegger and Ernst Krieck, in forming the new antiintellectual atmosphere (see, e.g., Kolnai 1938, Farías 1990).

In 1938 Merton wrote a brilliant and timely piece, titled "Science and the social order," on the latter subject (see Merton 1973). In it he summarized as follows the ethos of science : "intellectual honesty, integrity, organized skepticism, disinterestedness, impersonality," all of which "are outraged by the set of new sentiments that the [Nazi] State would impose in the sphere of scientific research." Little did Merton suspect that the very existence of that ethos would be challenged thirty years later by the post-Mertonian sociologists of science, many of whom regard themselves as leftists and would consequently feel insulted if told that they have, albeit unwittingly, embraced a central part of the Nazi creed, namely the contempt for pure science and for ideas in general.

There is no point in summarizing here Merton's contributions to the sociology of science, for they are numerous and well known, and because his prose—unlike that of many of the new-style sociologists of science—is transparent and elegant, hence a delight to read. (See Barber 1952 for an early and succinct report on the accomplishments of the Merton school.) However, we must make two points.

The first is that Merton seems to have been the first to state that science has an ethos of its own, which comprises four "institutional imperatives": *universalism,* or nonrelativism; epistemic *communism,* or unrestricted sharing of scientific knowledge; *disinterestedness,* or freedom from economic or political motivations and strictures; and *organized skepticism,* or emphasis on methodical doubt, arguability and testability (Merton 1942, in Merton 1957 and 1973). This point was to be elaborated later on by Bronowski (1959) and the author (1961).

The second point is that the work of Merton and the people around him would now be described as *discourse analysis*. It consisted in analyzing scientific documents, especially publications, and it involved hardly any empirical research aside from the occasional questionnaire. (For a representative sample of that work see Barber and Hirsch 1962.) None of those scientists had the cheek to spend a year in a scientific laboratory watching and recording the overt behavior and the "inscriptions" produced by investigators whose actions they could not possibly understand for lack of specialized training.

In the hands of scholars who had a correct understanding of what science is all about, discourse analysis produced a number of classics, such as Merton's own "Singletons and multiples in science" (1961),"The Matthew effect in science" (1968), and "Age, aging and age structure in science," the latter written with Harriet Zuckerman (1972). Other gems that came from the same school are "The case of the floppy-eared rabbits: An instance of serendipity gained and serendipity lost," by B. Barber and R. C. Fox (1958), "The exponential curve of science," by D. J. Price (1956), and "Resistance to scientific discovery," by B. Barber (1961). (These papers are collected in Barber and Hirsch, eds. or in Merton 1973.)

All of these studies rightly asumed the *uniqueness* of basic science, which derives from its universalism, communism, disinterestednesss, and organized skepticism—a uniqueness denied by the new sociology of science. This is not to say that all such studies were flawless.

In my view some of them have been excessively externalistic, and they have unduly minimized the uniqueness of the contributions of such men of genius as Archimedes, Newton, Darwin, and Einstein. Thus, in his justly famous paper on singletons and multiples, Merton wrote that "scientists of genius are precisely those whose work in the end would be eventually rediscovered. These rediscoveries would be made not by a single scientist but by an entire corps of scientists. On this view, the individual of scientific genius is the functional equivalent of a considerable array of other scientists of varying degrees of talent" (1973: 366).

How can we know that this is indeed the case? I submit that we cannot. We only know that (a) the work of many a genius has often been recognized very slowly, and (b) in the case of some breakthroughs, such as in the genesis of the quantum theory, of the synthetic theory of evolution, of physiological psychology, and molecular biology, entire teams of men of genius worked in building a new discipline. To be sure, there are cases—those studied by Merton—which fit his hypothesis, but they are seldom cases of scientific breakthroughs.

To sum up, Merton's school sinned occasionally in holding that quantity can compensate for quality and, being structuralist, it occasionally exaggerated the power of the social matrix. But it practised a kind of synthesis of externalism and internalism, it never embraced constructivism and relativism, and it did not underrate the importance of ideas. This is why it produced a number of serious studies on science as an institution. In my opinion Merton's school has so far been the summit of the sociology of science. The moment it began to be displaced by the new sociology of science, in the mid 1960s, the discipline started to roll downhill, as will be argued in the next section.

8.4. The "Strong Programme"

A number of new, "post-Mertonian" directions in the sociology of science emerged in the 1960s and 1970s (see, e.g., Knorr-Cetina and Mulkay, eds. 1983). One of the most articulate of them is the so-called "strong programme" launched by Barry Barnes, David Bloor, and Steve Shapin, of the Science Studies Unit at the University of Edinburgh. Let us take a quick preliminary look at it before going into details.

Both the Western Marxist and the Mertonian sociologists and historians of science who worked from the 1930s onwards distinguished the conceptual content of science from its social context, and held that the latter influences the former without however fully determining it. Moreover, they exempted mathematics and natural science from the charge that these branches of learning are ideologically committed. By contrast, the new sociology of science, particularly the "strong programme," claims that *all* knowledge is shaped by society and moreover is somehow *about* society, that is, that it has a *social content*—whence ultimately there would be no content/context distinction.

This would hold even for mathematics: "if mathematics is about number and its relations and if these are social creations and conventions then, indeed, mathematics is about something social. In an indirect sense it therefore is "about" society. It is about society in the same sense as Durkheim said that religion is about society. The reality that it appears to be about represents a transfigured understanding of the social labour that has been invested in it" (Bloor 1976: 93). And Restivo (1991) assures us that "mathematics is social through and through." Likewise,

Randall Collins (1998: 862) contends that "mathematics is social discourse" just because it is communicable. The same argument could be used to prove that the AIDS virus is a social entity.

These extraordinary statements are of course merely programmatic: No serious effort has been made to gather evidence for them. (See Restivo 1983 and 1991 for a thorough discussion of the sources.) But there is no need to search for positive evidence when the evidence against it is so overwhelming. To begin with, mathematics is not just "about number and its relations" . Only number theory is about (whole) numbers, or rather number systems. Moreover, number theory is a smallish part of contemporary mathematics, which contains a large number of nonnumerical fields, such as logic, abstract algebra, category theory, and topology. However, this is a minor point that only goes to suggest that our sociologist of science is not familiar with the discipline he writes about.

The important point is the claim that every science, even pure mathematics, is about society. Even granting the trivial point that mathematics is a social creation, in the sense that it is constructed by a number of people who interact and learn from one another, it does not follow that mathematical axioms, definitions or theorems refer to society, let alone describe it. Let a theory of reference—a branch of philosophical semantics—determine what a given mathematical concept or proposition is about: This is no matter for decree. Now, any reasonable theory of reference will tell us that the statement "The number 2 is even" refers to the number 2; that the statement "The Poisson brackets are not asociative" refers to Poisson parentheses; and that "The derivative of a linear function is a constant" refers to linear functions. (For an exact theory of reference see Bunge 1974.)

If a reasonable theory of reference is applied to the mathematics of mathematicians—not to the mathematics imagined by the adherents of the new sociology of science—it will yield the unsurprising result that set theory is about sets, abstract algebra about algebraic systems, topology about topological spaces, geometry about manifolds, analysis about functions, and so on. If mathematics were about society it would be a social science, and consequently (a) it would not be applicable in physics, chemistry, biology, or psychology; (b) it would be tested empirically the way social science hypotheses are supposed to be; and (c) social science proper would be redundant.

In any event, a claim of the form "X refers to Y" must be substantiated with the help of a theory of reference, and the new crop of sociologists of science have not proposed or used any such theory: They proceed in this crucial matter in a dogmatic, hence unscientific, manner. This bodes ill for the "strong programme." But it is time to take a look at the latter.

David Bloor (1976) has proposed the following four principles of the "strong programme" in the sociology of science.

1. *Causality* : the sociology of science should be "concerned with the conditions which bring about belief or states of knowledge"; knowledge "emanates from society," it is "the product of collective influences and resources and peculiar to a given culture."

2. *Impartiality* "with respect to truth and falsity, rationality or irrationality, success or failure."

3. *Symmetrical* with regard to explanation: "The same types of cause would explain, say, true and false beliefs."

4. *Reflexive* : "In principle its patterns of explanation would have to be applicable to sociology itself."

Let the following critical remarks suffice for the moment.

1. *Causal analysis is not enough and moreover it is sometimes inappropriate*, because (a) it focuses on external conditions, ignoring the inquirer's motivations and cognitive problems, or attributes them all to external factors, thus making him appear as a mere pawn rather than as a creator; and (b) it overlooks chance—ever present inside the brain and out.

2. *Impartiality* is of course necessary as long as it is not construed as indifference between truth and error and as tolerance of antiscience and pseudoscience, or confusion of these with science—as it has actually happened with the claims of some members of the school with regard to the IQ and eugenics controversies, as well as to the scientific status of parapsychology, Velikovsky's speculations, and astrology. Impartiality is one thing, unconcern with truth is another.

3. *Symmetry* with regard to explanations is obviously mistaken in an externalist and relativist perspective, which requires that vested interests disguise reality and thus lead to error more often than truth. It is also wrong in the classical perspective, particularly when conjoined with the causality requirement, for it entails that it is either impossible or pointless to distinguish the "causes" of true belief from those of false belief. In either case the sociology of science would be a mere academic exercise rather than one of the three means we have to understand science and further its advancement.

4. *Reflexivity* is an honest but suicidal requirement : If the strong programme is viewed in its own light, it must be construed as a response to extrascientific interests of some kind, hence as no more creditable than an ideology. In any event, the principle does not seem to have been applied.

However, there is an even more important problem with this program, namely that its very first principle (Causality) *begs the question* whether in fact scientific ideas are caused by social circumstances. Should this matter not be left to unbiased research, or is it naive to demand from the new sociology of science that it abide by the ethos of science as sketched by Merton? What if a social psychologist were to show that a given social stimulus elicits idea a in person A, idea b in person B, and so on until person N, whereas it arouses no ideas at all in the remaining persons of his experimental group? After all, this is what the so-called Zeroth (or Harvard) Law of experimental psychology leads us to expect even for rats.

And what if an anthropologist of science specializing in following researchers around in their daily chores (and understanding what his subjects are about) were to show that they are sometimes helped and at other times hindered by their encounters with co-workers and colleagues, but that they get many of their problems and ideas and plans when on their own or in unlikely circumstances, such as the proverbial beach in Rio de Janeiro?

An ideologist or a politician attempts to prove *that* such and such is the case, whereas a scientist investigates *whether* this is indeed so, and tries to be objective even if, for some reason or unreason, he wishes that it were (or were not) so. An ideological program is a declaration of faith and a plan to reinforce and propagate the faith. A scientific program is a research project that starts with problems, not principles other than the general philosophical principles underlying all scientific research—for example, that the external world is real, lawful, and knowable.

In the light of the above it is more than doubtful that the "strong programme" in the sociology of science is more scientific than ideological. However, worse is to come: Other directions in the new sociology of science are even further removed from genuine science, in rejecting epistemological realism, as will be seen in the next chapter. However, before examining them we propose to take a closer look at externalism and at the way the new sociology of science handles the micro-macro problem.

8.5. Externalism

The externalist thesis in the sociology of science is that context determines content, or even that there is no difference between them; that the ideas, procedures and actions of an individual scientist are determined by his social environment or even that the latter "constitutes" the former. Since the expressions "social context," "determines," and "constitutes" are vague, the externalist thesis can be interpreted in various ways. In fact the following versions are distinguishable:

Moderate or weak externalism: Knowledge is socially conditioned.

Ml (Local): The scientific community influences the work of its members.

M2 (Global): Society at large influences the work of individual scientists.

Radical or strong externalism: Knowledge is social.

Rl (Local): The scientific community emanates or constructs scientific ideas, all of which have ultimately a social content.

R2 (Global) Society at large emanates or constructs scientific ideas— hence there are no inside-outside, micro-macro, content-context, and discourse-praxis distinctions.

The *local moderate* thesis Ml presupposes that the scientific community is self-regulating: that it sets its own agenda and settles its own affairs. This thesis is so mild as to be hardly distinguishable from the internalist thesis. The difference between the theses Ml and M2 is that, unlike the radical internalism inherent in the traditional history of science, which is individualistic, moderate global externalism (i.e., M2) postulates that individual scientists do not act on their own but as members of their scientific communities, observing the norms and standards prevailing in such systems, seeking recognition and rewards from their peers, and in most cases following the scientific fashion of the day. By and large, sociologists of science around the Merton school (section 8.3) embraced moderate local externalism, which is perfectly compatible with the internalist thesis that scientific research has its own rules and standards, and is driven mainly by curiosity. Moreover it is the necessary complement of internalism (see Agassi 1981; Bunge 1983a, chap. 3).

Some new-style sociologists of science regard Thomas S. Kuhn as a radical externalist and even as an externalist sociologist of science and the father of the new sociology of science (see, e.g., Barnes 1982a; Collins 1983). But in fact Kuhn was a moderate global externalist historian, far more interested in ideas than in their social circumstances. Indeed, he never referred to social structure in any detail, and he mentioned scientific communities only as the consecrators or desecrators of scientific ideas. Moreover he never studied any scientific community in particular and, as Mendelson (1977: 7) pointed out, Kuhn never even posed himself the problem of the possible relations between knowledge and institutional structures or the broader social structures and processes.

Why then has Kuhn sometimes been hailed as the founding father of the new sociology of science? For different reasons, namely because he is a relativist and conventionalist; because he is inclined to favor irrationalism over either empiricism or rationalism; and because he rejects the idea that logic and method are stronger than intuition, analogy, metaphor, social convention, or fashion. In short, he was perceived as the godfather of the new sociology of science. (See Merton 1977 for the difference between Kuhn and his acolytes.)

What I have called the *moderate global externalist* thesis goes much further: It asserts that science is subject to external social control rather than to the internal control exerted by the scientific community. This is a neo-Marxist view: Marx and Engels had occasionally been far far more radical (recall section 8.1). It asserts that science is a productive force, hence part of the economic infrastructure of society. More precisely, according to this school (a) every scientific problem is a problem of production or trade; (b) science is only a tool for solving economic problems; and (c) the dominant ideology, which expresses the material interests of the ruling class, orients the scientist's research.

The paragon of this school is Hessen's famous essay on "The social and economic roots of Newton's 'Principia'" (1931), which we first met in section 8.1. Hessen asked the question: "Where are we to seek the source of Newton's creative genius? What determined the content and the direction of his activities?" (p. 151). He saw that source not in Newton's brain, steeped in the culture of his time, but in modern capitalism, navigation, and warfare, all of which posed mechanical problems. These technical problems concerning machines, mining, transportation, gunnery, and the like, would constitute the "earthy core" of Newton's *Principia* (p. 171). Even Newton's later passion for alchemy would be a result of his interest in industry, particularly metallurgy (pp. 172 ff.). However, Hessen is not a complete economic determinist, for he acknowledges the influence of ideology (in particular religion)— though, like Marx, only in a distorting capacity (pp. 82 ff).

Though an externalist, Hessen was moderate by comparison with the externalists *à la mode* for, after all, he did acknowledge that scientific research is an *intellectual* activity accomplished by individuals. He claimed that science has economic (and secondarily also ideological) inputs and outputs, but not that its content is social or that it "emanates" from social groups. Hence he would not have accepted any of the radical externalist theses, to which we now turn.

Radical externalism is the thesis that all knowledge is social in content as well as in origin. In other words: Tell me in what kind of society you live and I'll tell you what you think. This view comes close to a generalization of the well-known Feuerbach-Durkheim thesis that all *religions* are symbolic transcriptions of actual social structures—a thesis confirmed by a number of studies (e.g., Frankfort, Wilson, and Jacobsen l946). If the same were true of *science* we should be able to read society off scientific theories, much as Durkheim (1972: 189) had claimed that "[i]t is through religion that we are able to trace the structure of a society."

But of course nobody has ever discovered anything about social structure by studying, say, Maxwell's equations or the way electromagnetic field intensities are measured. It so happens that natural science is not built in the image of society and with the aim of reinforcing the social order: Natural science is expected to explore and represent nature. (Reference: the entire scientific literature.)

A while ago we stated that radical externalism comes in two strengths: local and global. The *local radical externalist* thesis Rl is that every science and all of its objects are literally created by the corresponding scientific community. The classical statement of this thesis is Ludwik Fleck's *Genesis and Development of a Scientific Fact*, an obscure book originally published in 1935, which Kuhn rescued from oblivion (see the English translation of 1979, edited by J. Trenn and R. K. Merton, and prefaced by T. S. Kuhn). Fleck, a competent bacteriologist, seems to have been the first to address the sociogenesis of medical thought. The theme of his book is the history of medical and popular thinking about syphilis, which he called a "scientific fact" (see Bunge 1981 for a review).

Fleck denied that science studies independently existing things: He was a constructivist. In particular, he held that "syphilis, as such, does not exist." We shall examine this aspect of his work in the next chapter. What concerns us at this point is Fleck's thesis that every "scientific fact" is the product of a "thought collective" or community of people united by a "thought style." He rejects the idea that a person can think and quotes approvingly Ludwig Gumplowicz's dictum that "What actually thinks within a person is not the individual himself but his social community" (Fleck: 46-47). Hence every "scientific fact" (discovery or invention) would be a social fact. Moreover, the converse would hold as well. According to Fleck, there would be no such thing as the external world out there: "there" would be in here. Indeed, "objective reality can be resolved into historical sequences of ideas belonging to the collective" (p. 41). This collectivist form of subjectivism, adumbrated by the later Husserl (1931), has been adopted by a number of sociologists (e.g., Berger and Luckmann 1966) and sociologists of science (e.g., Latour and Woolgar 1979). But where is the evidence for its truth? We postpone the answer until chapter 9.

A more recent product of the same school of thought, and one often cited as a great achievement of the new sociology of science, is Paul Forman's long essay "Weimar culture, causality, and quantum theory, 1918-1927: Adaptation by German physicists and mathematicians to a hostile intellectual environment" (1971). The title says it all: The inventors of quantum mechanics did not overcome the antiintellectualist ideology rampant in postwar Germany but, on the contrary, they adapted to it. In particular, "the movement to dispense with causality in physics which sprang up so suddenly and blossomed so luxuriantly in Germany after 1918, was primarily an effort by German physicists to adapt the content of their science to the values of their intellectual environment" (p. 7).

Forman's much-cited paper has several fatal flaws. Firstly, it is true that the dominant philosophy in Germany at the time of the gestation of the quantum theory was antiscientific, vitalistic, and irrationalist. Suffice it to recall Husserl's later philosophy and that of his star pupil, Martin Heidegger. (Incidentally, both are heroes of the new sociology of science.) But this was definitely *not* the philosophy popular among physicists: the latter were overwhelmingly positivist and therefore proscience. Even Pasqual Jordan, a militant Nazi as well as an eminent contributor to the quantum theory, was a positivist. (There were of course a few exceptions: Einstein and Planck were realists, and Bohr did not convert to positivism till *ca.* 1935.) So much so, that the orthodox or Copenhagen interpretation of the mathematical formalism of quantum mechanics, which prevailed from about 1935 until recently, is universally considered to be positivistic. True, it can be shown that this interpretation is inconsistent with the mathematical formalism of the theory, and that it can be replaced advantageously with a strictly realist interpretation (Bunge 1967a, 1973, 1985a). Still, at the time of the birth of quantum mechanics positivism was a comparatively enlightened philosophy, not an obscurantist one like phenomenology, existentialism, or Hegelianism. After all, it was, and still is, attacked mainly because of its proscience stand, not because of its deep flaws.

Secondly, by focusing on Germany, Forman forgets that the quantum theory was fathered not only by the Germans Heisenberg, Born, and Jordan, but also by the Dane Bohr, the Austrian Schrödinger, the Frenchman de Broglie, the Englishman Dirac, and the citizen of the world Einstein. After all, the place that all the quantum physicists at the time flocked to in pilgrimage, and called "the Mecca of the quantum theory," was Copenhagen, not Göttingen, Berlin, Leipzig, or Munich. (Several of the pilgrims, among them my teacher, Guido Beck, went so far as to marry Danish girls.)

Thirdly, quantum mechanics was invented not as an "effort to adapt to the intellectual environment," as Forman claims, but to solve long-standing problems that had been intriguing physicists for nearly two decades before the birth of the Weimar Republic. How could anyone invent matrix mechanics, wave mechanics or quantum electrodynamics just to please a bunch of obscurantist philosophers? What is true is that positivism, not the increasingly popular *Lebensphilosophie* favored by Husserl and Heidegger among others, suggested the (operationalist) interpretation of quantum mechanics, as we saw a moment ago. It is also true that Bohr was initially influenced by his fellow countrymen Kierkegaard and Høffding in conceiving of his obscure complementarity "principle"—but this is not a principle because it does not entail anything, and it plays no role in any of the calculations anyway.

Fourthly and finally, what is so obscurantist about postulating that chance intertwines with causation instead of being nothing but our ignorance of the latter? Why should we distrust chance: just because of the popular confusions betwen causes and reasons, and between probability and indeterminacy? And what is so obscurantist about the first successful attempt to account for the very existence and the major properties of atoms, molecules, photons, crystals, nuclear and chemical reactions, and so much more?

Like Fleck before him, Forman is a radical externalist and relativist, though not a constructivist. But both have retained the inside-outside distinction: Fleck with reference to scientific communities, and Forman relative to the *intelligentsia* as a whole in a given country at a given time. Not so the radical global externalists. For them, just because scientific laboratories are public institutions open to laypersons (even to writers ignorant of natural science), they have no walls but mesh intimately with society at large, and what goes on in there is quite ordinary (e.g., Latour 1983).

Just because in a laboratory thought and action intertwine, "context and content merge" (Latour 1987). For the same reason there is no distinction between discourse and *praxis* (Woolgar 1986). And, just because scientific research involves some politicking and, when mistaken for technology, it can be seen as the most potent source of power in modern society, "science is politics pursued by other means" (Latour 1983: 168). Thus, ultimately the micro/macro distinction too dissolves in the big magma that the new sociologists of science call "science." More on this in the next section.

The radical externalist thesis, namely that all knowledge is social, to the extent that no distinction can be drawn between its content and its context, is false for the following reasons. Firstly, the fact that content is influenced by context does not prove that the two are undistinguishable, anymore than the fact that an organism cannot live if all its ties with its environment are severed does not refute the organism/environment distinction. (It is is a general truism that only different things can interact.) The cellular and organismic biologists, while not denying the existence and importance of the environment, focus on the organism not on its environment. In semantical terms, the *central referents* of biological statements are organisms, whereas the environment is their *peripheral referent.* Likewise, to the serious student of science the latter is the central referent of his statements, and society its peripheral referent.

The radical externalist draws no such semantic distinction: for him center and periphery become fused into one big mushy blob where scientific ideas drown. Such fusion is a convenient trick to avoid coming to grips with "technical" matters, such as the construction and test of scientific theories: it allows the student to shift from the nuts and bolts of research to its instruments, externalities and contingencies. It allows the outsider to deride the philosophers of science who ignore "science in the making." It even nourishes the illusion that an outsider is able "to explain to the insider how it all works" (Latour 1987: 15). Exemplary scientific modesty!

A second reason that the radical externalist thesis is false was anticipated in section 8.4, namely that any reasonable theory of reference will tell us that the referents of mathematical statements are mathematical objects, and those of physical statements physical objects—not social facts. What is the social content of a mathematical function, what that of a formula for a chemical reaction? The externalist gives no precise answers to these questions. The facts that the creation of such constructs requires learning from others and communicating with others, and that some of them are used in industry and trade via technology, does not turn those constructs into social facts, anymore than the social nature of the production and sale of a box of breakfast cereal turns the cereal itself and our eating and digesting it into social processes.

What holds for basic science holds, *mutatis mutandis,* for technology as well. In both fields intellectual creativity is a property of brains, not of social groups. The latter can only stimulate or inhibit intellectual creativity. For this reason the scattered and half-hearted efforts to pass off technology as a social contruction (e.g., Bijker, Hughes, and Pinch, eds. 1987) are unconvincing.

Technological designs, plans, proposals and recommendations must certainly fit the economic and political realities and possibilities. But it is well known that "demand-pulls" only result in improvements of existing artifacts: flaws call for fixes (see Petroski 1983). Radically new inventions, whether in technology or in science, are ultimately motivated by curiosity, the passion for solving problems, and the joy of tinkering. And, far from being children of the market, radical inventions beget new markets (see Bunge 1998).

To sum up, the externalists are right in holding that scientists do not live in a social vacuum. Consequently the detachment of scientific ideas and practices from scientists and their social circumstances is purely analytic—albeit indispensable if we are to understand and evaluate them *as* ideas or practices. But stating that social contingencies *constitute* scientific ideas and practices is like saying that, since we must breathe to stay alive, we are fully determined by the atmosphere or, in the case of radical externalism, that we are made up of air- —probably hot air at that. (For further criticisms of externalism see Shils 1982.)

8.6. The Micro-Macro, or Agency-Structure Question

Every science faces the problem of the relations between micro and macro levels, that is, between the part (e.g., the individual) and the whole (e.g., society). This problem is particularly central to social science (see, e.g., Knorr-Cetina and Cicourel, eds., 1981, and Alexander, Giesen, Münch, and Smelser, eds., 1987).

The two classical attempts to solve (or rather evade) this problem are individualism and holism, each of which has an ontological and a methodological aspect. (See,e.g., Krimerman, Ed., 1969, O'Neill, Ed., 1973, Bunge 1979a, 1985b.) Holists maintain that the individual is a pawn of society, and therefore favor the top-down (or macro-to-micro) approach: they are macroreductionists. By contrast, individualists hold that everything social is a resultant of individual actions, and therefore they favor the bottom-up (or micro-to-macro) approach: they are micro-reductionists. Whereas Marx and Durkheim were largely holists, Weber and Schutz were largely individualists.

Still, it may be argued that holism and individualism are ideal types. For instance, Marx did not deny but, on the contrary, extolled individual (though concerted) action, particularly when aimed at changing the existing social order. And even the most radical individualists admit that an individual is likely to behave differently in different social situations—but he will not even attempt to analyze the macrosociological concept of a situation in terms of individual actions.

In sum, a practicing social scientist can be neither a consistent holist nor a consistent individualist. Whether or not he knows it, he is a systemist, that is, someone who studies social systems, such as scientific communities, the way they are generated, maintained, reformed, revolutionized, or dismantled by individual actions, and the way these are in turn conditioned (in particular stimulated or inhibited) by the social structure. The systemist admits the micro-macro distinctions and relations and accepts some reductions (upward or downward) as legitimate, but he also stresses the limits of reduction set by the very facts that social systems are composed by individuals, and that individual actions are conditioned by the social environment (see Bunge 1979a, ch. 5; 1985b, ch. 4, 1991, 1996).

Where do the various schools in the sociology of science stand with regard to the individualism-holism-systemism trilemma? Obviously, in their general statements Marx and Engels were holists. (Recall section 8.2.) But when they judged individual scientists whom they respected, such as Ricardo or Darwin, they did not treat them as mere spokesmen for the bourgeoisie, and they did not assert that their ideas were formed out of components of the material infrastructure. As for the Western Marxist scientists, such as Bernal, they were even less holistic than Marx and Engels, for they did not deny individual creativity and they did not claim that every scientific statement has a social content. They stressed the influence of social context on content without obliterating the distinction between the two. (Recall section 8.3.)

As for Merton, although he used to be a functionalist-structuralist and therefore a holist of sorts, his outstanding contributions and those of his students to the sociology of science belong neither in the holist nor in the individualist camp. Indeed, they all deal with individual scientists or teams of scientists who share an approach, a stock of knowledge, and an ethos. Since those contributions concern individuals-in-society, as well as the social (in particular economic and ideological) inputs and outputs of the work of individual scientists and research teams, they establish micro-macro links instead of attempting to perform either macroreductions (characteristic of holism) or microcreductions (inherent in individualism). In short, the Merton school in the sociology of science may be characterized as systemist, although it is by no means sure that Merton himself would accept this characterization, if only because of his early opposition to Parsons's opaque talk of systems.

How about the new sociology of science? No matter how united it is on other issues, it is divided on the micro-macro one. Whereas a minority, particularly the ethnomethodologists, is individualist, the majority, particularly the advocates of the "new programme," is collectivist or at least cryptoholist. In contrast to other branches of sociology, there seem to be no systemists among the members of the new sociology of science—a bad sign.

Let us take a quick philosophical look at ethnomethodology. A major philosophical component of this school is phenomenology, which is fundamentally subjectivistic and therefore individualistic. Husserl, the father of phenomenology, demanded that the subject turn his gaze upon himself in order to trace the flow of his own consciousness, and place reality "in parentheses," that is, pretend that it does not exist. Moreover, according to this view the subject creates the social reality around himself, particularly his own everyday reality or *Lebenswelt*. True, the later Husserl (1931) assigned this task to the "intersubjective communities of individuals." Still, the basic idea is that reality is anything but self-existent: The real world is "inseparable from transcendental subjectivity" and moreover it is *"an infinite idea, related to infinities of harmoniously combined experiences"* (Husserl 1960: 62, emphasis in the original). This is why phenomenology "forms the *extremest contrast to sciences in the hitherto accepted sense,* positive, *'objective'* sciences" (op. cit., p. 30, emphasis in the original).

In short, Husserl himself emphasized that phenomenology involves a vigorous rejection of the epistemological realism peculiar to science and technology, and that characterizes the work of the founding fathers of sociology. Is it really necessary to explain why a discipline that does not even attempt to give an objective account of reality does not rate as scientific even if it calls itself such?

Berger and Luckman (1967), following Schutz (1932)—who followed Husserl, who followed Dilthey, who in turn followed Kant and Hegel— write therefore about the *construction of reality* rather than about the *study* of it. (See Outhwite 1986 for the pedigree of phenomenological sociology.) So do Harold Garfinkel (1967) and other members of the ethnomethodological school. Yet, although the putative philosophical godfathers of ethnomethodology are the later Husserl and even Heidegger, unlike these philosophers the ethnomethodologists are not apriorists but conduct empirical research on minutiae. There can be little doubt that Husserl and Heidegger, who felt contempt for science, would have strongly disapproved of such empirical research, much as the accompanying hermetic jargon would have delighted them.

Ethnomethodology opposes radical externalism because most of the latter's advocates take the reality of the external world for granted and all of them regard the individual as being fully a product of his social environment. This rejection of externalism would be sound if it did not ignore the large social systems and social issues altogether and if it were accompanied by an in-depth study of the peculiar activities of individual scientists and research teams. But, alas, this is not the case.

Indeed, what is peculiar to ethnomethodological studies is (a) the recording (audiotaping and videotaping) of minutiae of everyday life actions, that is, of what is familiar, not extraordinary; and (b) the arbitrary attribution to the subjects or actors of the assigning of a "general system of meaning" to every new situation they face—where, of course, the key term "meaning" (or its pragmatic equivalent, "interpretation") is left undefined, in the tradition of Dilthey and Weber. (See Bunge 1996 for the ambiguity of *Verstehen*, or interpretation, and is irrelevance to Weber's scientific work.)

The ethnomethodologist who studies science is only interested in the "worldly objects" (e.g., measuring instruments) that scientists use in their "embodied practice" (could there be a disembodied practice?) and in the signs they speak and write. He is not interested in the scientific ideas that confer a "meaning" upon that practice and upon the interactions among scientists as such. He cannot be interested because he does not understand them: He is an outsider and thus a methodological externalist though not an ontological one. Nor is he interested in the interactions between science and technology, or in the constraints and opportunities presented by industry and government. We shall come back to ethnomethodology in chapter 9.

However, most of the members of the new sociology of science are holists. To them, the group precedes and dominates the individual, and it forms and holds all beliefs. The view that belief systems can be imputed to social groups, in particular social classes, faces two difficulties. One of them has been pointed out by a charter member of the new sociology of science: Research has found that "[b]eliefs which seemed rationally indicated by the interests of one class were found to be disturbingly common among members of another; the dominant beliefs of a class were sometimes extraordinarily resistant to being made rationally intelligible in terms of any plausible version of its objective interests; sometimes so much diversity of belief and thought was found within a class as to preclude analysis of what were the dominant forms" (Barnes 1977: 45).

In short, social classes are not ideologically homogeneous. But we knew this long before the new sociology of science emerged. For instance, we knew that the French Revolution, though admittedly bourgeois, was in part the effect of writings and actions of a considerable number of people belonging to the lesser nobility or the small clergy. The Russian Revolution of 1917 was parallel: A number of members of the privileged classes, among them Lenin and Trotsky, participated in it. Moreover, it is questionable whether any revolution is possible unless the ruling class splits.

However, the main difficulty with the holistic views on imputation is that they presuppose that beliefs can be held by social groups, not just by members of social groups. A belief is a mental state or process, hence it can only be formed, entertained, held or abandoned by an individual mind or, better, brain. Hence the attribution of beliefs to social groups can only be elliptical. That is, the expression "Social group X believes Y" ought to be construed as short for "All (or most) of the (adult) members of X believe Y." (This is of course one of the valid tenets of methodological individualism.)

As we saw in section 8.5, Fleck (1935) was perhaps the first to assert that "thought communities," not individuals, construct science and even facts, such as syphilis infection. (The idea that only persons, natural or supernatural, create facts is of course much older. Remember not just George Berkeley but also Ernst Mach and Edouard Le Roy, the conventionalist philosopher who coined the famous phrase *Le savant crée le fait*.) According to Fleck, every *Denkkollektiv* has its own *Denkstil*, and the various thought styles are—as some would say today—mutually "incommensurable."

How did Fleck come by these ideas? Presumably he got their gist from Marxism, which was rather popular in Europe at that time. How did he confirm them? By focusing his study on the history of the Wasserman test for syphilis, and even so on a couple of cases of team work of a comparatively routine nature, and ignoring individual work altogether. He did not realize that, although discoveries and inventions can be anonymous and are subject to social influences, they are never collective. This is because they are mental proceses, and these can only occur in individual brains. Those who overlook the individual mind are unable to account for curiosity and creativity. Hence they cannot answer elementary questions of the form: "Even though many contemporaries of X's shared the same relevant data and the same interests and the same problems as X, why was it that only X hit on Y?"

Many practitioners of the new sociology of science share Fleck's holism. For example, Bloor (1976: 12) writes about "the knowledge of a society" construed as a "collective vision." And Latour (1983) claims that there is no difference between what he calls microactors and macroactors, or between the inside and the outside of a laboratory. He bases this thesis on his examination of Louis Pasteur's famous 1881 experiments on anthrax. The doors of Pasteur's laboratory opened to the public, and he himself went to a farm to perform a field experiment. Allegedly, these actions erased the border between scientists and the public. After all, "the belief in the 'scientificity' of science has disappeared" (p. 142).

But no sooner is the inside-outside distinction denied, than it is reasserted: By studying the anthrax bacillus in the laboratory, Louis Pasteur is able to "dominate" it, whereas outside, in the field, the given micro-organism is hard to study and control for being invisible and mixed up with many other micro-organisms (Latour: 147). Moreover, by overlooking the links between the science of microbiology, the technology of the design, control and use of vaccines, the vaccine industry, and the education campaign waged by hygienists and teachers, Latour concludes that "*Pasteur actively modifies the society of his time and he does so directly—not indirectly—by displacing some of its most important actors* [namely the veterinarians]" (p. 156, emphasis in the original). Then he makes the inductive leap: The laboratory "generates most new sources of power" (p. 160) and is thus a potent and direct agent of social change. Hence the humble title of the article: "Give me a laboratory and I will raise the world." A curious sociology this, which overlooks the links in the chain that relates the individual scientist to fellow scientists, industry, and government.

To conclude. Individualism does not work in the sociology of science because it minimizes or even ignores the very existence of the social systems (e.g., scientific networks and universities) to which every individual scientist belong. Consequenctly it fails to explain the peculiar behavior of individual researchers *qua* members of such systems—for example, the difficult position of the postdoctoral fellow sandwiched between the professor and his graduate students. Holism does not work either, because it minimizes or even denies individual initiative, creativity, dedication, and moral courage, turning all scientists into nine-to-fivers incapable of curiosity, initiative, doubt, passion, and the occasional rebellion.

Both holism and individualism are one-sided and therefore impoverishing. And the wavering between the two, detectable among both the ethnomethodologists and the advocates of the "strong programme," exhibits confusion. I submit that the right approach to all problems in every social science is the systemic one, for it suggests studying the ways people combine—cooperate in some respects and compete in others—to build, reform or destroy social systems, and the ways these function and interact in society at large (recall chapter 1).

Our next task will be to examine the most radical, outrageous, and obnoxious of all the theses of the new sociology of science, namely, social constructivism and relativism.

9

The Constructivist-Relativist
Sociology of Science

In the 1960s, a few philosophers of science claimed that there is
no absolute distinction between observational and theoretical concepts, for all of the former are "theory-laden," in the sense that all
observation is guided or misguided by some hypotheses, explicit or
tacit. There is a grain of truth in this thesis, namely that *scientific*
observations, unlike ordinary ones, are designed and conducted in
the light of hypotheses. Still, there are clear differences between
observational concepts, such as "blue," and theoretical ones, such
as "wavelength." The former belong in ordinary knowledge, whereas
the latter belong in scientific theories. True, the two are related, but
this does not entail that they belong in the same category. Furthermore, even advanced experimental science makes use of concepts
that are employed in a pretheoretical fashion, such as those of thing,
place, change, and color.

From the thesis about the theoretical load of empirical concepts it
seemed but a short step to proclaim "the abolition of the fact/theory
distinction" (Barnes 1983: 21). But it is not, for one may admit the
former and not the latter. That is, one may admit that the distinction
between observational and theoretical concepts is not absolute, or that
it is a matter of degree, and yet retain the fact/theory distinction, because the former is an epistemological distinction (it only concerns
knowledge) whereas the latter is an ontological one, as it concerns
reality as a whole. In other words, one may consistently assert that
the scientific observation of objective (theory-free) facts involves
(some) theoretical concepts, without mistaking constructs for things
or conversely. This elementary confusion is at the source of the
constructivist-relativist school in the new sociology and philosophy
of science.

9.1. Constructivism

When not in a philosophical mood, a physicist is likely to admit that the *concept* of an electron contained in (and elucidated by) any of the electron theories is theoretical, while at the same time admitting that there are electrons out there, whether or not we theorize about them. Likewise, a sociologist will admit that the *concepts* of social stratification are theoretical, while at the same time holding that modern societies are objectively stratified, and that every theory of social stratification attempts to represent such an objective feature. In short, whereas all except the radical empiricists agree that constructs (concepts, hypotheses and theories) *are* constructed, only subjectivists claim that all facts are constructed as well. Thus, while *epistemological* and *psychological* constructivism are in order up to a point, *ontological* constructivism is not, for it flies in the face of evidence.

Indeed, if facts and theories were the same, no fact could be used to test a theory, and no theory could be used to guide the search for new facts. Since theory-testing and theory-steered exploration are facts (not theories) of daily scientific life, it follows that the denial of the distinction between them is contrary to fact (though not contrary to subjectivistic theory). Moreover, if fact and theory were identical, facts would have theoretical properties (e.g., consistency and explanatory power) and theories would have physical, chemical, biological, or social properties (e.g., viscosity and chemical reactivity). This not being the case, the postulated fact-theory identity is a mere sophism.

Yet, this sophism and the epistemological relativism that comes with it are characteristic of the "strong programme" we first met in the previous chapter, section 8.4. Its advocates claim that reality is a human construct, and that all constructs have a social content. In particular, the phrase *the social construction of scientific facts* has become commonplace in the new sociology of science, particularly since it was adopted as the subtitle of the first edition of Latour and Woolgar's oft-quoted *Laboratory Life* (1979).

Where the constructivists write about "the social construction of scientific facts," most scientists, realist philosophers and sociologists of science would refer to the process of interaction among scientists (either face-to-face or via the literature). This interaction starts with an observation, a conjecture or a critical remark, and ends up in one or more statements. These are generally accepted (as sufficiently true), at least for the time being, for having passed all of the required tests.

Thus, whereas Latour and Woolgar (1986: 152) claim that "TRF [Thy-rotropin Releasing Factor] is a thoroughly social construction," a real-ist would say that the molecular composition and biological function of TRF were *discovered* by scientists working over a decade in two rival (yet often cooperating) research teams.

There is more than careless use of key terms such as "fact" and "con-struction" in the writings of the constructivists. There is also deliberate neglect of the "technical" aspect of the research process, that is, the problems, hypotheses, arguments, experimental designs, and measure-ments that accompany the exchanges of views, plans and findings among the members of research team(s), and without which such exchanges are wholly unintelligible. There is even explicit refusal to employ such methodological terms as "hypothesis," "proof," and the like, presum-ably for being the stigmata of the internalists (see, e.g., Latour and Woolgar 1986: 153).

Such neglect of the meanings and truth values of the "inscriptions" produced in the laboratory is not accidental. It is a product of a deliber-ate choice: that of studying the tribe of scientists as if it were an ordi-nary social system such as a tribe of hunters and gatherers, or a fishing village. In the case of an ordinary social system even a traveler or an investigative journalist can learn something from untutored observa-tion for being familiar with the basic cross-cultural human activities: he undertakes an in-depth study only if he wishes to understand the political organization, the mythology, or the ceremonies of the group.

But a scientific research team is very different from a primitive tribe. Not that the former's operations are mysterious, but they have an ex-tremely specialized and sophisticated function: that of producing *sci-entific* knowledge through processes that, unlike gathering, hunting, or fishing, are not in full view. The layman visiting a laboratory can only observe behavioral manifestations of the mental processes locked in the brains of the researchers and their assistants. To the layman the problems that trigger the research activity are even less intelligible than its results. Hence he is bound to take only a superficial look, much as the behaviorist psychologist limits his task to describing overt behav-ior. We shall insist on this point in section 9.3.

Despite this obvious limitation, Latour and Woolgar (1986: 153) claim that "observation of actual laboratory practice" yields a material that "is particularly suited to an analysis of the intimate details of scientific activity." They do not explain how an outsider, who does not even un-derstand the language of the "tribe" whose daily life he "shares" (for being in the same rooms) can have access to such intimate details, which happen to take place inside the skulls of the subjects of study. Nor do they explain how mere conversational exchanges and "negotiations" can "create or destroy facts."

Not only do these anthropologists of science fail to apologize for butting into a research group engaged in a project that they cannot understand, but they believe such ignorance to be a merit: "We take the apparent superiority of the members of our [*sic*] laboratory in technical matters to be insignificant, in the sense that we do *not* regard prior cognition...as a necessary prerequisite for understanding scientists' work. This is similar to an anthropologist's refusal to bow before the knowledge of a primitive sorcerer" (Latour and Woolgar 1986: 29).

No wonder that those ill-equipped observers conclude that scientists do not engage in any peculiar thought processes, that scientific activity is "just one social arena," and a laboratory just "a system of literary inscriptions." How would they know if they do not understand what scientists are up to? And, given their deliberate confusion between facts and propositions, how would they know when "a statement splits into an entity and a statement about an entity"—or when the converse process, during which reality is "deconstructed"—in ordinary parlance, a hypothesis is refuted? On the strength of such elementary confusions and borrowings from antiscientific philosophies, they conclude that "'out-there-ness' [i.e.,the external world] is the *consequence* of scientific work rather than its *cause* " (Latour and Woolgar 1986: 182).

One might think that Latour and Woolgar are not subjectivists but merely philosophical unsophisticates who misuse the word "fact" to designate a statement held to be true without qualification, such as "The Earth is a planet." Indeed, they do state that "A fact is nothing but a statement with no modality [i.e., no indication that it is entertained as a hypothesis, or that it has been confirmed] and no trace of authorship" (Latour and Woolgar 1986: 82). That is, one might think that, for want of philosophical sophistication, this is a confusion on a par with the vulgar confusions of "ecology" with "environment," "meteorology" with "weather," "sociological" with "social," "ontology" with "reference class," and "methodology" with "method." But, since on pages 174 ff. they launch an attack on realism, one is forced to take their subjectivism seriously.

Latour and Woolgar leave no doubt as to their subjectivism when they state that "reality is the consequence rather than the cause of this construction," so that "a scientist's activity is directed, not toward 'reality', but toward these operations on statements" (*op. cit.* p. 237). This would hold not only for the social world but also for nature: "Nature is a usable concept only as a by-product of agonistic activity" [whatever this may be]" (*loc. cit.*).

Other members of the school concur. In particular, H. M. Collins (1981: 3) writes that "the natural world has a small or non-existent role in the construction of scientific knowledge." And, just because laboratories are chock-full of artefacts, living as well as inanimate, Knorr-Cetina (1983: 119) claims that "nowhere in the laboratory do we find the 'nature' or 'reality' which is so crucial to the descriptivist interpretation of inquiry."

In short, according to constructivism reality is not independent of the inquiring subject but a product of it: Scientific research is "the process of secreting an unending stream of entities and relations that make up 'the world'" (Knorr-Cetina 1983: 135). And a major philosophical mentor of the new sociology of science wrote: "*Scientific entities* (and, for that matter, all entities) *are projections and are thus tied to the theory, the ideology, the culture that projects them*" (Feyerabend 1990: 147, emphasis in the original). Regrettably he did not explain how there can be a projection without a screen—in this case the autonomous external world.

The new sociology of science has replaced the concept of discovery with that of social construction. Accordingly, Christopher Columbus and Captain Cook, Michael Faraday and Ramón y Cajal, and all the others who thought they had made discoveries, were under a delusion: They only participated in some social constructions. As Garfinkel and his students say, even the celestial bodies are "cultural objects" (Garfinkel, Lynch, and Livingston 1981). And indeed every object is "an icon of laboratory temporality" [whatever this may mean] (Lynch, Livingston, and Garfinkel 1983). Moreover, what holds for the furniture of the world is alleged to hold for the entire world . Arthur Schopenhauer's old formula "The world is my representation" reads now "The world is our construction."

Constructivism is not an invention of the new sociology of science: it inheres in idealism. Some of the practitioners of the school realize this. For example, H. M. Collins (1981) admits that the new sociology of science has been influenced by such idealist philosophies as phenomenology, structuralism, poststructuralism, deconstructionism, and the glossocentrism of the second Wittgenstein and the French school of general semiotics. And Woolgar (1986: 312) explains that the discourse analysis he, Latour, Knorr-Cetina, and others practice is indebted to poststructuralism (in particular Foucault), which "is consistent with the position of the idealist wing of ethnomethodology that there is no reality independent of the words (texts, signs, documents, and so on) used to apprehend it. In other words, reality is constituted in and through discourse." The world is a huge book, and even *"praxis* cannot exist outside discourse" (*loc. cit.*)

According to the textualist (or hermeneutic) version of idealism, *to be is to be an inscriber or an inscription*. Remember Heidegger (1953: 11): *"Im Wort, in der Sprache werden und sind erst die Dinge"* ["Only in the word, in language, become and are things"]. Hence, if one wishes to understand the world all one has to do is to read texts, or to treat human action as a discourse, and subject them to hermeneutic or semiotic analysis. This would hold in particular for the world of science, which would be just a heap of inscriptions (Latour and Woolgar 1979). How very convenient!

Since doing science or metascience—or anything else for that matter—is only a matter of wordmanship or language games, any literate person can play the game. The consequence for the fact/fiction and the truth/falsity distinctions is obvious: "the distinctions between fact and fiction are thereby softened because both are seen as the products of, and sources for, communicative action" (Brown 1990: 188). Why should then anyone worry about the very concept of truth (other than consensus), let alone with empirical tests for truth?

The textualist (or hermeneutical) approach is so convenient that it allows one to tackle even the most abstruse scientific ideas with the sole tools of semiotic analysis. Thus Latour (1988) has performed such an analysis of the special theory of relativity (SR)—though not as expounded in any scientific publications, but in Einstein's earliest popularization book, and in its English version of 1920 at that—*Relativity: The Special and the General Theory* . Since Einstein's popular exposition of SR revolves around a bunch of travelers who board trains, measure times, and send signals, Latour concludes that SR is not about the electrodynamics of moving bodies (the title of Einstein's 1905 founding paper), or even about space and time. He reveals to us that what counts in SR is certain human activities (p. 11). He goes so far as to suggest that Einstein chose the wrong title: "His book could well be titled: 'New Instructions for Bringing Back Long-Distance Scientific Travellers'" (p. 23). Moreover, Einstein's work would be similar to the Smithsonian Institution's initial plan for setting up a nationwide network of weather observers in order "to build up meteorological phenomena [*sic*]." Apparently, the profound changes introduced by SR in our concepts of space and time, as well as in the relation between mechanics and electrodynamics, are invisible from the constructivist viewpoint.

Not content with distorting the content of SR, Latour goes on to vindicate the old philosophical misinterpretation of SR (and of quantum mechanics) as a confirmation of *epistemological* relativism, a form of subjectivism according to which all scientific facts are created by "independent and active observers." Hence the title of his paper: "A relativistic account of Einstein's relativity." It did not occur to him that, in order to evaluate any claims concerning the role of the observer in a scientific theory, it is necessary (a) to axiomatize the theory, so as to separate the scientific grain from the philosophical chaff, and (b) to analyze the theory with the help of some theory of reference, so as to ferret out its genuine referents (see, e.g., Bunge 1974).

If this task is performed it can be *proved,* not just *claimed*, that SR and quantum mechanics are about independently existing physical things, *not* "about the ways of describing any possible experience" (Latour, op. cit., p. 25). In particular, by proving that the referents of relativistic mechanics are bodies interacting via an electromagnetic field (as suggested by the title of Einstein's founding paper), one disproves the extraordinary claim that the speed of light and the Lorentz transformations are "part of the normal business of building a society" (Latour, loc. cit.). Societies are built by people, mostly without blueprints, they have been in existence long before the birth of science, and—for better of for worse—their emergence and breakdown is utterly foreign to the theories of relativity.

Paradoxically, despite their antirealism the proponents of the new sociology of science claim that only their own "empirical studies" supply an adequate (realistic, true) account of scientific research. Woolgar (1986) has noticed this paradox, but it does not seem to bother him. After all, only old-fashioned students of science care about logic.

9.2. Relativism

If there is no independent reality, if the entire world is a social construction, and if facts are statements of a certain kind, there can be no objective truth. In other words, if there is nothing "out there" which was not previously "in here," the very expression "correspondence of ideas with facts" makes no sense. And if there is no objective truth, then scientific research is not a quest for truth. Or, to put it in a somewhat milder way, "what counts as truth can vary from place to place and from time to time" (Collins 1983: 88). This is the kernel of epistemological relativism. It is part and parcel cultural relativism, which is in turn a philosophical component of cultural nationalism (see Jarvie 1984; Trigger 1998).

If epistemological relativism were true there should be, at least potentially, as many "alternative" mathematics as social (or ethnic or other) groups: masculine and feminine mathematics, white and black, Western and Eastern, and so on. As Bloor (1976) and Restivo (1983) remind us, this was indeed a thesis of the once-popular obscurantist and pompous philosopher of history Oswald Spengler's, and one that met with Ludwig Wittgenstein's approval. But it was also a favorite Nazi thesis: for example, whereas Aryan mathematics is concrete and intuitive, hence congenial with the blood-and-soil myth, Jewish mathematics is abstract and counterintuitive.

The above thesis about "alternative" mathematics can be proved to be false by showing that mathematical statements do not refer to anything real (in particular social) and are not justified (in particular proved) by recourse to empirical operations, in particular social actions (see, e.g., Bunge 1985a, chap. 1). What is true is that mathematics cannot flourish in a backward society, whose members have neither the education nor the motivation or the means to devote themselves to the purest of all pure sciences.

It is also true, though perhaps of no interest to our relativist sociologist, that modern mathematics contains a large number of "alternative" mathematical theories *alongside* the "canonical" ones. Examples: intuitionist logic, nonstandard set theories, modulo arithmetics, non-Euclidean geometries, and nonstandard analysis. Hence mathematical truth *is* relative , as has been known for more than a century. (For example, the equality "12+1 = 1" is true in clock arithmetic though false in number theory. Another old example: Within a disc there are infinitely many parallels to any given straight line. A third: the internal angles of a spherical triangle do not add up to two right angles.)

However, every mathematical truth is relative to some *theory*, not to society. And any departures from the canonical, standard, or classical mathematical theories are prompted by purely intellectual reasons, mainly the wish to generalize, that is, to overcome restrictions of earlier theories. (Example: If the inverse operation is dropped, a group collapses into a semigroup, and the latter is generalized to a groupoid if the associativity condition is removed.) Any such changes are brought about by pure intellectual curiosity: They are not responses to social pressures, industrial needs, or ideological demands. They are answers to conceptual problems, not social issues. If mathematical problems were social problems, the latter would mostly be soluble and, moreover, they would get solved along with the advancement of mathematics—which, alas, is impossible.

Social structure has nothing to do with "deviant" mathematical theories. Not only do all of them fail to refer to anything social, but they are cultivated along with their standard counterparts in the same mathematical community regardless of economic or political factors—except of course that poor societies cannot afford to support much mathematical research, and that dictators may dislike certain branches of mathematics. Incidentally, two provincial governors under the 1976–1983 Argentine military dictatorship unwittingly adhered to the "strong programme" by banning modern mathematics (including the vector calculus), which it regarded as subversive.

Epistemological relativism is of course nothing new: it was stated long ago in a concise formula: *Veritas filia temporis.* It is a naive reaction to the variety of cultures and to the multiplicity of conflicting views about the same facts. This multiplicity of coexisting or successive representations of the world inspires skepticism, particularly in the light of the externalist view that social circumstances and interests determine or even constitute all scientific statements.

Philosophers have disposed of these arguments long ago. The multiplicity of simultaneous or successive mutually incompatible theories about one and the same domain of facts only goes to prove that scientific research does not guarantee *instant, complete, and definitive truth.* But, as observational and experimental tests show, we often do hit on *partially true* hypotheses. And, as the history of science shows, if a hypothesis is interesting and sufficiently true, it will stimulate further research that may result in truer or deeper hypotheses. What holds for hypotheses and theories holds also, *mutatis mutandis*, for experimental designs. There *is* scientific progress after all because there *is* such thing as objective (though usually only partial) truth.

As for the suspicion that, if a scientific project has been motivated or distorted by material or ideological interests, it cannot yield objectively true results, it is an instance of what philosophers have called the *genetic fallacy* . In fact, it consists in judging a piece of knowledge by its birth (or baptism) certificate. (The *argumentum ad hominem* is a special case of the genetic fallacy.) A hypothesis, datum, or method may be correct (true in the case of a proposition) regardless of the motivation of the research that produced it. Or it may be false even if produced with the purest of intentions. In short, the correctness of an idea is independent of its origin and utilization, and it must be established by strictly objective means. The same holds for the content of an idea. For instance, Durkheim held that all logical ideas, in particular that of class inclusion, have a social (in particular religious) *origin*, but he did not claim that they also have a social (in particular religious) *content*.

Another source of relativism, and one already used by Kuhn (1962), is the perception of ambiguous figures studied by the Gestalt psychologists. If I now see a human face, and now a vase, what is there really to be seen and how can I claim that either perception is the correct one? The constructivist replies: "The nicest feature of this example is that we can see how foolish it is to ask which of these it *really* is" (Collins 1983: 90). But of course an ambiguous figure is, *by definition*, one that can be interpreted in two different ways, neither of which is truer that the other. Psychologists know that the ambiguity resides neither in the real face nor in the real vase, but in the brain, which switches automatically, every thirty seconds or so, from one perception to the other.

(Incidentally, Kuhn the historian of science was not a constructivist/relativist, as his work on the origins of quantum physics attests. But his philosophical comments are so ambiguous that they can be construed as lending support to the new sociology of science. As Merton [1977: 108] wrote, they have been used by "varieties of acolytes [in particular subjectivists and would-be Marxists] who have transmuted those ideas to accord with their own ideological dispositions.")

Collins suggests that such ambiguity affects *all* scientific problems, data, hypotheses, and methods. But neither he nor anyone else has advanced any *evidence* showing that this is indeed the case. Moreover, any scientist or philosopher of science knows that ambiguity and vagueness will happen but must be corrected. We all know that fortune tellers thrive on ambiguity, but it has never occurred to serious students of science that scientists must put up with it.

Although the practitioners of the new sociology of science do not have much use for the concept of truth, they cannot ignore the fact that everyone makes mistakes. Only, they do not *define* the concept of a mistake or error in terms of departure from truth, as it is done in the theory of errors of observation and in epistemology: They simply leave it undefined.

Moreover, some proponents of the new sociology of science would seem to value error more than truth. For example, Latour (1983: 164–165) assures us that scientists "can make as many mistakes as they wish or simply more mistakes than any others "outside" who cannot master the changes of scale. Each mistake is in turn archived, saved, recorded and made easily readable again.... When you sum up a series of mistakes, you are stronger than anyone who has been allowed fewer mistakes than you." Thus the laboratory "is a technological device to gain strength by multiplying mistakes" (p. 165). If the reader suspects that Latour is mistaking science for politics, she is right. In fact, Latour and Woolgar (1979: 237) wrote that "there is little to be gained by maintaining the distinction between the "politics" of science and its 'truth.'" In short: As Hegel and the legal positivists said, might makes right.

What is alleged to hold for truth would also hold for controversy. According to the relativist, all scientific controversies are conceptually unending, because there is no objective truth. Hence *"even in the purest of sciences*, if debate is to end, it must be brought to a close by some means not usually thought of as strictly *scientific* " (Collins 1983: 99, emphases in the original). In other words, there are no crucial observations or experiments, no new predictions, no logical or mathematical proofs, no decisive counterexamples, no tests of (internal or external) consistency, and so on. There is only either the arbitrary choice of the "core set" or clique in power, or a negotiation and final compromise between the rival factions. "Politicking" would be the name of the scientific game.

Even the choice of citations would be a political matter: authors would not quote other people's works to pay intellectual debts but only to strengthen their own position or weaken that of their rivals (Latour 1987: 37–38). But this is one more dogmatic statement; no social constructivist has ever bothered to put it to the test. Such investigation would involve finding the statistical correlations between citation frequency and such variables as social ties and cited author eminence and institutional eminence. Now, the only existing study of this type (Baldi 1998), referring to an area of astrophysics, refutes the social-constructivist thesis that the perceived worth of one's contributions depends on one's position in the relevant social network rather than the other way around. Instead, the study corroborates the commonsensical view that investigators cite a work to acknowledge intellectual debt as well as to support their own claims.

Philosophers have taken care of epistemological relativism or skepticism with the help of purely logical arguments, or by listing some of the lasting findings of science—e.g., the heliocentric theory of the planetary system, the circulation of the blood, the existence of electromagnetic fields, atoms, and genes, and the evolution of biospecies. These and most of the truths of logic and mathematics are surely some of the many full (not just partial) and eternal truths established since the beginning of the modern era—*pace* such distinguished skeptics as Hume, Engels, and Popper.

The sociologist Tom Bottomore (1956: 56) used the very same argument of the externalists to refute relativism, by stating that "if all propositions are existentially determined [as Mannheim used to say] and no proposition is absolutely true, then this proposition itself, if true, is not absolutely true, but is existentially determined." Two decades later Bloor (1976: 14), in formulating the "strong programme," thought that he disposed of this argument by claiming that it presupposes that social causation implies error (e.g., ideological bias). But it does not, for Bottomore admitted, for the sake of the argument, that the externalist thesis is true. He only pointed out that, even if actually true, the thesis cannot be absolutely true but only true in (or relative to) a given social group or society. If so, why should he or I, members of a different tribe, adhere to that thesis? After all, what Bottomore was doing *avant la lettre* was to apply to the externalist sociology of science the fourth demand of the "strong programme," namely the condition that "In principle its patterns of explanation would have to be applicable to sociology itself" (recall chap. 8, section 8.4).

However, epistemological relativism is not totally false but does have a grain of truth. Indeed, scientific research proceeds by assuming that all *propositions de fait* are *in principle* fallible and corrigible. The scientific researcher adopts tacitly what may be called *methodological* (or *moderate*) *skepticism* in contrast to *systematic* (or *radical*)*skepticism*. He doubts only where there is some (logical or empirical) *reason* to doubt, and he never doubts *everything at once,* but weighs what is in doubt in the light of the bulk of his background knowledge. And he does not doubt some of the very philosophical principles that the new sociology of science rejects, among them those of the independent existence of the external world, and its objective intelligibility. In short: Most of the truths about the world are likely to be only *partial*; but they are *truths* nonetheless, not just fables (see Bunge 1991b).

Furthermore, scientific truths, whether total or partial, are supposed to be *universal* rather than the property of this or that group. There are no such things as proletarian science or Aryan science, black mathematics, or feminine philosophy: these are just political or academic rackets. To be sure, learning prospers more in some groups or societies than in others. But so does superstition.

Many values and norms are culture-bound: scientific findings are not. That is, whereas axiological and ethical relativism is partly justifiable, epistemological relativism is not. If a view is only acceptable to the members of some social group, then it is ideological, not scientific. Even when an idea originates within a special group, to count as scientific it must be *universalizable* . Unless this criterion of scientificity is accepted, it becomes impossible to distinguish science from ideology, pseudoscience, or antiscience—which is of course one of the claims of the new sociology of science, as we shall see in sections 9.5 and 9.6. (See Archer 1987; Siegel 1987; Livingston 1988; Boudon 1990; Wolpert 1992; and Trigger 1998 for further criticisms of epistemological relativism.)

9.3. Cryptobehaviorism and Overt Pragmatism

Positivism-bashing has become fashionable, and the proponents of the new sociology of science take pleasure in this sport. Now, there are two kinds of antipositivist: enlightened and obscurantist. Enlightened antipositivism attacks the narrowness of positivism and seeks to overcome its limitations, in particular its attachment to empiricism, its phenomenalist metaphysics, and its slighting of theory. By contrast the obscurantist antipositivism criticizes what was best in positivism: its (unrequited) love of science and mathematics, its conceptual clarity and use of formal methods, its demand for tests, and its criticism of obscurantism.

Regrettably, most of the students of society and philosophers of social science who denounce positivism have adopted an obscurantist stand. Many of them reject positivism for believing that it is the same as natural science. Lukács (1923), one of Mannheim's heroes, was among the first to equate positivism with natural science, and to write vehement denunciations of both. Ironically, most of the members of the new sociology of science are positivists in as much as they spend much of their time collecting data which they cannot assimilate for want of theory. This holds in particular for the ethnomethodologists.

The ethnomethodologist audiotapes and videotapes "the detailed and observable practices which make the incarnate production of ordinary social facts, for example, order of service in a queue, sequential order in a conversation, and the order of skillfully embodied improvised conduct" (Lynch, Livingston, and Garfinkel 1983: 206). His data are the audible or visible traces left by people who presumably behave purposefully and intelligently. This is the only clue he can go by for, lacking the specialized knowledge of the scientist, he cannot understand what makes the latter tick: what are his problems and ambitions, his principles, values, and methods, his conjectures, plans, and decisions—in sum, everything that goes on inside his skull.

In what does the ethnomethodologist's procedures differ from those of the radical empiricist, in particular the behaviorist psychologist? Only in that the former is inordinately fond of obscure jargon and of notoriously opaque philosophers such as Husserl and Heidegger, neither of whom held science proper in esteem. (See, e.g., Husserl [1960], Sects. 3 to 5, on the opposition between "genuine science," i.e., phenomenology, and science; and Heidegger [1953], chap. 1, on the subordinate position of science *vis-à-vis* philosophy and poetry.] Aside from this, the ethnomethodologist's practice does not differ from that of the empiricist and, in particular, the behaviorist—as even Atkinson (1988), a sympathizer of the school, has admitted.

What are the findings of the ethnomethodological studies of science? Essentially two. (See Lynch, Livingston, and Garfinkel 1983 for a summary.) One is that "something more" is involved in research, than what can be formulated in even the most detailed of instruction manuals. This "something more" is of course the set of tacit assumptions and of bits and pieces of know-how or procedural knowledge, both of them well known to psychologists, philosophers, and engineers.

The other "finding" is that, no matter how elementary a scientific experiment may be, it cannot be performed without a minimum of theory—this being why a partially paralyzed chemistry student could do his lab exercises with the help of an able-bodied ethnomethodology student, largely ignorant of chemistry, who acted as the former's hand. But did we not know this all along, at least those of us who have had a scientific training? Neither result is new, and in both cases the philosopher of science might have supplied what escaped the ethnomethodologist, namely an answer to the question: Precisely which are the explicit and tacit assumptions involved in a given experiment?

Epistemological constructivism and relativism imply conventionalism and instrumentalism. The particular brand of conventionalism favored by the new sociology of science may be called *social conventionalism*, for it comes combined with radical externalism. If all cultures are equivalent, if neither is superior to the other, and if there are not even different kinds of knowledge (e.g., scientific and ideological), then the adoption of any one idea is a social convention and a matter of usefulness to a given community.

Social conventionalism holds, in particular, that (a) "proper usage [of, e.g., classificatory terms] is agreed usage"; and (b) "*different* [conceptual] *nets stand equivalently as far as the possibility of 'rational justification' is concerned. All systems of verbal culture are equally rationally-held* " (Barnes 1983: 33, emphasis in the original). Barnes reaches these conclusions from an examination of the ways different *preliterate* peoples classify animals, and from his readings of Wittgenstein's *Philosophical Investigations* (1953), which of course was only concerned with *ordinary* language.

Barnes generalizes to *all* knowledge, even mathematical, scientific and technological knowledge, what he believes to have found in the literature on primitive ordinary knowledge. (Durkheim and Mauss [1903], who were among the first to note that primitive classifications mirror the tribe's social structure, particularly in the case of totemism, did not commit Barnes's error.)

Barnes does not bother to look into the way *contemporary* systematists or chemists classify, or the way physicists build theories and check them. Presumably, he would not be budged by the objection that statements such as "Whales are fish" and "There are witches" are false—period. This is not surprising, for all relativist anthropologists are epistemological relativists, conventionalists, and subjectivist. (See, e.g., Shweder 1986: 172: Since belief in witches influences behavior, witches "are, in some important sense, real and objective.") Magic thinking seems to have taken hold of those who are supposed to study it scientifically. Must we conclude that they have been bewitched?

Social conventionalism, an offspring of the marriage of externalism and constructivism, implies instrumentalism or pragmatism. This was realized by the later Durkheim (1955), who in a posthumously published work retreated from the realism of his fundamental work *Les règles de la méthode sociologique* (1895). In that work we find this revealing passage: "If the objective of thought were simply to "reproduce" reality, it would be the slave of things; it would be chained to reality. It would have no role except to "copy" in a servile fashion the reality it has before it. If thought is to be freed, it must become the creator of its own object; and the only way to attain this goal is to accord it a reality that it has to make or construct itself. *Therefore, thought has as its aim not the reproduction of a given reality, but the construction of a future reality.* It follows that the value of ideas can no longer be assessed by reference to objects but must be determined by the degree of their utility, their more or less 'advantageous' character" (Durkheim 1972: 251, emphasis in the original).

Not surprisingly, instrumentalism or pragmatism is central to the new sociology of science. Thus Barnes (1977: 2) states that knowledge is "developed actively and modified in response to practical contingencies." Theoretical problems and developments are not within the purview of pragmatism. Latour and Woolgar (1979: 171) write: "A useful maxim is Heidegger's observation that "*Gedanke ist Handwerk*": Thinking is craftwork. At other places they pooh-pooh ideas in general and "stories about minds having ideas." There would be nothing special about laboratory research, and no essential difference between their activity and that of their informants: "The only difference is that they have a laboratory" (p. 257). And Knorr-Cetina (1981: 7) claims that "If there is a principle which seems to govern laboratory action, it is the scientists' concern with making things 'work,' which points to a principle of success rather than of truth." Good constructivist that she is, she combines pragmatism with subjectivism and, borrowing a phrase from Nelson Goodman (1978), claims that scientific research is a "way of world-making" (Knorr-Cetina 1983).

Like Monsieur Jourdain, who did not know that he had been talking prose all his life, the proponents of the new sociology of science have reinvented William James's pragmatist concept of truth as efficiency (or cash value). Thus Bloor (1976: 35) declares that the realist notion of (factual) truth as the matching of ideas to reality can be dispensed with: "It is difficult to see that much would be lost by its absence." What matters in a theory is that it should "work." (But what exactly it is for a theory to "work" he does not explain.)

The truth is that every conceptual or empirical (observational or experimental) test of a hypothesis is a test for its *truth*, regardless of its credibility or of its potential usefulness. If the hypothesis passes the tests we declare it (sufficiently) true (*pro tempore*). Once this happens the hypothesis is available for further argument, tests, or applications. In short, truth precedes "social convention," not the other way round.

The practitioners of the new sociology and philosophy of science have also unwittingly reinvented Bridgman's operationalist concept of meaning as a set of laboratory operations. Thus Latour (1988: 26): "we refuse meaning to any description that does not portray the *work* of setting up laboratories, inscription devices, networks; we always relate the word 'reality' to the specific trials inside specific laboratories and specific networks that measure up the resistance of some actants." Clearly, on this view all of mathematics, theoretical science (in particular theoretical physics, chemistry, biology, psychology and sociology) is meaningless. But by the same token so is the new sociology of science, since it does not engage in laboratory work but only in occasional visits to laboratories.

Instrumentalism or pragmatism does not "work" for science because scientific theories and experiments aim at constructing maximally consistent, true, and deep accounts of the real world. If they did not, there would be no point in checking or perfecting such accounts. Only technological theories, designs, and plans are tested for efficiency, that is, effectiveness together with low cost, low risk, and significant benefit. Yet, although technology is pragmatic, in the sense that it pursues practical rather than cognitive success, pragmatism fails to deliver a faithful picture of modern technology, for the latter feeds on disinterested inquiry. Modern technology, unlike prescientific "craftwork," can only "work" if there is some truth to its underlying science. To be sure, occasionally an artifact or a process is designed on scant scientific knowledge. (However, the steam engine and the airplane are the only important modern examples of this kind of process.) If efficient and important, the invention is bound to elicit scientific research that will ultimately vindicate its design.

Pragmatism is inconsistent with rationalism but it goes well with intuitionism and even stronger forms of irrationalism, such as existentialism. Not surprisingly, the new sociology of science contains some intuitionist theses. For example, it holds that scientists do not proceed rationally, critically, and objectively, but guided by the prevalent cultural paradigms and fashion—class bias included—as well as by analogies and metaphors. (At this point, suitable quotations from Thomas S. Kuhn [1962], Mary Hesse [1980], or Richard Rorty [1979] will be produced.)

Now, it is true that there is no fruitful scientific endeavor without intuitions of various kinds. Information and rigor are not enough to "discover" new problems, hypotheses, experimental designs, or methods. However, intuition is powerless without logic, just as reason is (outside mathematics) powerless without observation or experiment. The creative scientist manages to combine all three (see Bunge 1962). Hence intuitionism is as inadequate a philosophy of science as are radical rationalism and radical empiricism. And, of all the varieties of intuitionism, phenomenology is the worse, for postulating the existence of the *Wesensschau*, or the ability to "see" essences in a direct and immediate fashion, which exempts the phenomenologist from the hard tasks of building theories, in particular mathematical models, and putting them to tests of any kinds.

In short, the new sociology of science suffers from behaviorism and pragmatism. As we know from the history of psychology, the former is a guarantee of psychological shallowness because it overlooks mental processes and, *a fortiori*, it does not look into their neural mechanisms (see, e.g., Bunge and Ardila 1987). As for pragmatism, we know from the philosophy of science that it does not account for scientific research because it minimizes the role of theory and it identifies meaning with operationality, and truth with efficiency. No wonder then that new sociology of science is characteristically shallow, as will be seen anon.

9.4. Ordinarism

A major tenet of the new sociology of science is that there is nothing peculiar, let alone extraordinary, about science: that it is just one more "social construction," one more "way of world-making," one more "political arena." What can one expect from research conducted with this presupposition, which was called "ordinarism" in the Introduction? Can we expect it to teach us what *distinguishes* science from other fields of human endeavor, such as technology and ideology, or industry and government, and how it *interacts* with them? Obviously not, since the new sociology of science denies such differences and therefore the very possibility of such interactions. Can we expect it to discover the social factors that stimulate, and those that inhibit, the advancement of science? Clearly not, since it construes social factors themselves to be constructions, in particular scientific constructions. Nor can we expect it to *discover* anything else, since it denies the very possibility of discovering anything existing out there, for the simple reason that there is no such thing as "out there." If we take constructivism at its word, we can only expect it to deliver what it makes up itself. And if we take relativism at its word, we can only expect its deliveries to be no better than fables.

So, why believe anything the new sociologists of science tell us?

Francis Bacon, not one of the heroes of this school, believed that he had hit on a handful of rules whereby ordinary people could make scientific findings. In fact, the plan for the House of Solomon, which he laid out in *The New Atlantis*, specified that it would be staffed by only a few dozen diligent and meticulous but otherwise quite ordinary men. The advocates of the new sociology of science (e.g., Knorr-Cetina 1981; Latour 1983) agree with the grandfather of positivism and go even further, by asserting that there is nothing special about science, "nothing of any cognitive quality." Thus Latour (1983: 162): "Scientific fact is the product of average, ordinary people and settings, linked to one another by no special norms or communication forms, but who work with inscription devices." Never mind what the inscriptions mean and how their content is checked for consistency and truth: only the "technology of inscribing (writing, schooling, printing, recording devices)" matters. "To take up Feyerabend's saying: 'in the laboratory anything goes, except the inscription devices and the papers'" (Latour 1983: 161).

The constructivist/relativist view of scientific research is a sociologized version of Bacon's. According to it scientists are only busy with collecting (or rather constructing) data, making inscriptions, "negotiating" with one another, and changing their "rules" (even their "rules for seeing") in mysterious ways (see, e.g., Collins 1983). Somehow the spotting of problems, the conception of hypotheses, the design of experiments, and the checks for truth do not occur in the "Wittgensteinian/ phenomenological/Kuhnian model of scientific activity," as Collins (1983) calls it.

Because the new sociology is externalist and pragmatist (recall chapter 8), it pays no attention to scientific theories—or, when it does, it mistakes them for heaps of inscriptions that can be subjected to "semiotic analysis," as Latour (1988) has done with special relativity. And because the new sociology of science overlooks or misinterprets scientific theories, it fails to give an adequate (true) account of laboratory operations, all of which actually presuppose some theories and some of which are designed to test theories.

Thus Latour and Woolgar (1979) and Knorr-Cetina (1981) believe that the essence of laboratory work is the manipulation of artifacts. In the process scientists would not discover or invent anything (not even the instruments themselves). They would only acquire and accumulate "new skills in manipulating things," in particular laboratory equipment (Knorr-Cetina 1981; Latour 1983). Actually the handling of laboratory equipment is often left to lab technicians, or even to automated devices, for instruments, however sophisticated, are only means—means to produce items of objective knowledge about the world. When the means are systematically mistaken for the ends, something fundamentally wrong is happening, not only in morality but everywhere.

Presumably, on this operationalist view of scientific work, Newton did not investigate the motion of bodies (the referents of mechanics), but was busy handling measuring instruments—which, alas, he did not care for. And, withdrawn though he was, he was actually engaged in "negotiating" with Leibniz and the Cartesians. His ultimate victory over them was presumably a result of his superior ability in outmanoeuvring his rivals: he was the better politician. Likewise, presumably Crick and Watson should be presented as spending their time in Cambridge making measurements [which actually they never did] and "negotiating" with Rosalind Franklin and other crystallographers, as well as with with Linus Pauling via his son, while being all the time under the delusion that they were intent on discovering the composition and structure of the hereditary material. If only they had been familiar with the constructivist-relativist program they would have known what they were actually doing. Nothing like consulting your right science therapist to get rid of your delusions.

The advocates of the new sociology of science claim over and over again that, far from neglecting the "technical content" of the scientific projects they study, they provide "detailed accounts of the 'nuts and bolts' of scientific activity" (Pinch 1985: 3). This they manage not by undergoing a normal lengthy scientific apprenticeship but by visiting scientific laboratories. Thus Pinch (1985: 5) tells us that he became "familiar" with the tricky problem of solar neutrinos "having visited the site of the experiment [Raymond Davis's] and having spent several days talking with and 'observing' the experimental group." No solid background in theoretical or experimental physics is needed to accomplish this task. All one needs is enough pluck to ask to be invited to visit a laboratory, and sufficient command of a natural language to understand the popularized version that the host is willing to hand out to the bold explorer. Evidently, although this passes for participant observation it is only veranda observation.

Indeed, in order to participate effectively in a scientific project, in any capacity other than that of mere lab technician, it is necessary to understand the problem that is being investigated. For example, to understand the so-called problem of solar neutrinos one must be able to read the complex mathematical formulas for the neutrino flux. And to understand the experimental design one must understand, among other things, the principle of neutrino detection that is being employed, which calls for some complex theoretical atomic physics. Otherwise the problem, which is that of explaining the discrepancy between the measurement data and the theoretical calculation, cannot be understood, let alone expounded. Admittedly, Pinch does a good job at popularizing the whole thing, but he fails to account for the real "nuts and bolts" because this would require highly specialized knowledge. Science is not that ordinary after all.

Ironically, Pinch's analysis is, except for a few side remarks, a thoroughly epistemological and therefore *internalist* account of the way observational data are interpreted in the light of theories—alas, a superficial analysis because he only mentions some of the theories involved in the project without analyzing any of them. Pinch claims to have sketched a theoretical integration of case-study findings in terms of two allegedly new concepts: those of externality and evidential context. What he means by "externality" or "externalization of observation" is "the chain of interpretations involved in making an observation." He claims, rightly so, that empirical results must be "seen" in the light of theories, but he does not attempt to show how such an "interpretation" is performed by means of fragments of theory and indicator hypotheses (for which see Bunge 1973, 1983b, 1996).

As for the "evidential context of observation," it is just a misnomer for the purpose of an observation: is this being carried out to find new facts, to obtain new data to be inserted into a theoretical calculation, to test a theory, or to check the results of another observation? In short, Pinch has been reinventing the very philosophy of science he and his comrades at arms have so vehemently denounced as being unfaithful to science. But, because they mistrust logic, they have not succeeded in building a clear and consistent philosophy of science.

The practitioner of the new sociology of science does not bother to learn the language of the tribe he claims to study. Once or twice in a lifetime he or she visits a biology laboratory without knowing any biology, he writes about the sociology of mathematics without having undergone a training in mathematics, and so on. He is thus a pre-Malinowski veranda observer rather than a genuine participant observer. And yet he claims to possess a quick and fool-proof method for acquiring "native competence" in any science, that is, for mastering the tacit as well as the explicit rules of any scientific "game." The recipe is this: "Tacit knowledge is best acquired through face-to-face contact" with scientists—never mind their subject matter (Collins 1983: 92). However, Collins admits that "The method of full participation can rarely be attained [*sic*] in practice…but a series of depth interviews can be an acceptable substitute" (1983: 93). Shorter: To master a field of research one need not undergo any training in it, let alone conduct original research: A stint at scientific journalism suffices.

No wonder that the findings of the sociologists of science who believe that scientific research is an ordinary endeavor are ordinary themselves. In fact, their correct findings are that scientific research is not performed in isolation but in the midst of a social network; that every member of a research team exchanges information, questions, valuations, proposals, etc., with other members; that scientists make statements of different kinds (e.g., tentative and assertive); that there is an ongoing transformation of one kind into another; and that "the fate of what we say and make is in the later user's hands" (Latour 1987: 29).

Side by side with such platitudes we find egregious mistakes, such as the assertions that every statement has a social content; that "a statement becomes a fact" when "freed from the circumstances of its production" (Latour and Woolgar 1979); that reality is constructed and "deconstructed "in the same way as a literary text; that "the whole process of fact construction has been shown to be accountable inside a sociological framework" (Latour 1980: 53); that even the notion of a contradiction, as well as the operations of instrument calibration and statistical analysis, can and must be be construed in sociological terms (Collins 1983: 101); that "inferences from the general to the particular actually have an inductive character" (Barnes 1982: 101)—and so on and so forth.

In short, as the old chestnut goes, what is true in the new sociology of science is not original, and what is original is false. (See also Gieryn 1982.)

9.5. Ideology and Science

A good number of adepts of the new sociology of science have adopted the thesis of the Frankfurt school (e.g., Marcuse 1964; Habermas 1971; Adorno and Horkheimer 1972), that science (including mathematics) and technology have an ideological content, and even that they have become the ideology of contemporary capitalism, so that they discharge the function of legitimating the powers that be (recall chapter 7). What is the *evidence* for this bold thesis? Its defenders do not say. The very notion of evidence is alien to dogmatists.

Now, it is well-known that modern science and technology have evolved hand in hand with capitalism, and that ideology infiltrates the *social* sciences, particularly economics. (The historical point is hardly arguable. For the second point see, e.g., Robinson and Eatwell 1974; and Galbraith, 1987.) But science and technology should be just as useful—if not more, as Bernal (1939) argued—in a (genuinely) socialist society. As for economics, recall that economic theories and methods, unlike economic policies, must be ideology-free if they are to count as scientific—by definition of "science" and "ideology." Since the econometric methods and models, the input-output models, and the bioeconomic models are portable from one society to another, there is no reason to suspect that they are ideologically contaminated. In any event, no *evidence* has been produced to show that they are.

The charge that pure mathematics and basic natural science are ideological and political weapons of capitalism is even more groundless. What, pray, is the economic or political content of the Pythagorean theorem, or of Euclid's theorem that there are infinitely many prime numbers? What is the social content of the assertions that the hydrogen atom has a single proton, that carbon has four valences, that the ribosomes synthesize proteins, that the brain is composed of many subsystems, each with a specific function, that children resemble their ancestors, or that lead is toxic? To be sure, mathematics and science can be *utilized* for economic or political purposes. But the fact that they can be utilized for good as well as for wrong social goals is surely an argument in favor of the thesis that they are intrinsically neutral.

If every mathematical or scientific statement is imputed some (undefined) social content, it follows that all scientific controversies (a) have an ideological component and (b) are terminated by means other than experiment, calculation, or logical argument. These theses are, indeed, favorites with the new sociology of science. Again, we ask: What is the *evidence*? The only supposed evidence is that *some* scientific controversies have indeed had ideological overtones because one of the views in conflict was a component of the ideology of the ruling class. This was of course the case with the trial of Galileo, the evolutionism-creationism controversy, the claim that there are superior human races, the Lysenko scandal, and a few others. However, the final verdict has been scientific, not political.

Only a very primitive inductivist will leap from *some* to *all* without paying attention to counterexamples. Now, it so happens that the ideology-free scientific controversies by far outnumber the ideology-laden ones. Here is a random sample of heated controversies of the first kind: Those over cold fusion in 1989; the ongoing controversy on the existence of black holes; the polemics between gradualists and saltationists in evolutionary biology; the dispute in the 1930s and 1940s over the (electrical or chemical) nature of inter-neuronal contacts; the controversies over the interpretation of the quantum theory since its inception in 1926; the spirited debate over special relativity during the decade that followed its invention in 1905; the controversies about the very existence of atoms and the discussions on set theory around 1900; the polemics between field theorists and partisans of action at a distance in mid-nineteenth century; and the conflict between Newtonians and Cartesians in the seventeenth and eighteenth centuries.

This is not deny that some of these controversies had some *philosophical* components. For instance, the last-cited one did have such a component, but it so happens that the two rival views, Cartesianism and Newtonianism, were ideologically progressive at the time, for both were mechanistic. However, the point is that the above-quoted scientific controversies were *ideology* -free and were terminated by strictly scientific means. (In particular, the Newtonians won by showing that they could calculate, in particular predict, the real trajectories of bodies in a number of cases, whereas the Cartesians were unable to do anything of the sort.) The above counterexamples, which can easily be multiplied, refute the thesis of the new sociology of science, that in *all* cases consensus in science depends on who elbows hardest, shouts louder, or lies best.

It cannot be denied that in *some* cases ideological or sociopolitical factors do interfere with the normal course of scientific controversy. But this is not the case with *all* of them. In particular, it is not the case with the Pasteur-Pouchet controversy over spontaneous generation, used by some members of the to confirm their theses. True, Pasteur was a Catholic—but then his opponent was a Protestant, hence he should have sided with Pasteur to remain faithful to the book of Genesis. But the important point is that Pasteur was *right* in denying the possibility of near-instant emergence of organisms out of inorganic matter—particularly in the aseptic conditions which he produced. And he cannot be blamed for not having anticipated Oparin's 1922 hypothesis on the abiotic origin of life. Whatever the philosophical merits of Pouchet's hypothesis may have been, it was conclusively refuted by Pasteur on purely scientific grounds. (For this whole matter see Roll-Hansen 1983.)

Our last example will be Pinch's version of the early phase of the controversy over hidden variables in quantum mechanics triggered by David Bohm's famous 1952 paper (Pinch 1979a). The technical part of this account is correct, though shallow, in failing to distinguish the two philosophical aspects aspects of the controversy. One of thee consists of the ontological problems of determinism and of whether or not each physical property has a "sharp" value at all times. (With hindsight, particularly after the 1981 experiments by Aspect et al. that resulted in the refutation of Bell's inequalities, we can see that Bohm, as well as Einstein and de Broglie, were mistaken on this point.) The second philosophical component is the epistemological question whether quantum mechanics is about physical reality or about the operations of an experimenter. (In my opinion Bohm, Einstein, and de Broglie were right on this point. See, e.g., Bunge 1967a, 1979b, 1985a,1988b.) However, here we must concentrate on the allegedly sociological aspect of Pinch's version.

The originality of Pinch's analysis lies in his claim to be sociological just because he employs Pierre Bourdieu's expressions "social capital" and "investment strategy" involved in a superficial analogy between the production of knowledge and that of commodities, that had been suggested earlier by Louis Althusser (Bourdieu 1975). The idea is that scientific activity is a struggle to gain scientific ascendancy ("capital recognition"). Such struggle is conducted in the light of "investment strategies," and occasionally "subversion strategies" as well. Thus we are told that "in 1943 he [Bohm] increased his social capital by obtaining a Ph.D.... In 1945 he acquired more capital by his appointment to the position of assistant professor at Princeton" (Pinch 1979a: 179). The publication of his well-known textbook on quantum mechanics "provided Bohm with further capital and helped him to establish a relation with the quantum elite" (p. 180). By 1952 Bohm "had accumulated considerable social capital," and "then switched to a subversion strategy with the publication of his heterodox paper" (p.181).

Does this representation of David Bohm as a "social capitalist" engaged in hoarding and attempting takeovers throw any light on his attempt to recast quantum mechanics in terms of hidden variables? Not at all, for it misses Bohm's strongest motivation, which was philosophical—as I happen to know for having spent one semester with him in São Paulo, in 1953, discussing precisely the matters raised by his epoch-making 1952 paper. At the time Bohm was working on three tough scientifico-philosophical problems. One was the attempt to derive the quantum-mechanical probabilities from some function(s) other than the state (or *psi*) function. The second was to elucidate the relations between causation and chance via the concept of a level of organization. (Bohm had read my 1951 paper on this subject, had liked it, and therefore had gotten me a fellowship to give me the chance to discuss face-to-face the objections to his theory which I had raised in a letter.) Bohm's third problem at the time was to apply his own alternative theory to solving the problem of measurement, which Wolfgang Pauli—in accordance with the operationalist dogma—had declared was necessary to endow Bohm's theory with a physical meaning. (Incidentally, the problem of constructing a general theory of measuremnt is still open. Moreover, it is likely to be insoluble.)

Pinch's version of the story is wide of the mark because it overlooks the philosophical ideas that motivated Bohm at the time. Moreover, he makes no room for Bohm's disinterested and passionate quest for truth, or for the courage it took to challenge orthodoxy without hope of overcoming and with no wish to gain power of any kind—and furthermore without any hope of augmenting whatever "social capital" (i.e., academic prestige) he had earned before. Needless to say, nor does the Bourdieu-Pinch approach shed any light on Bohm's later switch to Oriental mysticism. (For criticisms of Bourdieu's approach see Bourricaud 1975 and Knorr-Cetina 1983.)

Besides, the publication of his textbook did not allow Bohm to join the "quantum elite": he was already a member of it. What the book did was to draw Einstein's attention to him. As Dave told me, Einstein summoned him to his office and told him: "Yours is the best book on standard quantum mechanics. But this theory is wrong, because it does not attempt to represent physical reality. I believe it should be replaced or supplemented with hidden variables [that is, dispersion-free functions]. Why don't you examine this possibility? I would be very much interested in discussing such work with you." Obviously, Dave could not refuse this offer. Very soon, the seed that Einstein planted germinated, and the old debate over hidden variables, which von Neumann had terminated by decree two decades earlier, was reopened. In the process Bohm lost rather than increased his "social capital." In fact, he was ostracized from the physics community until the famous paper on the Aharonov-Bohm effect appeared.

At the beginning of this section we mentioned one of the roots of the belief that all science is tainted by ideology. Another root the transposition of the Feuerbach-Durkheim interesting hypothesis that *primitive cosmogonies and religions* are modeled on the corresponding societies. The drafter of the "strong programme" (Bloor 1976, chap. 2) believes that what holds for primitive cosmogonies and religions holds also for modern science. But why should it, given that science, far from being a belief system, is a research field, hence one where belief is the final (and even so only *pro tempore*) stage of hypotheses and data?

The claim that scientific controversies can only be resolved by extra-scientific means has a third root, namely the thesis of the "under-determination" of theory by data, popularized by W. V. Quine but actually known to the ancient Greek astronomers. According to it, any set of empirical data may be accounted for by two or more theories, which are then said to be "empirically equivalent." Conventionalists such as Pierre Duhem, and some empiricists, such as Philipp Frank, have used this alleged fact against scientific realism and in favor of the view that scientific controversies are settled by recourse to some nonscientific (but still conceptual) criterion, such as simplicity (see, e.g., Bunge 1963). The members of the new sociology of science use it in support of their claim that scientific controversies are resolved by nonconceptual means, such as political manoeuvres. In point of fact the problem of empirical underdetermination is not as bad as it looks, and there is no evidence that scientists solve in nonconceptual ways.

For one thing, the usual underdetermination situation concerns hypotheses (single propositions), not comprehensive theories (systems of hypotheses). Unlike the former, the latter are supposed to account for a number of apparently disparate collections of data. What amounts to the same thing, scientific theories are supposed to predict facts which, *prima facie*, look unrelated. Hence a classical test to which rival theories are subjected is to ascertain which of them predicts more accurately the greater variety of facts. This is how Maxwell's field electromagnetic theory came to be preferred to the Ampère-Gauss-Weber action at a distance theory, Einstein's relativistic mechanics to classical mechanics, quantum electrodynamics to classical electrodynamics, and so on.

Still, it is true that predictive power is not enough: Scientific theories are made to pass a whole battery of additional tests, but all of these are conceptual (Bunge 1963, 1967b, 1983b). One of them is what I call the test of external consistency, that is, compatibility with the bulk of the background knowledge. Another is compatibility with the world view prevailing in the scientific community—which may be at variance with the ideology of the ruling class. This is not surprising, for a scientific world view grows hand in hand with science itself. For example, if two rival psychological learning theories are compatible with the same experimental data, but one of them makes reference to some neurophysiological process while the other does not, it is only natural to prefer the former, and this for the following reasons. First, because the former theory will help explore neurophysiological learning mechanisms and may thus come to enjoy additional empirical support. Second, because the hypothesis that mental functions are brain functions, rather than functions of an immaterial mind, is consistent with the naturalistic world view prevalent in the contemporary scientific community. In short, philosophy does play a role in (some) scientific controversies. But politics does not or, when it does, this is a sign that one of the parties is political, not scientific.

There must be something very wrong with a study of science that is incapable of telling science from ideology and, worse, that conflates the two. The source of this confusion is the naive pragmatist epistemology according to which knowledge "is whatever men take to be knowledge . It consists of those beliefs which men confidently hold to and live by" (Bloor 1976: 2)—with the proviso that the word "knowledge" should be reserved "for what is collectively endorsed, leaving the individual and idiosyncratic to count as mere belief" (p. 3). Shorter: Knowledge is whatever belief enjoys social sanction. (For two different criticisms of the view that knowledge is a kind of belief see Popper 1972 and Bunge 1983a.)

According to this definition of "knowledge," abstruse but well-confirmed scientific theories, such as quantum mechanics, do not qualify as knowledge because they are not collectively endorsed. On the other hand, superstitions do qualify for being popular.

Let us not quibble over the correct definition of the concept of knowledge. What is crucial here is whether or not the student of science should draw any distinction between truth and falsity. According to the proponents of the "strong programme," the sociologist is not interested in the true/false distinction: He must give "equal time" to all theories, and his own theories "will have to apply to both true and false beliefs" and "regardless of how the investigator evaluates them" (Bloor 1976: 3). Consequently the new style sociologist of science is both unable and unwilling to distinguish science from nonscience. However, this problem deserves a separate section.

9.6. Nonscience

Most of the new-style sociologists of science do not admire, trust, or love science. They regard it as an ideology, a domination tool, an inscription-making device with no legitimate claim to universal truth, and just one more kind of social construction on a par with trench digging if not worse. They regard scientists as skilled craftsmen but somewhat unscrupulous wheeler-dealers and unprincipled politicians. In short, they laugh at Merton's characterization of the scientific ethos.

The members of the new sociology of science regard all facts, or at least what they call "scientific facts," as social constructions. But in matters of knowledge the only genuine social constructions are the scientific forgeries committed by two or more people. A famous forgery of this kind was the Piltdown fossil man, "discovered" by two people in 1912, certified as authentic by a number of experts (among them Teilhard de Chardin), and only unmasked as a fake in 1950. According to the existence criterion of the school, we should admit that the Piltdown man did exist—at least between 1912 and 1950—because the scientific community believed in it. Are we prepared to believe this, or rather to suspect that the new sociology of science is incapable or even unwilling to tell hot air from cold?

Because the members of the new sociology of science deny that there is any conceptual difference between science and other human endeavors, some of their evaluations of science overlap with that of the counterculture, to the point that the school is in some important respects a component of it. Let us take a look at a few examples.

Michael Mulkay (1969), an early leader of the school, waxes indignant over the way the scientific community treated Immanuel Velikovsky's allegedly revolutionary *Worlds in Collision* (1950). He scolds scientists for their "abusive and uncritical rejection" of Velikovsky's speculation and for clinging to the "theoretical and methodological paradigms"—among them the laws of celestial mechanics. He claims that the astronomers had the duty to put Velikovsky's fantasies to the test.

Mulkay's complaint ignores that (a) the burden of the proof rests on the would-be innovator; (b) empirical tests are unnecessary when a theory violates well-confirmed theories or successful methods, on top of which it does not solve any outstanding problems; (c) nearly all of Velikovsky's claims have been proved wrong (the exception being his conjecture that there had been collisions between galaxies, a lucky guess for which he offered no evidence); and (d) scientists have more important tasks than to devote their energies to testing the fantasies of an outsider without any scientific credentials. This is why the eminent and mild-mannered American astronomer Harlow Shapley, chastised by Mulkay, rejected Velikovsky's book out of hand. However, a number of scientists, headed by Carl Sagan, did take their time to criticize in detail Velikovsky's fantasies, and the American Association for the Advancement of Science devoted an entire symposium to them (Goldsmith, ed. 1977).

Second example: Yaron Ezrahi (1971) claimed that Arthur Jensen's "findings" on the innate intellectual inferiority of blacks were rejected by the American scientific community for ideological reasons. And he held that the geneticists were particularly vehement in their criticisms of Jensen's work, at least in part, for being concerned with their own "public image and support." He did not bother to analyze the very IQ tests from which Jensen's conclusions were derived. Had he done so he would have learned that (a) at that time such tests were culture-bound and thus bound to favor whites over blacks; and (b) no IQ test will be fully reliable unless backed up by a well-confirmed theory of intelligence—which is still to come (Bunge and Ardila 1987).

Another two vocal members of the new sociology of science, H. M. Collins and T. J. Pinch, have mounted a spirited defense of astrology and parapsychology (see Pinch and Collins 1979; Pinch 1979b; Collins and Pinch 1982; and Pinch and Collins 1984). They have defended, in particular, (a) the "Mars effect" (linking the position of Mars at time of birth with athletic prowess) announced by the French psychologists Michel and Françoise Gauquelin; (b) the research of J. B. Rhine—whom they call "an arch-exponent of careful statistical method"—on telepathy, psychokinesis, and the like; and (c) the 1974 work of R. Tharg and H. Puthoff on "remote viewing." At the same time they have attacked the Committee for the Scientific Investigation of Claims of the Paranormal (of which I am proud to be a member) and its journal *The Skeptical Inquirer* for taking the defense of what they call "the standard model of science," which they dub "ideology."

Of course Collins and Pinch do not propose an alternative "model" of science. They only call for a "re-appraisal of scientific method" to make room for astrology, parapsychology, psychoanalysis, and other "extraordinary sciences." It would go against the grain of the new sociology of science to propose its own clear-cut criteria of scientificity, since it holds science to be an "ordinary social construction." But how is it possible to discuss rationally the scientific status of an idea or practice unless it is in the light of *some* definition of scientificity, whether Popper's (1935), Merton's (1957) classical ones, my own (Bunge 1983b), or someone else's? As for the truth values of the alleged findings of astrologers, parapsychologists, psychoanalysts, and the like, how can we discuss them in a constructivist/relativist framework, where truth is said to be a social convention? How would it help to quote, for example, any of the authoritative studies included in *A Skeptic's Handbook of Parapsychology*, edited by Paul Kurtz (1975)?

Volume III (1979) of the *Sociology of the Sciences Yearbook*, edited by Helga Nowotny and Hilary Rose, is devoted to "counter-movements in the sciences." Most of the contributors to this volume sympathize with antiscience and with the counterculture generally, whereas others favor the recognition of astrology, parapsychology, and psychoanalysis as sciences or at least as "controversial sciences." Since they do not offer a new and precise definition of "science" to accommodate such "controversial sciences," theirs must be rated as just an ideological *cri de coeur*.

Some of the contributors to this volume write about the "myth" of science and attack rationality. Others restrict themselves to criticizing what they see as limitations of science. And still others denounce science—which they mistake for technology—as the handmaiden of capitalism. But all of these authors share the conviction that "science is a social relation," although they do not explain what they mean by this. (Whether science is conceived as a body of knowledge, an activity, or a community of researchers, it is not a *relation*, although it is *related* to a host of other items by so many relations.)

Not surprisingly, most of the contributors to the volume under review are gullible: the one believes in UFOs, another in astrology, a third in telepathy, a fourth in all of these. Some of them, in particular Hilary Rose (1979), link antiscience with the Left, and would not be impressed by the historical evidence that the Right has always been suspicious of science and opposed to public scientific education, if only because ignorant people are easy to fool. On second thought there should be nothing surprising about that because Rose, who chides the eminent physicist and sociologist of science J. D. Bernal for having had faith in science, substitutes a quotation from Mao for a scientific analysis of the relations between science and society. Apparently the New Left is just as antiscientific as the Old Right (see Gross and Levitt 1994; Sokal and Bricmont 1998).

There are several other examples of this convergence of Left and Right in the cultural sphere. One of them is the birth, in the 1970s, of the "radical philosophy" movement, where neo-Marxists joined with phenomenologists and existentialists in their rejection of scientism. Another case is the common abhorrence of science and science-oriented philosophy by both leftists and right-wingers in the Third World. A third instance is what Hirschman (1981) has dubbed "the unholy alliance" between neo-Marxist and orthodox economists against development economics, as well as against the industrialization of Latin America.

Another example of this unholy alliance is Hilary and Steven Rose's (1974) criticism of biological psychiatry and the concomitant use of drugs to treat depression, schizophrenia, and other serious mental disorders that resist the methods of clinical psychologists. They oppose biological psychiatry because it looks for "a biological rationale for problem of the social order." By the same token they favor the antipsychiatry movement of Laing, Cooper, and Esteson, regarding it as "politically destabilizing." Why not go all the way and, for the same reason, favor medical quackery over "orthodox" medicine? What is most surprising is that Steven Rose is a neurobiologist. But his is not the first case of a scientist misled by ideology, nor will it be the last.

Our last case will be Lynch's ethnomethodological study "Sacrifice and the transformation of the animal body into a scientific object: Laboratory culture and ritual practice in the neurosciences" (1988). Taking his cue from Durkheim's studies in the sociology of religion, Lynch claims that the killing of laboratory animals at the end of a run of experiments is part of a ritual practice whereby the body of the animal is transformed into "a bearer of transcendental significances." Characteristically, he omits to present any evidence for this extraordinary claim. It was bad enough when Latour and Woolgar (1979) compared the scientific laboratory to a political committee. Now that the laboratory bench is presented as a sacrifice altar, it should not be surprising if laboratory scientists were to put a ban on visitors from the enemy camp. The popular misperceptions of science are bad enough without the help of the new sociology of science.

To conclude this section. The failure to distinguish science from pseudoscience is an indicator of philosophical shallowness and it is pratically as well as theoretically disastrous. This is particularly so in the field of social studies, because pseudoscientific views on society can become the conceptual basis of, and justification for, atrocious governmental (or antigovernmental) policies. Think of the myth of the superiority of the "white race" in relation to slavery, colonialism, and apartheid ; of monetarism and, in general, neoclassical economics as a weapon against social justice; or of the myths of the dictatorship of the proletariat and of "democratic centralism" as tools of Stalinism.

9.7. Conclusions

There are two possible lines of criticism of the sociology of knowledge and, in particular, of the sociology of science: destructive and constructive. The former, espoused by most of the classical students of science, denies the very possibility and desirability of the discipline, and insists on maintaining a radical internalist perspective. This view is lopsided because in actual fact cognition and in particular scientific research cannot be detached from the knowing brain or her society: every knower is an animal embedded in a natural and social environment.

Externalism is of course an extreme reaction against internalism. In most respects this reaction goes too far, for maintaining the classical distinction between the constitutive or cognitive and the contingent or social, only to claim (without proof) that the latter determines the former, or even that the cognitive is the contingent in a different linguistic wrapping, one stripped of all the "modalities" or references to the scientist's beliefs and actions (Latour and Woolgar 1979). This thesis spares the new-style student of science the task of studying scientific ideas and experimental designs, so that in fact he never acquires an intimate knowledge of any research project: he looks at science from afar, as if he were a journalist or an administrator.

However, in another respect the new sociology of science does not go far enough in investigating the social circumstances of scientific research. Indeed, in most cases it restricts its interest to investigating what it calls "local accounting procedures" (Knorr 1977; Krohn 1980; Collins 1983), such as particular laboratories, as if the particular site were more important than both the generic features of scientific research and the structure of society at large (see Gieryn 1982). In this regard, the new sociology of science is a retreat from the Marxist variant. On the other hand, it fits in with the thesis of the "interpretive" (or hermeneutic) anthropologists, like Geertz (1983), that all knowledge is local.

As a result of this parochial (site-centered) perspective, the new sociology of science has failed to address such non-local and topical questions as (a) the deliberate underfunding of social science research by the U.S. conservative governments, and of scientific research in general by the British conservative governments; (b) the current decline of epistemic communism, that is, the increasing reluctance of experimental scientists to share data, ideas and materials as a consequence of heightened competition and commercial pressures (Marshall 1990); (c) the increasing frequency of exaggerated claims and unabashed publicity, and the mounting number of cases of fraud and plagiarism, particularly in the biomedical sciences, as a result of the stiff competition for research grants and jobs; (d) the decline in the number of native scientists and science students in North America and Great Britain as a result of the philistinism fostered from above, combined with the antiintellectual atmosphere; and (e) the prosperity of the antiscientific and pseudoscientific doctrines, movements and industries, and the concomitant resurgence of irrationalist philosophies, in all industrialized countries, West and East.

The new sociology of science has failed to address these problems because it is part of them: Indeed, it has been criticizing what it calls "the myth of science." It is mainly nonsociologists, in particular members of the staffs of *Science* and *Nature*, as well as contributors to *Free Inquiry* and the *Skeptical Inquirer*,who have been carefully monitoring and analyzing the above-mentioned trends. In short, the new sociology of science sees politics and ideology where there is none, namely in the content of science, both formal and factual, while failing to perceive them where they hinder its development.

How can the emergence of the new sociology of science be accounted for? A sociologist might be tempted to explain it as a "perverse" effect of the rapid increase in the demand for teachers of STS (Science, Technology, and Society) that accompanied the postwar explosion of science and technology. Suddenly there were too many job opportunities in this field, and they could not be missed by lengthening the course of study of science that in earlier times had been deemed necessary to become a serious student of science. Externalism provided the perfect excuse for not bothering with science as a body of knowledge.

But why did a subjectivist (constructivist) and relativist trend, and moreover one that feels no respect for science, come to the fore in the 1960s and 1970s? In my view *this* event, and the concomitant revival of antirealist and irrationalist philosophies, can be explained in externalist terms, namely as follows. The new sociology of science was born together and in interaction with the student revolts in both the U.S. and Western Europe, which culminated in the events of May of 1968. Those rebels fought not only the American involvement in Vietnam (once students began to be drafted). They revolted against the "establishment" as a whole, and in Western Europe against the rigid university hierarchy in particular.

Misled by Herbert Marcuse, Jürgen Habermas, and other "critical theorists," those young people, whose good intentions there is no reason to doubt, perceived science and technology as the ideology of the "establishment." Consequently they blamed science and technology (which, like their mentors, they confused with one another) for the sins of some political and business leaders—mainly war-mongering, environmental degradation, economic exploitation, and even political oppression.

But, since people have got to believe in something, many of those rebels embraced irrationalist doctrines, such as Oriental mysticism, existentialism, occultism, and radical skepticism, in particular epistemological anarchism, centered in the popular slogan "Anything goes," coined at the right time by the philosopher Paul K. Feyerabend (1975). In turn, the adoption of these antiscientific doctrines turned many young people away from the study of science and technology, and favored the nonscientific approach to the sociological, historical and philosophical studies of science and technology. The current dismal state of scientific literacy, and the decline in the number of science and engineering students, are partly results of the revolt against "the myth of science," for one does not study science or technology if one dreads, hates or despises it (see Bunge 1989). Another result of the revolt against science is the new sociology of science and, in general, the recent crop of constructivist, relativist and irrationalist social studies. (For a representative sample see Fiske and Shweder, eds. 1986.)

To recapitulate. Until the mid-1960s science was generally regarded as being characterized by a unique set of rigorous standards and by an ethos of its own. From then on a growing number of students of science have claimed this to be a myth and, of course, in their own work they have refused to abide by those standards and by that ethos. The result has been an utterly grotesque picture of science. This result suggests the following morals.

M1: If you wish to learn about science, start by studying some science.

M2: Ignore philosophy, and you'll reinvent bad philosophy.

M3: Where anything goes, nothing goes well.

10

In Praise of Intolerance toward Academic Charlatanism

Up until the mid-1960s, whoever wished to engage in mysticism or freewheeling, intellectual deceit or antiintellectualism, had to do so outside the hallowed groves of academe. For nearly two centuries before that time the university had been an institution of higher learning, where people cultivated the intellect, engaged in rational discussion, searched for the truth, applied it, or taught it to the best of their abilities. To be sure, once in a while a traitor to one of these values was discovered, but he was promptly inactivated by ridicule or ostracism. And here and there a professor, once tenured, refused to learn anything new, and thus became quickly obsolete. But he seldom lagged more than a couple of decades, was still able to engage in rational argument, as well as to distinguish genuine knowledge from bunk, and did not proclaim the superiority of guts over brains, or of instinct over reason—unless of course he happened to be an irrationalist philosopher.

This is no longer the case. Over the past three decades or so, many universities have been infiltrated, though not yet seized, by the enemies of conceptual rigor and empirical evidence: those who proclaim that there is no objective truth—whence "anything goes"; who pass off political opinion as science; and who engage in bogus scholarship. These are not unorthodox original thinkers: They ignore or even scorn rigorous thinking and experimenting altogether. They are not misunderstood Galileos punished by the powers that be for proposing daring new truths or methods. On the contrary, nowadays many intellectual slobs and frauds have been given tenured jobs, are allowed to teach garbage in the name of academic freedom, and see their false or even meaningless writings published by scholarly journals and erstwhile prestigious university presses. Moreover, many of them have acquired enough power to censor genuine scholarship. They have mounted a Trojan horse inside the academic citadel with the intention of destroying higher culture from within.

The academic enemies of the very *raison d'être* of the university, namely the search for and dissemination of truth, can be grouped into two bands: the antiscientists, who often call themselves "postmodernists," and the pseudoscientists. The former teach that there are no objective and universal truths, whereas the academic pseudoscientists smuggle fuzzy concepts, wild conjectures, or even ideology as scientific findings. Both gangs operate under the protection of academic freedom, and often at the taxpayer's expense too. Should they continue to use these privileges, misleading uncounted students and misusing public funds in defaming the search for truth, or should they be expelled from the temple of higher learning? This is the main problem to be tackled in the present chapter. But first let us sample the production of the academic antiscientists and pseudoscientists, restricting ourselves to the humanities and social studies.

10.1. Academic Antiscience

Academic antiscience is part of the counterculture movement. It can be found in nearly all departments of any contemporary faculty of arts, particularly in the advanced countries. Let us take a look at a small sample of the antiscientific reaction inside the gates of academia: existentialism, phenomenology, phenomenological sociology, ethnomethodology, and radical feminist theory.

Example 1: Existentialism. Existentialism is a jumble of nonsense, falsity, and platitude. Let the reader judge for himself from the following sample of Heidegger's celebrated *Sein und Zeit* (1986 [1927]), dedicated to Edmund Husserl, his teacher and the founder of phenomenology. On human existence or being-there (*Dasein*): "Das Sein des Daseins besagt: Sich-vorweg-schon-sein-in-(der Welt-) als Sein-bei (innerweltlich begegnendem Seienden)" (p. 192). On time: "Zeit ist ursprünglich als Zeitigung der Zeitlichkeit, als welche sie die Konstitution der Sorgestruktur ermöglicht" (p. 331). I dare anyone to make sense of these word-plays, or even to translate them into good German. Other famous formulas of Heidegger's, such as *"Die Welt weltet"* ("The world worlds"), *"Das Nichts nichtet "* ("Nothingness nothings"), *"Die Sprache spricht"* ("Language speaks"), and *"Die Werte gelten"* ("Values are valuable"), are translatable and have the virtue of brevity, but are just as nonsensical.

Not content with writing nonsense and torturing the German language, Heidegger (1976 [1953]: 20, 37) heaped scorn on "mere science" for being allegedly incapable of "awakening the spirit." He also denigrated logic, "an invention of school teachers, not of philosophers" (op. cit. : 92). Last, but not least, Heidegger was a Nazi ideologist and militant, and remained unrepentant till the last (see op. cit: 152). (No mere coincidence here: The training of obedient soldiers ready to die for an insane criminal cause starts by discouraging clear critical thinking.) In short, existentialism is no ordinary garbage: it is unrecyclable rubbish. Its study in academic courses is only justified as an illustration of, and warning against, irrationalism, academic imposture, gobbledygook, and subservience to reactionary ideology.

Example 2: Phenomenology. This school, the parent of existentialism, is characterized by opaqueness. Let the reader judge from this sample of its founder's celebrated attack upon the exact and natural sciences: "I as primaeval I [*Ur-Ich*] construct [*konstituire*] my horizon of transcendental others as cosubjects of the transcendental intersubjectivity that constructs the world" (Husserl [1935] 1954: 187). Phenomenology is also a modern paragon of subjectivism. In fact, according to its founder, the gist of phenomenology is that it is a "pure egology," a "science of the concrete transcendental subjectivity" (Husserl 1931: 68). As such, it is "in outmost opposition to the sciences as they have been conceived up until now, i.e., as *objective* sciences" (ibid). The very first move of the phenomenologist is the "phenomenological reduction" or "bracketing out" (*epoché*) of the external world. "One must lose the world through *epoché* in order to regain it through universal self-examination" (op. cit.: 183). He must do this because his "universal task" is the discovery of himself as transcendental (i.e., nonempirical) ego (op. cit.: 76).

Having feigned that real things, such as chairs and colleagues, do not exist, the phenomenologist proceeds to uncover their essences. To this end he makes use of a special intuition called "vision of essences" (*Wesensschau*)—the nature of which is not explained, and for which no evidence at all is offered. The result is an *a priori* and intuitive science (op. cit., sect. 34). This "science" proves to be nothing but transcendental idealism (op. cit.: 118). This subjectivism is not only epistemological but also ontological: "the world itself is an infinite idea" (op. cit.: 97).

How could anyone think that this wild fantasy could shed any light on anything except the decadence of German philosophy? This extravagance can only have at least one of two negative effects on social studies. One is to focus on individual behavior and deny the real existence of social systems and macrosocial facts: these would be the products of such intellectual procedures as aggregation and "interpretation" (guessing). The other possible negative effect is to alienate students from empirical research, thus turning the clock back to the times of armchair ("humanistic") social studies. The effect of the former move is that *social* science is impossible; that of the second is that social *science* is impossible. Either or both of these effects are apparent in the two schools to be examined next.

Example 3: Phenomenological sociology (e.g., Schutz 1932, Berger and Luckmann 1967). This school is characterized by spiritualism and subjectivism, as well as by individualism (both ontological and methodological) and conservatism—ethical and political. The first two features are obvious. Indeed, according to phenomenology, social reality is a construction of the knower, not a given, for all social facts would be "meaningful" (have a purpose) and the subject of "interpretation" (guessing), whence everything social would be spiritual and subjective, or at most intersubjective, rather than material and observer-independent.

The ontological individualism of phenomenology derives from its subjectivism. Because individuals are said to "interpret" themselves and others, without ever facing any brute social facts, the task of the sociologist is to grasp "subjective meaning structures" rather than to construct or test models of social systems or processes. In particular, he must study the *Lebenswelt* or everyday life of individuals, skirting such macrosocial issues as gender and race discrimination, mass unemployment, social conflict, and war. The phenomenological sociologist claims to grasp directly the objects of his study, alleging that they are ordinary. Moreover, let us remember that he is graced with the "vision of essences," which gives him instant insight. Hence he can dispense with statistics, mathematical modeling, tedious argument, and empirical test. In short, phenomenological sociology is avowedly nonscientific and an invitation to sloth.

Example 4: Ethnomethodology (e.g., Garfinkel 1967, Goffman 1963). This is the offspring of the union of phenomenology with symbolic interactionism. The members of this school practice what phenomenological sociologists preach: They observe at first hand and record trivial events in the *Lebenswelt* or everyday life, focus on symbols and communication, and skirt any important activities, processes and issues, particularly large-scale social conflicts and changes. They engage in participant (short range) observation but shun experimentation, which they disapprove of on philosophical grounds. Lacking theories of their own, the ethnomethodologists invoke the murky pronouncements of hermeneutics, phenomenology, and even existentialism—all of them declared enemies of science. Obviously, an unscientific philosophy, which opposes the search for objective truth, could hardly inspire scientific research. Mercifully the ethnomethodologists make no use of these doctrines in their empirical work. As a matter of fact, in field work they behave as positivists—even while vehemently denouncing positivism—inasmuch as they spend most of their time collecting data which they are unable to interpret correctly for want of theory.

In fact, the ethnomethodologist audiotapes and videotapes "the detailed and observable practices which make the incarnate [?] production of ordinary social facts, for example, order of service in a queue, sequential order in a conversation, and the order of skillfully embodied [?] improvised conduct" (Lynch, Livingston, and Garfinkel 1983: 206). Possible English translation: "The ethnomethodologist records observable ordinary life events." The data thus collected are audible or visible traces left by people who presumably behave purposefully and intelligently. These traces are the only clues the ethnomethodologists can go by, for, lacking a theory, they cannot tell us what makes people tick—that is, they cannot explain the behavior they observe and record. Their practice does not differ from that of the empiricist and, in particular, the behaviorist—as even Atkinson (1988), a sympathizer of the school, has admitted. In short, they behave like positivists even while engaging in positivism-bashing—actually a devious way of attacking the scientific approach.

Only the ethnomethodologists's convoluted lingo suggests intimate contact with their philosophical mentors. For example, Garfinkel (1967: 1) starts one of his books by stating that ethnomethodology "recommends" that "the activities whereby members [of a team?] produce and manage settings [?] of organized everyday affairs are identical with members' procedures for making those settings 'account-able'[?]. The 'reflexive'[?] or 'incarnate'[?] character of accounting [?] practices and accounts makes up the crux of that recommendation." Or consider the same author's (1967: 11) definition of ethnomethodology as "the investigation of the rational [intelligible?] properties of indexical [context-dependent] expressions and other practical actions as contingent [?] ongoing accomplishments [outcomes?] of organized artful [purposive?] practices of everyday life." Why use extraordinary prose to describe ordinary accounts of ordinary life?

This is not to deny the importance of observing everyday-life occurrences, such as casual encounters and conversations—the favorite material of ethnomethodologists. Such observation, a common practice of anthropologists, yields raw material for the scientist to process in the light of hypotheses and with a view to coming up with new hypotheses. But that empirical material is of limited use unless accompanied by reliable information concerning the role that the observed subject enacts, for example, boss or employee. The reason is that such roles—in other words, the systems in which the protagonists are embedded—largely determine the "meaning" (purpose) of everyday actions and the content of conversations (Collins 1987). But ethnomethodologists overlook the macrosocial context and are not interested in any large social issues. This fact, combined with the absence of tests of the proposed "interpretations" (hypotheses) and the lack of theory, explains the paucity of findings of ethnomethodology.

A characteristic product of this school is Lynch's study "Sacrifice and the transformation of the animal body into a scientific object: Laboratory culture and ritual practice in the neurosciences" (1988). Taking his cue from Durkheim's studies in the sociology of religion, Lynch claims that the killing of laboratory animals at the end of a run of experiments is part of a ritual practice whereby the body of the animal is transformed into "a bearer of transcendental significances." Characteristically, he presents no evidence for the extraordinary claim that the laboratory bench is just a sacrificial altar.

Example 5: Radical feminist theory. The word "feminism" nowadays denotes three very different objects: the movement for women's emancipation from male domination; the scientific study of the feminine biological, psychological, and social condition; and radical feminist "theory." While the first two are legitimate and laudable endeavors, the third is an academic industry that makes no use of science. It is moreover hostile to science and is characterized by pseudoproblems and wild speculation. Some radical feminist theorists have promised a "successor science" that would eventually replace or at least complement what they call "male dominated science." Others, more consistent, are dead against all science, for believing that reason and experiment are weapons of male domination. They hold that the scientific method is part of the "male-stream." They denounce precision (in particular quantitation), rational argument, the search for empirical data, and the empirical testing of hypotheses, as so many tools of male domination. They are constructivist-relativists: they denounce what they call "the myth of objectivity." (More on this in section 10.3.)

For example, the feminist theorists Belenky, Clinchy, Goldberger, and Tarule (1986) hold that truth is context-dependent, and that "the knower is an intimate part of the known"—just because some of the women they interviewed felt so. Sandra Harding (1986: 113) goes as far as to assert that it would be "illuminating and honest" to call Newton's laws of motion "Newton's rape manual." (The rape victim would be Mother Nature, which of course is feminine.) Moreover, basic science would be indistinguishable from technology, and the search for scientific knowledge would be just a disguise for the struggle for power—as Herbert Marcuse (1964) and Michel Foucault (1975) had claimed earlier on the strength of the same empirical evidence, namely none.

The radical feminist philosophers are interested in power not in truth. They want to undermine science, not to advance it. In this way they do a double disservice to the cause of feminine emancipation: They discredit feminism for making it appear to be barbaric, and they deprive it of a strong lever, namely the scientific research of the spurious causes and the pernicious effects of gender discrimination. Moreover, their attack on science alienates women from scientific studies and thus reinforces their subordinate position in modern society (Patai and Koertge 1994: 157).

To sum up, our antiscience colleagues are characterized by their appalling ignorance of the very object of their attack, namely science (see Gross and Levitt 1994). Lacking intellectual discipline and rigor, they have been utterly barren. This has not prevented them from misleading uncounted students, encouraging them to choose the wide door, incapacitating them to think straight and get their facts right, and in many cases even write intelligibly. (More on antiscience, particularly in social studies, in Bunge 1996.) Why should any serious and socially responsible scholar tolerate barbarians intent on discrediting genuine scholarly pursuits and even destroying modern culture?

10.2. Academic Pseudoscience

To paraphrase Groucho Marx: The trademark of modern culture is science; if you can fake it, you've got it made. Hence the drive to clothe groundless speculations, and even old superstitions, with the gown of science. The popular pseudosciences, such as astrology, pyramidology, graphology, ufology, "scientific" creationism, parapsychology, psychoanalysis, and homeopathy, are easy to spot, for they are obviously at variance with what is being taught at the science faculties. (Psychoanalysis would seem to refute this assertion but it does not. Indeed nowadays psychoanalysis is only taught in some psychiatry departments, which are part of medical schools, not of science faculties.) On the other hand, the academic pseudosciences are harder to spot partly because they are taught at university departments the world over. A second reason is that these pseudosciences abide by reason or at least seem at first sight to do so. Their main flaws are that their constructions are fuzzy and do not match reality. (Some of them, such as neo-Austrian economics, even claim that their theories are true a priori.) Let us take a small sample.

Example 1: Pseudomathematical symbolism. Pitirim Sorokin, one of the founders of American sociology and an early critic of what he called "quantophrenia" (1956), sometimes indulged in the latter. For example, he defined the freedom of an individual as the quotient of the sum of his wishes by the sum of his means for gratifying them (Sorokin 1937, vol. 3 : 162). But, since he did not bother to define wishes and means in a mathematically correct way, he "divided" words. In sum, the symbols he used in this case were mere shorthand for intuitive notions.

Example 2: Subjective probability in jurisprudence. The so-called New Evidence Scholarship, born in the mid-1960s, claims to use probability to measure credence and in particular the credibility of legal evidence. In this connection there is even talk of "trial by mathematics" (see Tillers 1991 and the subsequent papers). I submit that probability hardly belongs in legal argument, because it only measures the likelihood of random events, not the plausibility of a piece of evidence, the veracity of a witness, or the likelihood that a court of law will produce the just verdict. Consequently, talk of probability in law is pseudoscientific. Worse, the American and other criminal codes require the death penalty when "there is a probability that the defendant would commit criminal acts of violence"—as if such a "probability" (actually a mere plausibility) could be either measured or calculated. Thus sometimes not only property and freedom but even life hang on epistemologies that would not stand a chance in science or engineering, and whose ony function is to justify an academic industry.

Example 3: "Scientific" racism. Racism is very old, but "scientific" racism is a nineteenth century invention that culminated with the Nazi *Rassenkunde* and the accompanying extermination camps. The American version of this doctrine was introduced by some psychologists on the basis of flawed IQ measurements, and it was entrenched in the

American legislation restricting the immigration from Southern Europe and other regions (see, e.g., Gould 1981). It was muted for a while in the wake of the revelation of the Nazi horrors, but it was resucitated in 1969 by the Harvard professor Arthur Jensen, who, on the basis of some IQ measurements, asserted the innate intellectual inferiority of African Americans. This "finding" was unanimously rejected by the scientific community. In particular the Genetics Society of America warned against "the pitfalls of naive hereditarian assumptions" (Russell 1976).

Yaron Ezrahi's (1971), a member of the constructivist-relativist pseudosociology of science, claimed that this denial was due to ideological reasons. He held that the geneticists were particularly vehement in their criticisms of Jensen's work for being concerned, at least in part, with their own "public image and support." Ezrahi did not bother to analyze the very IQ tests from which Jensen had derived his "conclusions." Had he done so he might have learned that (a) such tests were indeed culture-bound and thus likely to favor whites over blacks, and (b) no IQ test will be fully reliable unless backed up by a well-confirmed theory of intelligence—one which is overdue (see, e.g., Bunge and Ardila 1987).

Undaunted by such methodological criticisms, Richard Herrnstein and Charles Murray (1994) repeated the racist claim in their best-seller *The Bell Curve* , without adding any new evidence. Their book was promoted by the American Enterprise Institute and widely publicized by right-wing journalists, who saw in this book the "scientific" basis for their proposal to eliminate all the social programs aimed at giving a chance to African American children. The idea is of course that no amount of money, particularly if public, can correct for an allegedly genetic deficiency. This time around geneticists and psychologists were slow to react: perhaps they took the book for what it is, namely a political tract. On the other hand some journalists and sociologists did point out the methodological flaws of the book, uncovered its ideological sources, and denounced its implications for public policy (see Lane 1994 and the March 1995 issue of *Contemporary Sociology*).

Example 4: Feminist technology . Since technology is the art and science of getting things done, maintained, and repaired, psychotherapy and jurisprudence should be regarded as technologies. Now, in recent years these technologies have acquired a sex: there is now talk of feminist psychotherapy and feminist jurisprudence. Let us take a quick look at the former. A *forte* of feminist psychotherapy is "recovered memory therapy," consisting in "enhancing" a woman's memory—if necessary with the help of hypnosis and drugs—until she "remembers" having been sexually abused by her father during childhood. The patient is then encouraged to take her father to court, in order to punish him and extract from him the maximum possible monetary compensation—to be shared with the therapist. This racket flourished during the past decade in the U.S., until the American Medical Association, and above all the False Memory Syndrome Foundation, warned the courts of law that they were being taken in. Thanks to this reaction the number of lawsuits of that type has started to decline. This is not to deny that many children are sexually abused by their relatives. What are objectionable are the therapist's planting false memories into her patient, and the "theory" that underlies this practice: the former is unscrupulous, and the latter is false. Indeed, the "theory" in question is psychoanalysis, a pseudoscience according to which we never forget anything unless repressed by the "superego." This hypothesis is false: psychologists know that memory is not photographic but fading, selective, distorting, and even constructive. They also know that many people are suggestible, so that unscrupulous psychotherapists can successfully plant false memories in their brain.

To sum up, academic pseudoscience is just as toxic as academic antiscience. Why should serious and socially responsible scholars tolerate it? Being a travesty of scientific research, it should be dissected and exposed, as well as taught only to exemplify bogus science. (More on pseudoscience in social studies in Bunge 1996.)

10.3. Two Kinds of Ignorance: Straight and Willful

No chemistry department would hire an alchemist. A department of crystallography is no place for believers in the psychical power of crystals. No engineering school would keep someone intent on designing a perpetual motion machine. An astronomical observatory is no place for people who believe that the planets are pushed by angels. A biology department would close its doors to anyone who rejects genetics. No one who denies the existence of Nazi concentration camps or Communist labor camps would be able to teach history at a decent university. Likewise, no mathematics department would tolerate anyone holding that logic is a tool of male domination or that quantity is masculine. No Jungian psychology is taught in any self-respecting department of psychology. Whoever believes in homoeopathy cannot make it into an accredited medical school. To generalize: Neither proven falsities nor lies are tolerated in any scientific or technological institution. And for a good reason too: namely because such institutions are set up with the specific purpose of finding, refining, applying, or teaching truths.

Walk a few steps away from the faculties of science, engineering, medicine, or law, towards the Faculty of Arts. Here you will meet another world, one where falsities and lies are tolerated, nay manufactured and taught, in industrial quantities. The unwary student may be offered courses in all manner of nonsense and superstition. Some professors are hired, promoted or given power for teaching that reason is worthless, empirical evidence unnecessary, objective truth nonexistent, basic science a tool of either capitalist or male domination, and the like. We find people who reject all the knowledge painstakingly acquired over the past half millennium. This is the place where students can earn credits for learning old and new superstitions of nearly all kinds, and where they can unlearn to write, so as to sound like phenomenologists, existentialists, deconstructionists, ethnomethodologists, or psychoanalysts. This is where taxpayers' moneys are squandered in the maintenance of the huge industry of cultural involution centered around the deliberate rejection of rational discussion and empirical testing. This fraud has got to be stopped in the name of intellectual honesty and social responsibility.

Let there be no mistake: I am not proposing that we only teach what can now be ascertained as true. On the contrary, we must doubt our learning and must continue teaching that we are all ignorant in most respects and to some degree or other. But we must also teach that ignorance can be gradually overcome by rigorous research: that falsity can be detected, that partial truth can be perfected—the way Archimedes illustrated with his method for computing successive approximations to the exact value of the area of the circle.

We should also realize and teach that there are two kinds of ignorance: natural and willful, traditional and postmodern. The former is unavoidable and its admission mandatory: it is part of being a curious learner and an honest teacher. By contrast, willful or postmodern ignorance is the deliberate refusal to learn items relevant to one's interests. Examples: The refusal of the psychotherapist and the philosopher of mind to learn some experimental psychology and neuropsychology; the refusal of the literary critic with sociological interests to learn some sociology; and the refusal of the philosopher of science to learn a bit of the science he pontificates about. All these are instances of willful ignorance. This is the only intolerable kind of ignorance, for it is a form of dishonesty. And yet this kind of ignorance is being peddled nowadays in many faculties of arts.

Willful ignorance comes in two guises: naked or naive, and disguised or contrived. Naked or *indocta ignorantia* is the clear rejection of science, or—what amounts to the same—the denial of any differences between science and nonscience, in particular pseudoscience. This is what the irrationalists and the relativist-constructivists preach: it is part of the radical feminist and environmentalist "theories," as well as of existentialism, poststructuralism, general semiotics, philosophic hermeneutics, deconstructionism, and similar obscurantist fads.

The first to deny the difference between science and nonscience was Paul K. Feyerabend, one of the philosophical godfathers of the "new" philosophy and sociology of science. He has been listened to for being wrongly believed to know some physics. But in fact his ignorance of this, the one science he tried to learn, was abysmal. Thus he misunderstood the only two formulas that occur in his *Against Method* (1978 [1975]: 62), the book that earned him instant celebrity. The first formula, which he calls 'the equipartition principle', is actualy the Maxwell-Boltzmann distribution function for a system of particles in thermal equilibrium. (Incidentally, the constant occurring in the correct formula is not R, the universal gas constant, but Boltzmann's far more universal k. This is no small mistake, because it renders Feyerabend's formula dimensionally wrong.) The second formula, Lorentz's, does not give "the *energy* of an *electron* moving in a *constant magnetic* field" (my emphases), as Feyerabend claims. Instead, the formula gives the *force* that an *arbitrary electromagnetic* field $<E, B>$ exerts on a particle with an *arbitrary* electric charge. (Incidentally, the constant c is missing in Feyerabend's copy—which, again, makes his formula dimensionally incorrect.) To top it all, Feyerabend substitutes the second formula into the first and, not surprisingly, he gets an odd result that, in a mysterious way, leads him to speculate on the (nonexistent) magnetic monopoles imagined by his teacher Felix Ehrenhaft. But the substitution cannot be made, because (a) the second formula does not give us an energy, which occurs in the first one; (b) the first formula refers to a system of particles whereas the second concerns a single particle; and (c) unlike the energy, which is a scalar, the force is a vector, and therefore it cannot occur by itself in the argument of an exponential function, which is only defined for scalars. (More on Feyerabend's scientific incompetence in Bunge 1991a.) None of Feyerabend's critics detected these elementary errors—a disturbing indicator of the present state of the philosophy of science. In sum, one of the gurus of the new philosophy of science was guilty of *indocta ignorantia*. Ironically, he was also seen as a guru of the student leftist movement.

However, irrationalism, in particular the distrust of science, has no political color: it is found left, center, and right. Still, in most cases it is passive: Babbit is not Torquemada, but just indifferent to and suspicious of intellectual pursuits. On the other hand, militant philistinism is strong in the New Left, the Old Right, and the religious wing of the New Right. This is no coincidence: all of these groups are authoritarian. And, as Popper (1945, chap. 24) pointed out half a century ago, authoritarianism is incompatible with rationalism in the broad sense, that is, "the readiness to listen to critical arguments and to learn from experience." Indeed, the citizens of a democracy are expected to form their own opinions on matters of public interest, to debate them in the agora, and to participate to some extent in the management of the commonwealth. Rationality is thus a necessary component of democratic life, just as irrationalism is a necessary ingredient of the *dressage* of a faithful loyal subject of a totalitarian regime. Remember Mussolini's commandment: "Believe, obey, fight." So much for academic antiscience.

Academic pseudoscience is a different ball game: it is far more subtle and therefore harder to diagnose and uproot. Indeed, it wears some of the accoutrements of genuine science, in particular an esoteric jargon that fools the unwary, or even a symbolic apparatus that intimidates the innumerate (chap. 4). It looks like science but is not scientific because it does not enrich knowledge and, far from having a self-correcting mechanism, it is dogmatic. Because it misleads the innocent, academic pseudoscience is at least as damaging as outright antiscience.

10.4. Conclusions

Academic freedom was introduced to protect the search truth and teaching of it. I submit that the academic charlatans have not earned the academic freedom they enjoy. They have not earned it because they produce or circulate cultural garbage, which is not just a nonacademic activity but an antiacademic one. Let them do that wherever they please except in schools, for these are supposed to be places of learning. We should expel the charlatans from the university before they deform it out of recognition and crowd out the serious searchers for truth.

The academic charlatans should be criticized, nay denounced, with the same rigor and vigor that Julien Benda (1927) attacked the intellectual mercenaries of his time in his memorable *La trahison des clercs*—which, incidentally, earned him the hatred of the so-called "organic intellectuals" of all political hues. Spare the rod and spoil the charlatan. Spoil the charlatan and put modern culture at risk. Jeopardize modern culture and undermine modern civilization. Debilitate modern civilization and prepare for a new Dark Age.

In former times, higher learning was only a refined form of entertainment and a tool of social control. Today it is all that and more: Scientific knowledge, science-based technology and the rationalist humanities are not only intrinsically valuable public goods but also means of production and welfare, as well as conditions of democratic debate and rational conflict resolution. The search for authentic knowledge should therefore be protected from attack and counterfeit both inside and outside academia.

To protect genuine research and scholarship I propose adopting the following

Charter of Intellectual Academic Rights and Duties

1. Every academic has the duty to search for the truth and the right to teach it.

2. Every academic has the right and the duty to question anything that interests him, provided he does it in a rational manner.

3. Every academic has the right to make mistakes and the duty to correct them upon detecting them.

4. Every academic has the duty to expose bunk, whether popular or academic.

5. Every academic has the duty to express himself in the clearest possible way.

6. All academics have the right to discuss any unorthodox views that interest them, provided those views are clear enough to be discussed rationally.

7. No academic has the right to present as true ideas that he cannot justify in terms of either reason or experience.

8. Nobody has the right to engage knowingly in any academic industry.

9. Every academic body has the duty to adopt and enforce the most rigorous known standards of scholarship and learning.

10. Every academic body has the duty to be intolerant to both coun-

terculture and counterfeit culture.

To conclude. Let us tolerate, nay encourage, all search for truth, however eccentric it may look, as long as it abides by reason or experience. But let us fight all attempts to suppress, discredit or fake this search. Let all genuine intellectuals join the Truth Squad and help dismantle the "postmodern" Trojan horse stabled in academia before it destroys us.

References

Adorno, T. and M. Horkheimer. 1972 [1947]. *Dialectic of enlightenment*. New York: Herder and Herder.

Agassi, J. 1998 [1964]. The nature of scientific problems and their roots in metaphysics. In M. Bunge, ed., *Critical approaches to science and philosophy : In honor of Karl R. Popper,* pp. 189–211. New Brunswick, NJ: Transaction Publishers.

———. 1981. *Science and society*. Dordrecht-Boston: Reidel.

Albert, H. 1994. *Kritik der reinen Hermeneutik*. Tübingen: J. C. B. Mohr (Paul Siebeck).

Alexander, J. C., B. Giesen, R. Münch, and N. J. Smelser, eds. 1987.*The micro-macro link*. Berkeley: University of California Press.

Allais, M. 1979. The so-called Allais paradox and rational decision under uncertainty. In M. Allais and O. Hagen, eds., *The expected utility hypothesis and the Allais paradox*, pp. 437–581. Dordrecht and Boston: Reidel.

Allison, P. D. 1992. The cultural evolution of beneficient norms. *Social Forces* 71: 279–301.

Arato, A.and E. Gebhardt, eds. 1978. *The essential Frankfurt school reader*. Oxford: Basil Blackwell.

Archer, M. 1987. Resisting the revival of relativism. *International Sociology* 2: 235–250.

Arrow, K. 1992. I know a hawk from a handsaw. In M. Szenberg, ed., *Eminent economists: their life philosophies,* pp. 42–50. Cambridge: Cambridge University Press.

Athearn, D. 1994. *Scientific Nihilism. On the Loss and Recovery of Physical Explanation*. Albany: State University of New York Press.

Atkinson, P. 1988. Ethnomethodology: A critical review. *Annual Review of Sociology* 14: 441–465.

Arrow, K. J. 1994. Methodological individualism and social knowledge. *American Economic Review* 84 (2): 1–9.

Baldi, S. 1998. Normative versus social constructivist processes in the allocation of citations: A network-analytic model. *American Sociological Review* 63: 829–846.

Barber, B. 1952. *Science and the social order*. Glencoe, IL: Free Press.

Barber, B. and W. Hirsch, eds. 1962. *The sociology of science*. New York: The Free Press.

Barnes, B. 1977. *Interests and the growth of knowledge*. London: Routledge and Kegan Paul.

———.1982a. *T. S. Kuhn and social science*. New York: Columbia University Press.

———. 1982b. On the implications of a body of knowledge. *Knowledge: Creation, Diffusion, Utilization* 4: 95–110.

———. 1983. On the conventional character of knowledge and cognition. In Knorr-Cetina and Mulkay, eds., pp. 19–51.

———, ed. 1972. *Sociology of science: Selected readings*. London: Penguin Books.

Baumol, W. J. and J. Benhabib. 1989. Chaos: Significance, mechanism, and economic applications. *Journal of Economic Perspectives* 3: 77–105.

Beaumont, J. G., P. M. Kenealy, and M. J. C. Rogers, eds. 1996. *The Blackwell Dictionary of Neuropsychology.* Oxford: Blackwell.

Becker, G. S. 1976. *The economic approach to human behavior.* Chicago: University of Chicago Press.

———. and K. M. Murphy. 1988. A theory of rational addiction. *Journal of Political Economy* 96:675–700.

Belenky, M. F. , B. McV. Clinchy, N. R. Goldberger, and J. M. Tarule. 1986. Women's ways of knowing: The development of self, voice, and mind. Basic Books. New York, NY.

Benda, J. .1927. La trahison des clercs, 2nd ed. Paris: Grasset, 1946.

Berger, P.L. and T. Luckmann 1966. *The social construction of reality.* New York: Doubleday.

Berlin, I. 1957. Two concepts of liberty. In *Four essays on liberty.* Oxford: Oxford University Press, 1969.

Bernal, J. D. 1939 *The social function of science.* New York: Macmillan.

Bernard, C. 1865. *Introduction à l'étude de la médecine expérimentale.* Paris: Flammarion, 1952.

Berry, B. J. L., H. Kim, and H.-M. Kim. 1993. Are long waves driven by techno-economic transformations? *Technological Forecasting and Social Change* 44: 111–135.

Bijker, W. E., T. P. Hughes, and T. Pinch, eds. 1987. *The social construction of technological systems.* Cambridge, MA: MIT Press.

Blatt, J. M. 1983. How economists misuse mathematics. In A. S. Eichner, ed., *Why economics is not yet a science,* pp.166–186. Armonk, NY: M. E. Sharpe.

Bloor, D. 1976. *Knowledge and social imagery.* London: Routledge and Kegan Paul.

Borkenau, F. 1934. *Der Uebergang vom feudalen zum bürgerlichen Weltbild.* Paris: Alcan.

Bottomore, T. 1956. Some reflections on the sociology of knowledge. *British Journal of Sociology* 7: 52–58.

Boudon, R. 1979. *La logique du social.* Paris: Hachette. Engl. transl.: *The logic of social action: An introduction to sociological analysis.* London: Routledge and Kegan Paul, 1981.

Boudon, R. 1990. On relativism. In P. Weingartner and G. Dorn, eds. *Studies on Mario Bunge's Treatise,* pp. 229–243. Amsterdam: Rodopi.

Boudon, R. 1995. *Le juste et le vrai.* Paris: Fayard.

Boudon, R. 1998. Etudes sur les sociologues classiques. Paris: Presses Universitaires de France.

Boudon, R. and M. Clavelin, eds. 1994. *Le relativisme est-il irrésistible? Regards sur la sociologie des sciences.* Paris: Presses Universitaires de France.

Bourdieu, P. 1975. The specificity of the scientific field and the social conditions of the progress of reason. *Social Science Information* 14: 19–47.

Bourricaud, F. 1975. Contre le sociologisme: une critique et des propositions. *Revue française de Sociologie,* XVI suppl.: 583–603.

Braiman, Y., J. F. Lindner, and W. L. Ditto. 1995. Taming spatiotemporal chaos with disorder. *Nature* 378:465–467.

Braudel, F. 1969. *Ecrits sur l'histoire.* Paris: Flammarion.

Brock, W. A. and W. D. Dechert. 1991. Non-linear dynamical systems: Instability and chaos in economics. In W. Hildenbrand and H. Sonnenschein, eds., *Handbook of mathematical economics,* vol. IV, pp. 2209–2235. Amsterdam-New York: North Holland-Elsevier.

Brodbeck, M. , ed. 1968. *Readings in the philosophy of the social sciences.* New York: Macmillian.

Brown, C. 1994. Politics and the environment: Nonlinear instabilities dominate. *American Political Science Review* 88: 292–303.

Brown, R. H. 1990. Rhetoric, textuality, and the postmodern turn in sociological theory. *Sociological Theory* 8: 188–197.

Bukharin, N. et al. 1931. *Science at the cross roads.* Repr. with foreword by J. Needham and introduction by P. G. Werksey. London: Frank Cass, 1971.

Bunge, M. 1944. Presentación. *Minerva* 1:1–2.

———. 1951. What is chance? *Science and Society* 15:209–231.

———. 1959. *Causality: The place of the causal principle in modern science.* 3rd rev. ed. New York: Dover, 1979. Translated into German, Hungarian, Italian, Japanese, Polish, Russian, and Spanish.

———. 1961. *Etica y ciencia.* Buenos Aires: Siglo Veinte.

———. 1962. *Intuition and science.* Englewood Cliffs, NJ: Prentice-Hall. Repr.: Westport, CT: Greenwood Press, 1975.

———. 1963a. *The myth of simplicity.* Englewood Cliffs, NJ: Prentice-Hall.

———. 1963b. A general black box theory. *Philosophy of Science* 30: 346—358.

———. 1964. Phenomenological theories. In M. Bunge, ed., *The critical approach to science and philosophy. In honor of Karl R. Popper,* pp. 234–254. New York: The Free Press. Repr.: New Brunswick NJ: Transaction Publishers, 1998.

———. 1967a. *Foundations of physics.* Berlin-Heidelberg-New York: Springer-Verlag.

———. 1967b. *Scientific research ,* 2 vols. Berlin-Heidelberg-New York: Springer-Verlag. Rev. ed.: *Philosophy of science,* 2 vols., New Brunswick, NJ: Transaction Publishers, 1998.

———. 1968a. The maturation of science. In I. Lakatos and A. Musgrave, eds., *Problems in the philosophy of science,* pp. 120–137. Amsterdam: North-Holland.

———.1968b. Les concepts de modèle. *L'âge de la science* I:165–180.

———.1969a. Models in theoretical science. *Proc. XIVth Intern. Congress of Philosophy* III: 208–217.

———. 1969b. Four models of human migration: An exercise in mathematical sociology. *Archiv für Rechts-und Sozial Philosophie* 55: 451–462. Repr. in *Method, Model, and Matter* pp. 131–142. Dordrecht: Reidel, 1973.

———.1973a. *Method, model and matter.* Dordrecht: Reidel.

———.1973b. *Philosophy of physics.* Dordrecht: Reidel.

———. 1974. *Treatise on basic philosophy,* vol. 1: *Sense and reference.* Dordrecht: Reidel.

———.1976. A model for processes combining competition with cooperation. *Applied Mathematical Modelling* 1:21–23.

———.1977. *Treatise on basic philosophy,* Vol. 3: *The furniture of the world.* Dordrecht: Reidel.

———. 1978. A systems concept of society: Beyond individualism and holism. *Theory and Decision* 10: 13–30.

———. 1979a. *Treatise on basic philosophy,* Vol. 4: *A world of systems.* Dordrecht-Boston: Reidel Academic Publishers.

———. 1979b. The Einstein-Bohr debate over quantum mechanics: Who was right about what? *Lecture Notes in Physics* 100:204–219.

———. 1980a.*The mind-body problem.* Oxford-New York: Pergamon Press.

———. 1980b. *Ciencia y desarrollo.* Buenos Aires: Siglo Veinte.

———. 1981a. *Scientific materialism.* Dordrecht-Boston: Reidel.

———. 1981b. Review of Fleck's book. *Behavioral Science* 26: 178–180.

———1983a. *Treatise on basic philosophy,* vol. 5: *Exploring the world.* Dordrecht-Boston-Lancaster: Reidel.

———. 1983b. *Treatise on basic philosophy,* vol. 6: *Understanding the world.* Dordrecht-Boston: Reidel Academic Publishers.

———. 1985. *Treatise on basic philosophy,* vol. 7: *Philosophy of science and Tech-*

nology, part II: *Life science, social science and technology*. Dordrecht-Boston: Reidel.

————1988a. Two faces and three masks of probability. *In* Probability in the sciences. E. Agazzi, ed. pp. 27–50. Reidel. Dordrecht-Boston.

————1988b. Niels Bohr's philosophy. *Philosophia Naturalis* 25:399–415.

————.1989a. *Treatise on basic philosophy*, vol. 8: *Ethics*. Dordrecht: Reidel.

————.1989b. Game theory is not a useful tool for the political scientist. *Epistemologia* 12: 195–212.

————.1989c. The popular perception of science in North America. *Transactions of the Royal Society of Canada*, ser. V. vol. IV:269–280.

————. 1991a The power and limits of reduction. In E. Agazzi, ed., *Reductionism in the sciences*, pp. 31–49. Dordrecht-Boston: Kluwer.

————1991b. A skeptic's beliefs and disbeliefs. *New Ideas in Psychology* 9:131–149. Criticisms: ibid. pp. 151–244. Author's replies : ibid. pp.245–283.

————. 1995a. The poverty of rational choice theory. In I. C. Jarvie and N. Laor, eds., *Critical rationalism, metaphysics, and science*, vol. 1, pp. 149–168. Dordrecht-Boston: Kluwer Academic Publishers.

————. 1995b. Rational choice theory: A critical look at its foundations. In J . Götschl, ed., *Revolutionary changes in understanding man and society*, pp. 211–218. Dordrecht-Boston: Kluwer Academic Publishers.

————.1996. *Finding philosophy in social science*. New Haven, CT: Yale University Press.

————.1998. *Social science under debate*. Toronto: University of Toronto Press.

Bunge, M. and R. Ardila 1987. *Philosophy of psychology*. New York:Springer-Verlag.

Clark, C. M. A. 1992. *Economic theory and natural philosophy: The search for the natural laws of the economy*. Aldershot, UK/Brookfield, VT: Edward Elgar.

Cohen, I. B., ed. 1990. *Puritanism and the rise of modern science: The Merton thesis*. New Brunswick, NJ: Rutgers University Press.

Coleman, J. S. 1990. *Foundations of social theory*. Cambridge, MA: Harvard University Press.

Collins, H. M. 1981. Stages in the empirical programme of relativism. *Social Studies of Science* 11:3–10.

Collins, H. M. 1983. An empirical relativist programme in the sociology of scientific knowledge. In Knorr-Cetina and Mulkay, eds., pp. 85–113.

Collins, H. M. and T. J. Pinch 1982. *Frames of meaning: The social construction of extraordinary science*. London: Routledge and Kegan Paul.

Collins, R. 1987. Interaction ritual chains, power, and property. In Alexander et al., eds., pp. 193–206.

Collins, R. 1998. *The sociologies of philosophies: A global theory of intellectual change*. Cambridge, MA: Harvard University Press.

Costantino, R. F., J. M. Cushing, B. Dennis, and R. A. Desharnais. 1995. Experimentally induced transitions in the dynamic behavior of insect populations. *Nature* 375: 227–230.

Cross, J. G., and M. J. Guyer. 1980. *Social traps*. Ann Arbor: University of Michigan Press.

Crowther, J. G. 1941. *The social relations of science*. New York: Macmillan.

Curtis, M., ed. 1997 [1970]. *Marxism: The inner dialogues*, 2nd ed. New Brunswick, NJ: Transaction Publishers.

D'Abro, A. 1939. *The Decline of mechanism (in modern physics)*. New York: Van Nostrand.

Dahl, R. A. 1985. *A preface to economic democracy*. Berkeley: University of California Press.

Damasio, A. R., H. Damasio, and Y. Christen, eds. 1996. *Neurobiology of decision-making.* Berlin-Heidelberg: Springer.

Dasgupta, P., and D. Ray. 1986. Inequality as a determinant of malnutrition and unemployment: Theory. *The Economic Journal* 96: 1011–1034.

Deininger, K., and L. Squire. 1996. A new data set measuring income inequality. *World Bank Economic Review* 10: 565—91.

Di Tella, T. S. 1986. *Sociología de los procesos políticos,* 3rd. ed. Buenos Aires: Eudeba. Engl. transl.: *Latin American politics: A theoretical approach.* Austin: University of Texas Press, 1990.

Dixon, W. J. and T. Boswell. 1996. Dependency, disarticulation, and denominator effects: Another look at foreign capital penetration. *American Journal of Sociology* 102:543–62.

Dumont, L. 1996.*Homo hierarchicus.* Essai sur le système des castes. Paris: Gallimard.

Durkheim, E. 1972. *Selected writings.* A. Giddens, ed. New York: Cambridge University Press.

———.1988 [1895]. *Les règles de la méthode sociologique.* Paris: Flammarion.

Durkheim, E. and M. Mauss 1903. De quelques formes primitives de classification. In M. Mauss, *Essais de sociologie* , pp. 162–230. Paris: ed. de Minuit, 1968.

Elster, J. 1989. *Nuts and bolts for the social sciences.* New York: Cambridge University Press.

Ezrahi, Y. 1972. The political resources of American science. In Barnes, ed., pp. 211–230.

Faludi, A. 1986. *Critical rationalism and planning methodology.* London: Plon.

Farías, V. 1990. *Heidegger and Nazism.* Philadelphia, PA: Temple University Press.

Featherstone, M., ed. 1988. Special issue on postmodernism. *Theory, Culture and Society* 5:195–576.

Feld, S. L. and W. S. Carter. 1998. When desegregation *reduces* interracial contact: A class-size paradox for weak ties. *American Journal of Sociology* 103: 1165–86.

Feyerabend, P. K. .1975. *Against method.* London: New Left Books.

———.1981 *Philosophical papers*, 2 vols. Cambridge: Cambridge University Press.

———.1990. Realism and the historicity of knowledge. In W. R. Shea and A. Spadafora, eds., *Creativity in the arts and science,* pp.142–153. Canton, MA: Science History Publications, U.S.A.

Fiske, D. W. and R. A. Shweder, eds. 1986. *Metatheory in social science.* Chicago: University of Chicago Press.

Fleck, L. 1979 [1935]. *Genesis and development of a scientific fact.* Foreword by T. S. Kuhn. Chicago: University of Chicago Press.

Fogel, R. W. 1994. Economic growth, population theory, and physiology: The bearing of long-term processes on the making of economic policy. *American Economic Review* 84:369–95.

Forman, P. 1971. Weimar culture, causality and quantum theory,1918–1927: Adaptation by German physicists and mathematicians to a hostile intellectual environment. In R. McCormmach, ed.,*Historical studies in the physical sciences* 3:1–115.

Foucault, M. 1979. *Discipline and punish.* New York: Vintage Books.

Fourier, J. B. J. 1888 [1822] *Théorie analytique de la chaleur.* In *Oeuvres,* vol. I, ed. by G. Darboux. Paris: Gauthier-Villars.

Frankfort, H., H. A. Frankfort, J. A. Wilson, and T. Jacobsen. 1949 [1946]. *Before philosophy: The intellectual adventure of ancient man.* London: Penguin.

Friedman, M. 1970. A theoretical framework for monetary analysis. In *Milton Friedman's Monetary Framework.* R. J. Gordon, ed., pp. 1–62. Chicago: University of Chicago Press.

Galbraith, J. K. 1987. *A history of economics .* London: Hamish Hamilton.

Garfinkel, H. 1967. *Studies in ethnomethodology.* Englewood Cliffs, NJ: Prentice-Hall.
Garfinkel, H., M. Lynch, and E. Livingston 1981. The work of a discovering science construed with materials from the optically discovered pulsar. *Philosophy of the Social Sciences* 11:131–158.
Geertz, C. 1973. *The interpretation of cultures.* New York: Basic Books.
———. 1983. *Local knowledge.* New York: Basic Books.
Gieryn, T. F. 1982. Relativist/constructivist programmes in the sociology of science: Redundance and retreat. *Social Studies of Science* 12: 279–297.
Glass, L. and M. C. Mackey. 1988. *From clocks to chaos.* Princeton, NJ: Princeton University Press.
Goffman, E. 1963. *Behavior in public places.* New York: Free Press.
Goldsmith, D., ed. .1977. *Scientists confront Velikovsky.* Papers from an AAAS Symposium. Ithaca, NY:Cornell University Press.
Goldsmith, M. and A. Mackay, eds. 1964. *The science of science.* London: Souvenir Press.
Goldstone, J. A. 1991. *Revolution and rebellion in the early modern world.* Berkeley: University of California Press.
Goodman, N. 1978. *Ways of world-making.* Indianapolis, IN: Hackett.
Gottschalk, L., ed. 1963. *Generalization in the writing of history.* Chicago: University of Chicago Press.
Gould, S. J. 1981. *The Mismeasure of man.* New York: W. W. Norton.
Granovetter, M. 1983. The strength of weak ties. In R. Collins, ed., *Sociological theory,* pp. 201–233. San Francisco, CA: Jossey-Bass Publishers.
Green, D. P. and I. Shapiro.1994. Pathologies of rational choice theory: A critique of applications in political science. New Haven, CT: Yale University Press.
Gross, P.R. and N. Levitt .1994. Higher superstition: The academic left and its quarrels with science. Baltimore, MD: Johns Hopkins University Press.
Gurr, T. R. 1970. *Why Men Rebel.* Princeton: Princeton University Press.
Habermas, J.1971 *Toward a Rational Society.* London: Heinemann.
Habermas, J. 1988 [1967]. *On the logic of the social sciences.* Cambridge, MA: MIT Press.
Haken, H. 1989. Synergetics: an overview. *Reports on Progress in Theoretical Physics* 52:515–553.
Hardin, G. 1985. *Filters against folly* . New York: Viking Penguin.
Harding, S. 1986. *The science question in feminism.* Ithaca, NY: Cornell University Press.
Harrison, B. and B. Bluestone.1988. *The great u-turn: Corporate restructuring and the polarization of America.* New York: Basic Books.
Harsanyi, J. C. 1956. Approaches to the bargaining problem before and after the theory of games: a critical discussion of Zeuthen's, Hicks' and Nash's theories. *Econometrica* 24:144–57.
Harvey, D. 1989. *The condition of postmodernity.* Oxford: Basil Blackwell.
Hebb, D. O. 1980. *Essay on mind.* Hillsdale, NJ: Lawrence Erlbaum.
Hedström, P. and R. Swedberg. 1998. Social mechanisms: theoretical status and use in sociology. In P. Hedström and R. Swedberg, eds., *Social Mechanisms.* Cambridge: Cambridge University Press.
Heidegger, M. 1986 [1927] *Sein und Zeit,* 16th ed. Tübingen: Max Niemeyer.
———.1987 [1953].*Einführung in die Metaphysik* , 5th. ed. Tübingen: Max Niemeyer.
Hempel, C. G. 1965. *Aspects of scientific explanation.* New York: The Free Press; London: Collier-Macmillan.
Herrnstein, J. W. 1990. Rational choice theory: Necessary but not sufficient. *American Psychologist* 45: 356–367.

Herrnstein, R. J. and C. Murray. 1994. *The bell curve: Intelligence and class structure in American Life*. New York: The Free Press.

Hesse, M. 1980. *Revolutions and reconstructions in the philosophy of science*. Brighton: Harvester Press.

Hessen, B. 1931. The social and economic roots of Newton's 'Principia'. In N. Bukharin et al. pp. 149–212.

Hicks, A., J. Misra, and T. N. Ng. 1995. The programmatic emergence of the social security state. *American Sociological Review* 60:329–349.

Hicks, J. 1979. *Causality in economics*. New York: Basic Books.

Hirschman, A. O. 1970. *Exit, voice, and loyalty*. Cambridge, MA: Harvard University Press.

———.1981. *Essays in trespassing: Economics to politics and beyond*. Cambridge: Cambridge University Press.

———. 1990. The case against "one thing at a time." *World Development* 18:1119–1120.

Homans, G. C. 1974. *Social behavior. Its elementary forms,* rev. ed. New York: Harcourt Brace Jovanovich.

Huntington, S. P. 1968. *Political Order in changing Societies*. New Haven, CT: Yale University Press.

Husserl, E. .1960 [1931]. *Cartesian meditations* . The Hague: Martinus Neijhoff.

———.1954 [1935]. Die Krisis der europäischen Wissenschaften und die tranzendentale Phänomenologie . *Husserliana* VI, pp. 314–348. Den Haag: Martinus Nijhoff.

Jacobs, S. 1990. Popper, Weber and the rationalist approach to social explanation. *British Journal of Sociology* 41:559–570.

Jarvie, I. C.1984. *Rationality and relativism*. London: Routledge and Kegan Paul.

Jasso, G. and K.-D. Opp. 1997. Probing the character of norms: A factorial survey analysis of the norms of political action. *American Sociological Review* 62: 947–64.

Kahneman, D., P. Slovic and A. Tversky, eds. 1982. *Judgment under uncertainty: Heuristics and biases*. Cambridge: Cambridge University Press.

Kauffman, S. A. 1993. *The origins of order.* New York/Oxford: Oxford University Press.

Kentor, J. 1998. The long-term effects of foreign investment dependence on economic growth, 1940–1990. *American Journal of Sociology* 103:1024–46.

Kiel, L. D. and E. Elliott, eds. 1996. *Chaos theory in the social sciences*. Ann Arbor: University of Michigan Press.

Knorr-Cetina, K. D. 1981.*The manufacture of knowledge: An essay on the constructivist and contextual nature of science*. Oxford: Pergamon Press.

———1983. The ethnographic study of scientific work: Towards a constructivist interpretation of science. In Knorr-Cetina and Mulkay, eds., pp. 115–139.

Knorr-Cetina, K. D. and A. V. Cicourel, eds. 1981. *Advances in social theory and methodology: Toward an integration of micro- and macrosociologies*. London: Routledge and Kegan Paul.

Knorr-Cetina, K. and M. Mulkay, eds. .1983. *Science observed: Perspectives on the social study of science*. London: Sage.

Koblitz, N. 1988. A tale of three equations; or, the emperors have no clothes. *Mathematical Intelligencer* 10:4–10.

Kolnai, A. 1938. *The War against the West*. London: Gollancz; New York: Viking Press.

Kosslyn, S. M. and O. Koenig. 1995. *Wet mind: The new cognitive neuroscience*, 2nd ed. New York: The Free Press.

Krimerman, L.I., ed.1969. *The nature and scope of social science*. New York: Appleton-Century-Crofts.

Krohn, R. G. 1971. *The social shaping of science*. Westport, CT: Greenwood Publ. Co.
————. 1980. Toward the empirical study of scientific practice. *Sociology of the Sciences Yearbook* IV: vii–xxv.
Krugman, P. 1996. *The self-organizing economy*. Cambridge, MA: Blackwell.
Kuhn, T. S. 1962. *The structure of scientific revolutions*. Chicago: University of Chicago Press.
Kurtz, P., ed. 1985. *A skeptic's handbook of parapsychology*. Buffalo, NY: Prometheus Books.
Lane, C. 1994. The tainted sources of 'the bell curve'. *New York Review of Books* XLI, no. 20:14–19.
Lang, S. 1981. *The file*. New York: Springer-Verlag.
Latour, B. 1980. Is it possible to reconstruct the research process? Sociology of a brain peptide. *Sociology of the Sciences Yearbook* IV: 53–76.
————.1983. Give me a laboratory and I will raise the world. In Knorr-Cetina and Mulkay, eds., pp. 141–170.
————.1987. *Science in action: How to follow scientists and engineers around society*. Cambridge, MA: Harvard University Press.
————.1988. A relativistic account of Einstein's relativity. *Social Studies of Science* 18: 3–44.
————. 1995. Who speaks for science? *The Sciences* 35: 6–7.
Latour, B. and S. Woolgar.1979. *Laboratory life: The social construction of scientific facts*. Beverly Hills, CA: Sage.
Latour, B. and S. Woolgar.1986. *Laboratory life: The construction of scientific facts*. Rev. ed. Princeton, NJ: Princeton University Press.
Livingston, P. 1988. *Literary knowledge*. Ithaca, NY: Cornell University Press.
Luhman, N. 1990. *Die Wissenschaft der Gesellschaft*. Frankfurt a. M.: Suhrkamp.
Lukács, G. 1971[1923]. *History and class-consciousness*. Cambridge, MA: MIT Press.
Lynch, M. E. 1988. Sacrifice and the transformation of the animal body into a scientific object: Laboratory culture and ritual practice in the neurosciences. *Social Studies of Science* 18:265–289.
Lynch, M., E. Livingston, and H. Garfinkel 1983. Temporal order in laboratory work. In Knorr-Cetina and Mulkay, eds., pp. 205–238.
MacKinnon, C. 1989. *Toward a feminist theory of the state*. Cambridge, MA: Harvard University Press.
Marcuse, H. 1964. *One-Dimensional Man*. Boston: Beacon Press.
March, J. G. and Z. Shapira. 1987. Managerial perspectives on risk and risk taking. *Management Science* 33: 1404–18.
Marshall, E. 1990. Data sharing: A declining ethic? *Science* 248:952–957.
Marx K. and F. Engels. 1986. *Selected works*. New York: International Publishers.
Marx, K. 1859. A contribution to the critique of political economy. In K. Marx and F. Engels, *Selected works*. New York: International Publishers, 1986.
Mendelson, E. 1977. The social construction of scientific knowledge. *Sociology of the Sciences Yearbook* 1: 3–26.
Merton, R. K. 1942. Science and democratic social structure. Repr. in 1957a, chap. XVI.
————.1957a. *Social Theory and Social Structure*, rev. ed. New York: The Free Press.
————. 1957b. The role set: Problems in sociological theory. *British Journal of Sociology* 8: 106–120.
————. 1970 [1938]. *Science, technology and society in seventeenth-century England*. New York, Harper and Row.
————.1973. *The sociology of science: Theoretical and empirical investigations*. Chicago: University of Chicago Press.

————. 1977. *The sociology of science: An episodic memoir.* Carbondale and Edwardsville: Southern Illinois Press.

————.1987. Three fragments from a sociologist's notebooks. *Annual Reviews of Sociology* 13:1–28.

Meyerson, E. 1921. *De l'explication dans les sciences,* 2 vols. Paris: Payot.

Mill, J. S. 1952 [1872]. *A system of logic,* 3rd ed. London: Longmans Green.

————. 1871. *Principles of political economy.*, 7th ed. In *Collected Works* , Vol. III. Toronto: University of Toronto Press; London: Routledge and Kegan Paul, 1965.

————. 1873. *The autobiography of John Stuart Mill* . J. J. Coss, ed. New York: Columbia University Press.

Moaddel, M. 1994. Political conflict in the world economy: A cross-national analysis of modernization and world-system theories. *American Sociological Review* 59:276–303.

Moessinger, P. 1996. *Irrationalité individuelle et ordre social.* Geneva: Droz.

Muller, E. N. 1995. Economic determinants of democracy. *American Sociological Review* 60: 805–21.

Mulkay, M. 1969. Some aspects of cultural growth in the natural sciences. In Barnes ed. 1972, pp. 126–142.

————.1979. *Science and the sociology of knowledge.* London: Allen and Unwin.

Nadeau, R. 1993. Confuting Popper on the rationality principle. *Philosophy of the Social Sciences* 23: 446–467.

O'Neill, J. , ed. 1973. *Modes of Individualism and collectivism.* London: Heinemann.

Outhwaite, W. 1986. *Understanding social science: The method called verstehen,* 2nd ed. Lewes: Jean Stroud.

Pareto, V. 1963 [1916]. *A treatise on general sociology,* 4 vols. New York: Dover.

Parsons, T. 1951. *The social system.* New York: Free Press.

Patai, D. and N. Koertge.1994. Professing feminism: Cautionary tales from the strange world of women's studies. New York: A New Republic Book, Basic Books.

Persson, T., and G. Tabellini. 1994. Is inequality harmful for growth? *American Economic Review* 84:600–21.

Petroski, H. 1983. *The evolution of useful things.* New York: Alfred A. Knopf.

Pierson, C. 1995. *Socialism after communism : The new market socialism.* University Park: Pennsylvania State University Press.

Pinch, T. J. 1979a. What does a proof do if it does not prove? *Sociology of the Sciences Yearbook* III: 171–215.

————.1979b. Normal explanations of the paranormal: The demarcation problem and fraud in parapsychology. *Social Studies of Science* 9: 329–348.

————.1985. Towards an analysis of scientific observation: The externality of evidential significance of observational reports in physics. *Social Studies of Science* 15: 3–36.

Pinch, T. J. and H. M. Collins .1979. Is anti-science not-science? *Sociology of the Sciences Yearbook* III: 221–250.

————.1984. Private science and public knowledge: The committee for the scientific investigation of the claims of the paranormal and its use of the literature. *Social Studies of Science* 14: 521–546.

Planas, P. 1996. *Karl Popper: Pensamiento político.* Bogotá: Fundación Friedrich Naumann.

Poincaré, H. 1901. Letter to L. Walras. In Correspondence of Léon Walras and Related Papers, W. Jaffé, ed., pp. 164–165. North Holland. Amsterdam, 1965.

Polanyi, K. 1944. *The great transformation.* New York: Rinehart.

Popper, K. R. 1960 [1944–45]. *The Poverty of Historicism,* 2nd ed. London: Routledge and Kegan Paul.

————. 1962 [1945].*The open society and its enemies*, 2 vols, 4th ed. London: Routledge and Kegan Paul.

————. 1959 Woran glaubt der Westen? In *Auf der Suche nach einer besseren Welt* pp. 231–254. München-Zürich: Piper, 1984.

————. 1967. The rationality principle. In D. Miller, ed., *Popper Selections* pp. 357–365. Princeton, NJ: Princeton University Press.

————. 1968. Epistemology without a knowing subject. In B. van Rootselaar and J. F. Staal eds. *Logic, Methodology and Philosophy of Science,* pp. 333–376. Amsterdam: North-Holland.

————. 1970a. Reason or revolution? *Archives européennes de sociologie* XI: 252–262.

————. 1970b. Normal science and its dangers. In I. Lakatos and A. Musgrave, eds. *Criticism and the growth of knowledge,* pp.51–58. Cambridge: Cambridge University Press.

————.1970c. The moral responsibility of the scientist. In P. Weingartner and P. Zecha, eds., *Induction, physics, and ethics* pp. 329–336. Dordrecht: Reidel.

————.1972. *Objective knowledge.* Oxford: Clarendon Press.

————.1974. Intellectual autobiography . In P. A. Schilpp, ed., *The Philosophy of Karl Popper*, vol. 1, pp. 1–181. La Salle, IL: Open Court. Repr. as *Unended Quest.* La Salle, IL: Open Court, 1976.

————. 1988. The open society and its enemies revisited. *The Economist* 307, no. 7547:19–22.

Popper, K. R. and J. C. Eccles. 1977. *The self and its brain.* New York: Springer.

Porter, T. M. .1986. *The rise of statistical thinking.* Princeton, NJ: Princeton University Press.

Pound, R. 1954 [1924]. *Introduction to the philosophy of law*, rev. ed. New Haven, CT: Yale University Press.

Price, D. de S. 1964. The science of science. In Goldsmith and Mackay eds. pp. 195–208.

Putnam, H. 1978. *Meaning and the moral sciences.* Boston-London: Routledge and Kegan Paul.

Ranelagh, J. 1991. *Thatcher's people.* London: HarperCollins.

Rapoport, A. 1989. *Decision theory and decision behaviour.* Dordrecht Boston: Kluwer.

Restivo, S. 1983. *The social relations of physics, mysticism and mathematics.* Dordrecht-Boston-Lancaster: Reidel.

————.1992. *Mathematics in society and history.* Dordrecht-Boston: Kluwer.

Rhees, R. 1969. *Without answers.* London: Routledge and Kegan Paul.

Robinson, J. and J. Eatwell. 1974. *An introduction to modern economics*, rev. ed. London: McGraw-Hill.

Roll-Hansen, N. 1983. The death of spontaneous generation and the birth of the gene: Two case studies of relativism. *Social Studies of Science* 13: 481–519.

Rorty, R. 1979. *Philosophy and the mirror of nature.* Princeton, NJ: Princeton University Press.

Rose, H. 1979. Hyper-reflexivity: A new danger for the counter-movements. *Sociology of the Sciences Yearbook* III: 277–289.

Rose, H. and S. Rose 1969. *Science and Society.* London: Allen Lane, Penguin Press.

Rose, H. and S. Rose 1974. Do not adjust your mind, there is a fault in reality. Ideology in the neurobiological sciences. In Whitley, ed., pp.148–171.

Rosenau, J. N. 1990. *Turbulence in world politics: A theory of change and continuity.* Princeton, NJ: Princeton University Press.

Russell, E. S. 1976. Report of the ad hoc comittee. *Genetics* 83:s99–s101.

Sarton, G. 1952. *A history of science: Ancient Greece through the golden age of Greece*, 2 vols. Cambridge, MA: Harvard University Press.

Schelling, T. C. 1978. *Micromotives and macrobehavior.* New York: W. W. Norton.

Schelting, A. von. 1934. *Max Webers Wissenschaftslehre.* Tübingen: Mohr.

Schutz, A. 1967 [1932].*The phenomenology of the social world.* Evanston, IL: Northwestern University Press.

Shils, E. 1982. Knowledge and the sociology of knowledge. *Knowledge: creation, Diffusion, Utilization* 4: 7–32.

Shweder, R. A. 1986. Divergent rationalities. In Fiske and Shweder, eds., pp. 163–196.

Siegel, H. 1987. *Relativism refuted: A criticism of contemporary epistemological relativism.* Dordrecht-Boston: Reidel.

Simmel, G. 1950 [1908]. *Soziologie.* Partial transl. in K. H. Wolff, ed., *The sociology of Georg Simmel.* Glencoe, IL: The Free Press.

Smelser, N. J. 1998. The rational and the ambivalent in the social sciences. *American Sociological Review* 63:1–15.

Smith, A. 1976 [1776]. *The wealth of nations.* Chicago: University of Chicago Press.

Sokal, A. and J. Bricmont. 1998. *Fashionable nonsense.* New York: Picador.

Sorokin, P. A. 1937. *Social and cultural dynamics*, vol. 3. Allen and Unwin. London.

———.1956. *Fads and foibles in modern sociology and related sciences.* Chicago, IL: Henry Regnery.

Soros, G. 1998. *The crisis of global capitalism (open society endangered).* New York: Public Affairs.

Sørensen, A. B. 1979. Theory and models of mobility. *IHS Journal* 3:B79–B97.

Stigler, G. J. and G. S. Becker. 1977. De gustibus non est disputandum. *American Economic Review* 67: 76–90.

Stinchcombe, A. L. 1968. *Constructing social theories.* Chicago: University of Chicago Press.

———. 1991.The conditions of fruitfulness of theorizing about mechanisms in social science. *Philosophy of the Social Sciences* 21:367–388.

Suppes, P. and J. L. Zinnes 1963. Basic measurement theory. In R. D. Luce, R. R. Bush and E. Galanter, eds., *Handbook of mathematical psychology*, vol. 1, ch. 1. New York and London: John Wiley and Sons.

Tellis, G. J. and P. N. Golder. 1996. First to market, first to fail? Real causes of enduring market leadership. *Sloan Management Review* 37, no. 2: 65–75.

Thompson, D. B., J. H. Brown, and W. D. Spencer. 1991. Indirect facilitation of granivorous birds by desert rodents: Experimental evidence from foraging patterns. *Ecology* 72: 852–863.

Tillers, P. 1991. Decision and inference. *Cardozo Law Review* 13:253–256.

Tilly, C. 1998. *Durable inequality.* Berkeley: University of California Press.

Tilly, C. and C. Tilly. 1998. *Work under capitalism.* Boulder, CO: Westview Press.

Tilman, D. 1987. The importance of the mechanisms of interspecific competition. *American Naturalist* 129:769–774.

Tocqueville, A. de. 1985. *Selected letters on politics and society.* R. Boesche, ed. Berkeley: University of California Press.

Touraine, A. 1994. *Qu'est-ce que la démocratie?* Paris: Fayard.

Trigger, B. G. 1998. *Sociocultural evolution: Calculation and contingency.* Oxford: Blackwell.

Tuchman, B.W. 1984. *The March of Folly.* New York: Ballentine Books.

Tuma, N. B. and M. T. Hannan. 1988. *Social dynamics: Models and methods.* San Diego, CA: Academic Press.

Tversky, A. 1975. A critique of expected utility theory: Descriptive and normative considerations. *Erkenntnis* 9: 163–173.

Wallace, W. L. 1983. *Principles of scientific sociology*. New York: Aldine.

Weber, M. 1922. *Wirtschaft und Gesellschaft. Grundriss der Vestehende Soziologie,* 3 vols, 5th ed. Tübingen: J. C. B. Mohr (Paul Siebeck).

Whewell, W. 1847. *The philosophy of the inductive sciences,* 2 vols. Repr.: London: Frank Cass, 1967.

Wolpert, L. 1992. *The unnatural nature of science.* London: Faber and Faber.

Index of Names

Index of Subjects